Wavetops at My Wingtips

Wavetops at My Wingtips

Flying with
RAF Bomber and Coastal Commands
in
World War II

Flt Lt Leslie Baveystock, DSO, DFC*, DFM

Airlife
England

This book is dedicated
to the memory of
Leslie Manser VC

Copyright © 2001 Leslie Baveystock

First published in the UK in 2001
by Airlife Publishing Ltd

Edited by Tom Harvey and Alan Lyon

British Library Cataloguing-in-Publication Data
A catalogue record for this book
is available from the British Library

ISBN 1 84037 310 5

This book contains rare photographs and the publishers have made every endeavour to reproduce them to the highest quality. Some, however, have been technically impossible to reproduce to the standard that we normally demand, but have been included because of their rarity and interest value.

Typeset by Phoenix Typesetting, Ilkley, West Yorkshire
Printed in England by MPG Books Ltd., Bodmin, Cornwall

Airlife Publishing Ltd

101 Longden Road, Shrewsbury, SY3 9EB England.
E-mail: airlife@airlifebooks.com
Website: www.airlifebooks.com

ACKNOWLEDGEMENTS

I must start by thanking Betty Baveystock for allowing us to proceed with the publication of this book. Her husband sadly passed away in 1997, when Tom Harvey was already preparing it for possible publication. Without her permission, we would not have the privilege of sharing in what is, by any standards, a remarkable story. I must also thank her for providing many of the photographs, especially those of the Resistance workers who assisted in the escape through France and Belgium.

Leslie Baveystock wrote his life story after he and Betty returned to New Zealand from a six-month trip to Europe in 1974. They hired a car and a small caravan and set off to see all the places where Les had served and, whilst in the UK, attended the Diamond Jubilee Celebrations of 201 Squadron at Royal Air Force Kinloss. During this visit, they also went over to Belgium, hoping to find some of the courageous people who had helped Les and his companions escape through Belgium and France to Spain. In this venture, they had a stroke of luck. It was quite by chance that they met René, who helped them to locate the farm near Bree where Les, Bob Horsley and Stan King were initially given a hiding place. René, having heard their story, decided that this was far better than the task which his family had given him, painting the house, and took two weeks off to help them with their quest. As he got into their car, he was asked if it was not too tight a squeeze and replied, 'Bob's Your Uncle'!! The Baveystocks then thought of the luck that they had just experienced. René was known thereafter as 'The Reluctant Painter'. The prologue and some of the photographs taken after the War bear witness to their success.

As the story develops, Les acknowledges, time and again, that it was all due to luck, from his early experiences in the Recruiting Office in Edgware, and throughout his flying training and operational flying. He would have been the first to admit the luck that his crews had in locating and sinking two U-boats. Other crews spent hundreds of hours over the Atlantic and in the Bay without a sniff of a contact. It was doubly sad but also lucky that he was given leave to bury his father as his second crew were killed whilst he was away.

The original book has been described to me by Betty Baveystock as a tome. Having worked from it in preparing the edited version, that is a very apt description. It was a continuous narrative without chapters. The original editing was carried out by the late Group Captain Tom Harvey RAF (retd). Tom was a remarkable man. In his last years, he lived and breathed 201 Squadron. He was one of the founders of the 201 Squadron Association and was its first chairman, a position he held until his sudden death in late 1998. Tom's dealings with everything to do with the association have been described as being tackled with the enthusiasm of a hungry fox approaching a chicken run, and so it was with editing Les's story. He did most of it; it was left for me to expand the chapter on Les's early life, to decide on the content of the chapters and to attempt to make the story flow more easily without using any words that were not in the original. I cannot thank him enough for his initial work, which broke the back of arranging the story for publication.

I must also thank Doctor Robert Kirby, whom I first met through the 207 Squadron Association and who is the historian of the Avro Manchester and its operations, for the unique photographs of the crashed Manchester, taken the day after the raid on Cologne. Others who have provided illustrations include Brian Landers, co-pilot in the sinking of U107, who also provided the Foreword, and a very new acquaintance, John Evans from Pembroke Dock, who provided some welcome information in the latter stages of producing the book.

Finally, luck also came into it when it came to trying to find a publisher, and I must thank Anne Walker and Peter Coles of Airlife Publishing for their advice to both myself and the 201 Squadron Association in our efforts to bring Leslie Baveystock's unique story to the attention of a wider audience.

Alan Lyon
Verl
Germany
February 2001

FOREWORD

I sometimes get asked what I did during the war – not so often these days – and when I say that I flew with the RAF the next question is frequently 'Were you on Fighters or Bombers?'. When I reply that I flew flying boats with Coastal Command the interest usually wanes and the impression is given that this did not involve much action. While this may be generally true compared with the other Commands, I am able to respond with a summary of the story, told here in his own words, of my old skipper, Leslie Baveystock, always known as 'Bav' or 'Bavey'.

I first came across him in the summer of 1944 on 201 Squadron based at Pembroke Dock in West Wales. I was then the second 'dickey' (the modern term is 'co-pilot') to Eddie ('Badly') Bent, a Canadian ex-lumberjack, who could throw a Sunderland around in the air like a Tiger Moth. 'Badly' was coming to the end of his operational tour of 800 hours and Bav took over his crew. We all knew of Bav because he was already the most decorated pilot on the squadron and, I believe, on the station. We knew that he had been awarded the DFM for his part in the first 1,000-bomber raid on Cologne (when he was second pilot on a Manchester to Leslie Manser, who was awarded a posthumous VC) and his subsequent escape without capture after bailing out on the Dutch/Belgian border. Then as a Sunderland captain he had gained the DFC for locating and attacking the German blockade runner *Alsterufer* which was subsequently sunk, and a bar to the DFC for sinking U955 on the night of the D-Day landings. After his latest success he was granted leave to attend his father's funeral, and sadly, while he was away, his crew, under the Flight Commander, Sqn Ldr 'Babe' Ruth, DFC*, failed to return from a sortie in the Bay of Biscay.

As I say, we knew of Bav but we did not really know him. He was not 'gung-ho' – very few Sunderland captains were – but his great strength was in his determination and in his mastery of detail about every aspect of the aircraft and the particular operation. This attention to detail even extended to the private lives of his crew. Bavey and I both had our wives staying unofficially in Pembroke Dock. I say 'unofficially' because in the build-up to D-Day we were not supposed to have wives within twenty or thirty miles of the station. There was, therefore, no 'living-out allowance', so that it was an expensive luxury – although well worth it! Bavey was over six years older than me – this does not seem much as I write this in my 80th year, but to a newly married twenty-three-year-old he was, if not a father figure, certainly avuncular. So I did not take exception when he took me aside one day and mentioned that he did not think it was advisable to have marital relations in the 24 hours before operations as it might affect one's alertness. Mind you, what with flying ops almost every other day and sleeping heavily in between, chance would have been a fine thing.

Whether this contributed to our alertness on 18 August 1944 I do not know, but I was very privileged to have sat beside Bavey when he won an immediate DSO for the sinking of U107.

Brian Landers
January 2001

CONTENTS

Bav in 1944.

PROLOGUE

Sunday, 15 September 1974

Slowly we drove through the beautiful Belgian countryside on the main road to the east, with Bree lying two or three kilometres behind us. It was much bigger than I had anticipated, much, much bigger. Of course, I had never seen it, but had only imagined it as a small Belgian village, not at all what it proved to be.

I looked around at the passing scene with more than the usual interest, searching for any familiar landmark, on the tranquil Sunday afternoon; but there was nothing I could see that stirred the faintest memory. After all, what was there to remember after the passage of thirty-two years?

Not only the years between, I reminded myself, but also my last time here during the hours of darkness, in a world whose lights had already been extinguished for almost three years.

This was a modern dual carriageway, not the country road of my imaginings. Then, ahead and to the right, rose the spire of a small church. Quickly I flashed my headlights to attract our new-found friend René, whose car we had been following. He stopped and we pulled up behind him. I got out and crossed to his car. 'The church,' I said, pointing, 'there was a church somewhere near the farmhouse. I can remember hearing church bells as I lay in the cornfield.' 'How far were you from the sound of the bells? Very far?' he asked. 'No,' I replied, 'it couldn't have been more than a mile at the most. Let us ask the priest.'

My wife had now joined us, and we strode up to the small house adjoining the church, and rang the bell. After a few minutes, the local priest appeared at the door. I was quickly reminded just how lucky we had been to meet René. With much pain and head scratching, I could get by with my schoolboy French; but these people spoke Flemish. So, thankfully, Betty and I stood listening as René and the priest talked, amid much pointing farther towards the east.

A few moments later René turned to us in triumph. 'You are right,'

1

he said, 'there is a family named Nijskens who own a farm about another kilometre along the road, where the double road finishes and becomes a single lane again.' After much handshaking we took our leave of the priest and continued our journey, feeling that soon our quest would end.

Back in the car again we followed René, and in no time at all the junction of the roads appeared ahead. We got out and looked around, only to find that there were two farmhouses, both fairly close. 'Can you remember which one it was?' asked René. I looked closely at them both, but again, nothing struck a chord in my memory. Then I remembered I had come into the farmhouse from the rear, and when I left, it had been in the dead of night; but what was there that I could possibly remember? I glanced up at the sun. Yes, I had come from the east, and the farm where I had hidden was on the north side of the road. So it had to be the second one. 'It must be that one,' I said, pointing to it. 'I am sure that I will be able to remember once I have a look at the courtyard at the rear.'

So, slowly our party walked up a farm track that led round the back. We ignored the sweeping driveway that curved round to the beautiful front part of the house, for this would tell me nothing. Then we rounded the curve in the track and looked into the courtyard surrounded by the usual cluster of farm buildings. All was quiet, for this was Sunday afternoon. For a moment I stood and looked, almost in disbelief. Somehow, nothing seemed quite real. I knew at once that this was the place, but I just could not absorb it all. It was like watching a film of long ago, in which the producer was telling the story with a sequence of flashbacks. I looked at the gateway that led to the farmland behind, its gate now hanging uselessly to one side. This was the entrance through which two dishevelled figures, wet through, tired and hungry, had found their way on that rainy Sunday morning more than half a lifetime ago. I think I half imagined that I would see those two same figures, and the woman, her eyes filled with surprise, gesticulating and, pointing to the wings on one of their blue battledresses, saying, 'RAF! RAF!'

No! This was 1974, not back in the dim past of 1942 when the world was an altogether different place. I turned to the others, feeling strangely excited. 'This is it, all right. That's the door into the outbuilding where we first hid and where I dried my clothes. And that door leads into their parlour where, after dark, we listened to the BBC account of the big raid on Cologne the night before: the raid on which our aircraft was one of forty-four reported as missing.'

We walked to the parlour door and René knocked. A moment or

two passed and then the door opened. An elderly man, white-haired and with a slight stoop from his years of bending and milking cows, appeared. He looked at us all with surprise, and René spoke to him. 'Are you Mr Nijskens, Sir?'

'Yes, yes, what do you want?'

'Sir, I bring you a visitor from thirty-two years ago', replied René with a smile.

I had been looking intently at the old man as René spoke, and I knew long before he replied that he was the younger brother in the family. Not only his face, but also his mannerisms and the way he moved convinced me. After the many long years he had changed but little. I had always carried a picture of him in my mind, for he had a rather elfish humour when he was younger, and despite a heavy frame, he moved quickly and lightly.

As René finished speaking, the old man turned to me. I clasped his hand and shook it vigorously. It was a marvellous moment, and he was so obviously delighted to see me. How I wished that we both spoke the same language so that I could adequately thank him. Instead, I could only continue to hold his hand in both of mine in a vain attempt to express my feelings.

After a few moments, Mr Nijskens resumed his conversation with René and we were all invited inside. We sat around the table and were provided with cool drinks. I looked round the room and the memory of it all came flooding back, as though it had been only yesterday. The room had changed little: the radio in the corner had gone, as had the old black stove that stood against the wall. A modern clean-burning model had now taken its place, but the atmosphere was the same. There was an indefinable feeling one often has in older buildings that seemed to defy itself.

Then René turned to us and began to translate his conversation. 'When you first arrived,' he said, 'Mr Nijskens was not completely sure about you, but when you turned your head he recognised the shape of your nose, and the fact that you had done all the talking with his brother. You were very excited then, and eager to escape; while your friend had hurt his foot and was a little frightened.'

We stayed for a while as René chatted away in Flemish, turning to us occasionally to interpret what he had learnt. We were sorry to hear that the woman who had first taken us in was in hospital and danger-ously ill with heart trouble. I had always believed that she was the brothers' sister-in-law, but in fact, she was their older sister. Nijskens's brother, the only one of the family who spoke a little English, was dead, killed by a bull on their farm shortly after the

3

war. Their parents had died many years ago. They had been in their seventies when I had last sat in that very same room. The news of his brother's death gave us quite a shock. What a tragic death for a man who had risked his and his family's lives by taking us in when the Germans were searching for us. This was a risk willingly undertaken without thought of gain or anything, except just the need to extend help to fellow beings in trouble; a Good Samaritan if ever there was one.

At last it was time to go. Mr Nijskens still ran the farm, and the cows were ready for milking. With his wife away, he had to do all the chores himself. So we rose and solemnly bade farewell. I clasped both his hands in mine, holding them tightly, and for a moment no language was necessary. Betty held his hand and kissed his cheek, and her gratitude to him required no other expression. Then with a few more handshakes from René and his friend, we had gone.

On our return to Zonhaven, we were immensely happy. Both Betty and I felt how wonderful it was to have made contact with the one person alive who, more than anyone else, had contributed to my escape back to England so long ago. An escape that not only saved me from three long tedious years in a prisoner of war camp, but also gave me another three years in the RAF, where my eternal good luck stayed with me; luck that resulted in a commission and four decorations, and a store of wonderful memories that would keep me warm in the twilight years of my life ahead.

We went to bed that night in the small caravan we had brought over from England. I dozed off to sleep determined to make a record of all the events that had culminated in the day's visit: a record that will not only give me much gratification, but someday may bring a smile and a chuckle to my grandchildren.

Auckland
September 1974

Chapter 1

My Early Days

On 17 October 1914, a few weeks after the start of the First World War, a new squadron was formed, known then as No. 1 Squadron, Royal Naval Air Service. On 1 April 1918, when the Royal Flying Corps joined with the RNAS to become the fully independent Royal Air Force, this squadron became No. 201 Squadron, RAF. Seven months later, on 5 November, I was born at No. 13 Rosemont Avenue, North Finchley. The house still stands today, but, for some reason or other, it seems to have shrunk terribly since I lived there. The two events were entirely unrelated; but thirty years later, in 1944 I was a member of that squadron, wining and dining as best as we could during wartime at the squadron's thirtieth birthday celebration, and a happy day it was for me, to be sure, for I had just completed my tour of operational flying which, due to the fortunes of fate, had been crowned with success. With the all the signs pointing to a fairly early end to the war, I guessed that with any luck at all I could look forward to being one of the fortunate few to survive the conflict. A further thirty years later, once again I was with my old squadron. Now a civilian, I was sitting at the VIP table as the squadron celebrated its Diamond Jubilee, wearing my miniature medals for the first and probably last time.

In the two wonderful days spent with 201, I was allowed at the controls of a Nimrod aircraft and flew it manually for some twenty minutes or more. Apart from the uncertainty of a different cockpit layout, I had no difficulty in holding steady courses on various compass headings. Despite the thirty years' lapse, I felt that with a few days' intensive training I would be fit again for a permanent job with them. Wishful thinking? Well, yes, perhaps so. But wait, what's happened to all the years between 1914 and 1974? I am forgetting already where my story begins.

I was named Leslie Harold, the Harold after my mother's brother. Alas, the name Leslie came from I know not where. I had a brother named Sidney, who was sixteen months older than me, but being the baby, I always got the maternal protection given to all last offspring, however big they grow. My young days were happy days, for my parents were fond of each other and our home was security for us. However, on starting school I developed a crippling stammer, especially when meeting new faces.

My father trained as a cabinet-maker and upholsterer, and ultimately he went into business making folding furniture such as deckchairs and card-tables in a factory situated in the East End of London. My brother had started at a Council school, but, although short of money, my parents transferred him to St Michael's Convent in North Finchley, where I was to join him. The nuns were kindness itself, but I was a small impressionable child and overawed by a huge picture of Christ that hung in the classroom. Quite unintentionally, the well-meaning nuns made me feel a bit of an outcast. Of course, most of the children were Roman Catholics, while my brother and I were C of E.

When my brother Sidney was eleven years old he left the Convent and went to Christ's College, Finchley, and I followed him a year later. Whilst I liked things such as geometry and algebra, I hated such subjects as history and French, so I didn't get very far up the educational ladder. One thing I did excel at was shooting. In the School Cadet Corps, I progressed into the School Team and gained my marksman's badge. This badge was the first step in building up my confidence. My scholastic progress at the college made it apparent I would have little chance of matriculating. Therefore, in 1930, at sixteen I left to join my father's business. It was about this time that I first met Betty, whose first name was for years spelt Elisabeth with an 's'; for years after it caused no end of bother making sure that everyone got the 's' right, especially on legal documents. It wasn't until some thirty years later that she got hold of her birth certificate and found that she had actually been registered with a 'z'. Even our marriage certificate was incorrect!! I met her originally because her stepfather was a business friend of my father and our families encouraged our friendship. Our romance did not start to blossom until some four years later when she came to visit me in hospital after an operation. We became engaged in the summer of 1937 and immediately began looking around for a house. A brand new one in Whetstone caught our eyes, and having put down a deposit, it was arranged that we would take it over in March 1938. Our original idea was that we would get married in June or July of that year, but once the house was ours we could see no point in waiting, and got married on 23 April.

Sidney had been a signaller in the School Cadet Corps, and his hobby was amateur radio, in which he graduated to become a radio 'ham.' He had sat up all night listening to the Morse signals coming from the ill-fated airship R101 telling of the storm that they were going through before the crash at Beauvais in France. He joined the Wireless Branch of the RNVR and completed a two-week course at Portsmouth. When the Munich crisis burst upon us in 1938, he, like many others, was mobilised for a time

The excitement of buying the house and our first year of marriage was heightened by the threat of war hanging over us, so in the latter part of 1938 I joined the new Auxiliary Fire Service, and at the same time put up an Anderson air raid shelter in the garden. At the end of August 1939, Sidney was again called up with the Reservists. This time, it would be six years before he finally came home, because the war started on 3 September.

During this period of inactivity the only real war was at sea. Almost at once the German U-boats commenced their attacks upon our shipping, and all our efforts and thoughts were with our Navy. Sidney had reported to Portsmouth and had been posted immediately as a full crew member to the destroyer HMS *Antelope*. Within hours they were at sea, and at the time of the actual declaration of war, he was far out in the Atlantic. He was one of four wireless operators, the other three being regulars, and at once found himself doing full watches of four hours on and four hours off. Unfortunately, he suffered from seasickness, and there were times when he didn't care if he lived or died. But survive he did, looking forward only to the day he would next be on leave. While on convoy duty *Antelope* destroyed two enemy U-boats. Listening on the hydrophones as the damaged vessels sank deeper, the operators could hear muffled explosions as the watertight compartments gave way under the enormous water pressure.

What with being over twenty-five years of age, in charge of our mill and a member of the Auxiliary Fire Service, I would have had no difficulty in being exempted from National Service when my age group was called up. Yet, somehow I felt that I just had to go into one of the actual fighting services. I don't really know why I felt this way, maybe just pride, with patriotism thrown in, or perhaps just for the sheer hell of it. The decision was hard to make because I neither fancied leaving Dad in the lurch nor wanted to leave Betty at this particular time, as she was pregnant by the end of 1939 and was expecting a baby by the next October. Without even having to talk very much about it to either Betty or my Dad, we seemed to arrive at an understanding that I should not try and get exempted but pick the service I wished to join, if at all possible. I realise now, much more than I did then, that they were both utterly unselfish in not trying to persuade me otherwise, or making me feel bad about my decision.

My first fancy, as with thousands of other young men, was to join the RAF. At the recruiting centre at Edgware they had all the volunteers they needed and were being too choosy to accept the likes of me. So I decided on the Navy, and naturally thought to become a wireless operator like Sidney. So I started taking lessons in Morse code from an old radio ham, a friend of Sid.

At home, we were treated to a series of defeats that seemed never ending, culminating in the fall of France and the epic of Dunkirk. The French surrender was our most serious setback. We relied heavily on the French Navy to help us contain the Italians and keep the Mediterranean open for our shipping heading to the Far East. It now seemed obvious that unless America joined in the war, we would never have a chance of regaining a foothold on the Continent. This necessitated a whole new look at our strategy; even to the man in the street, it seemed as if our only hope lay in the Royal Navy and RAF. We were a defeated nation, and many seriously wondered if our leaders would not be compelled to sue for peace on the best terms available.

That such did not happen can be attributed to one man – Winston Churchill. He rallied the nation as never before. His famous 'We shall fight on the beaches' speech thrilled every living soul old enough to understand in our beleaguered island. A determination to fight on against overwhelming odds came to us all.

The Battle of Britain was still to be fought and won, and at this time I was still working in our factory with my father. I was still doing three nights a week duty with the Auxiliary Fire Service, and when the night raids on the City of London started, I fully expected to be sent along to assist with the rest of the regular firemen. The Auxiliary firemen comprised two groups: one of unpaid volunteers, like myself, who still worked at daytime jobs; and the other group who had given up their usual jobs and worked full time. The authorities decided to send only full-time men into Central London, leaving unpaid members on standby in their own suburbs. Thus the volunteers could get a few hours' rest at night and still do their own jobs the next day. I was lucky not to be called into Central London, for it was terribly arduous work, fraught with danger, not just from the fires that raged everywhere, but also from the bombs and the falling shrapnel from our AA guns. Yet it began to rile me, and I looked forward to joining the Navy as Sidney had done.

In August, I received notice to attend a medical examination before being called up. I went along with dozens of others and was finally assessed Grade 1. I was then interviewed by the Officer-in-Charge of the Navy entrants. I told him that my brother was with HMS *Antelope* as a wireless operator, and that I was learning the Morse code. Somehow or other no mention was made of my civilian job, or the fact that I was in the Fire Service. At the end of the interview, I was told I had been accepted. I was given an official number and sent on deferred service, awaiting entry into the Wireless School. Feeling quite pleased, I went home and carried on with my job.

However, within a few days the RAF announced that they required a large number of men for aircrew duties, and that they would be interviewing volunteers immediately. Again, my thoughts turned to the RAF, and I wondered if I could manage to get a transfer, despite the fact that I was now more or less in the Navy. I took a couple of hours off from work and went over to the recruiting centre at Edgware, where I told the RAF staff my story. Much to my surprise, they seemed quite interested and agreed to put me forward to the Aircrew Selection Board; but it would require the formality of getting the Navy to release me. So the RAF officer took me along to the Navy Department and asked for my release. I think he assumed that this was just a formality, and gave the impression that, after all, the RAF at that time was more important that the RN. In fact, we got no change at all, and were told quite flatly that I was in the Navy for better or worse, and in the Navy I would have to remain.

I returned with the officer to his office, amid many apologies for his failure to accommodate me. Then he had a sudden thought: 'You know,' he said, 'I reckon we can beat the Navy yet.' He went on to explain how the prewar method of joining the RAF Volunteer Reserve (VR) still existed, alongside the compulsory call-up system. He said if I liked to sign up as a volunteer it would be okay, as long as I was accepted and actually in uniform before the Navy recalled me from my temporary leave.

Without wasting any time I filled in the necessary forms and had a further identical medical. Only one other formality remained, and that was to get the application approved by the National Service Officer. That was where we came unstuck; for in my application papers I had filled in precisely what my job was. Whereupon the officer told me that, being over twenty-five years of age and foreman of the furniture mill, I was in a reserved occupation and could not join up at all. For a few seconds the three of us just looked at each other. 'Well,' I said, 'that's just bloody silly', and groping in my pocket I pulled out the form the Navy had earlier given me and threw it on the desk. 'Have a look at that,' I said, 'and you'll see that if I can't get into the RAF, I'll be in the Navy anyway.' The National Service chap now seemed very sympathetic. Finally, it was agreed that I would fill in another set of forms, stating that I was in charge of the 'office', and not the mill. This way he had no objection.

A few days later I was summoned to RAF Headquarters, where I had another, much stricter, aircrew medical examination, followed by a short written examination on elementary maths. I sailed through these first two hurdles, and then joined a queue of other fellows, mainly younger than myself, who were waiting to go before the Selection Board. Earlier, we had been asked to indicate the choice of aircrew category we wanted. As we chattered together awaiting our turn for interview, it was obvious that everyone, including me, had opted for pilot as first choice, with most opting for navigator as second choice. In my case, I had opted for wireless operator/air gunner (WOp/AG) as second choice.

Unbeknown to me, this was a stroke of luck, for at the start of the interview each applicant was asked if he would accept the category of air gunner. As this was known to be the most dangerous job for aircrew, especially as a rear gunner, some fellows flatly refused. Immediately, they were rejected from aircrew duties, their mettle being automatically suspected. It was also my good fortune to have the magic letters 'VR' boldly marked across the top of the form in red pencil. This, in the eyes of the Board, was definitely one up on being a conscript.

After seeing some nine or ten fellows go through their interviews, we gleaned that only about one in five had been accepted for training as a pilot, the others either as navigators or WOp/AGs. At last, my turn came, and I went in quite resigned to my fate. I was told to take a seat facing three middle-aged officers. The officer in the centre, presumably the President, asked all the questions, while the other two just sat and listened. He looked at my papers, and asked me about my job and what I was like at sport. I answered as directly as I could, praying that I would show no trace of my earlier stammer. Then, having another look at my papers, he asked why I had opted for WOp/AG as my second choice. I replied that I was learning Morse, which seemed to impress them all.

He then remarked on my membership of the Cadet Corps and asked what sort of a shot I was. I paused, not knowing quite how honest I should be, for I reckoned I would definitely be a gunner if I told them I had been captain of our shooting team. So I just shrugged in an offhand sort of manner, and told them that I had been awarded the National Rifle Association's Skilled Shot Certificate. All three officers nodded their heads in approval, and for a moment, it seemed as if the interview was at an end. However, before I was dismissed I decided to say a few words for myself. 'Look,' I said, 'if you accept me as a wireless operator/air gunner, that's fine by me, and I will do my best in that role. My ambition is to be a pilot and I am sure I could do that job too.' My questioner looked up smiling, and asked, 'Have you done any flying at all?' ' No,' I replied, 'but I am sure that, if I had to, I could get a aircraft up in the air and down again. When I was younger, I spent a lot of time working on model aircraft and I know the theory behind it all.'

The interviewing officer merely nodded and told me to wait outside. A bell was rung and a warrant officer appeared and ushered me from the room. A few minutes later he reappeared clutching a small white card in his hand. He gave it to me saying, 'The Board instruct me to inform you that you have been selected for pilot training.' I just couldn't believe it!

Five minutes later I was on my way home, my feet barely touching the ground. Clutched in my hand was the small white card bearing my name and the magic words 'General Duties Pilot'.

Chapter 2

FLYING TRAINING

My call-up came at the end of September. I set off on my journey down to an RAF unit in Babbacombe, near Torquay, which turned out to be a reception centre for future aircrew. We were kitted-out in rough blue uniforms with all sorts of ancillary equipment, which we kept in two white regulation kit bags.

One morning we were all marched to a large public building with a theatre, for a special lecture of which we had been told nothing. After quite a long wait, an officer walked onto the stage, followed by an elderly very senior RAF officer. He was introduced to us with the considerable dignity befitting him, for he was none other than the 'Real Old Grand-daddy' of the Royal Air Force – Marshal of the RAF Lord Trenchard. He gave us one hell of a pep talk about the role that lay ahead of us. He went on to say that if anyone felt at this stage that he could not or might not be able to face up to this task, then he was to say so now. There was no doubt that the Marshal filled us all with the utmost zeal and patriotism.

Our next move was to No. 7 Initial Training Wing (ITW) at Newquay, for an agreeable eight weeks. The fellows I now shared my life with were for the most part a fine bunch. My closest friend was Bill Beck, chiefly I suppose because we were both married and about the same age. We went out together most evenings, making our way down to the local YMCA. There, for the sum of one penny we could buy ourselves a cup of tea.

The course at the ITW I found most interesting. After brushing up on elementary maths, we concentrated on Navigation, Meteorology, Hygiene, Aircraft Recognition, Gunnery and the Morse code. The latter included sending and receiving on both Aldis lamp and 'buzzer'; these I found very easy after my earlier instruction. We also spent much time learning the names of the parts and the method of stripping and reassembling both the VGO (Vickers Gas-Operated) and Browning machine-guns. At that time the Browning was used in both fighters and bombers with hydraulic gun turrets. Ship Recognition was another of our subjects. The course ran quite smoothly, and in spite of our being only 'erks', we were well treated. We had quite a few laughs one way and another, especially with our drill instructor. Exam success resulted in promotion direct to Leading Aircraftman (LAC), which gave us an immediate rise in pay from three shillings and threepence to five shillings and sixpence a day. This promotion was marked by the wearing of a badge with a two-bladed propeller on each tunic sleeve of our uniforms. The extra pay was very welcome, particularly for the married men; with no extra deductions we were two and a half times better off.

Following ITW, I was posted to No. 2 EFTS (Elementary Flying Training School) at Staverton, just outside Gloucester. The airfield itself was in the process of having runways built; so all our flying training took place at a small private airfield just outside Worcester. On alternate days one half of the course would stay at Staverton for ground school, while the other half either journeyed to Worcester by bus, or flew up with instructors in the Tigers. The first time I ever took to the air was on 10 March 1941. It consisted of a thirty-minute flight to Worcester with a rather elderly instructor named Plt Off Smith. We flew in a straight line, more or less, with both the instructor

A de Havilland Tiger Moth, the type of basic trainer in which 'Bav' first took to the air in 1941. *(Philip Jarrett)*

and myself holding the 'stick', to give me an idea of how the aircraft reacted to the controls. Two days later I flew with a Canadian instructor, Flt Lt Messiter. Word had already gone round the course that he regularly failed more pupils than the rest of the instructors put together. Perhaps this assessment did him an injustice, but somehow I doubt it. His ability to fly was not in doubt, but his miserable disposition, combined with an even more miserable temper, was completely demoralising. His rank made him senior to all the other instructors except our CO, who was a squadron leader, but still no match for him.

The result was that after a few lessons with Messiter, I was no closer to being able to fly than I had been after the one lesson with Plt Off Smith. He would nag away about the slightest thing that I did not perform to his satisfaction. After a while, I could not concentrate on what I was supposed to be doing. The rest of the fellows on the course just shook their heads, their usual comment being, 'You poor bastard, thank God I haven't got the blighter.' They all seemed to expect his pupils to fail, and I guess this sense of failure just crept into my bones. To make matters worse, I had just got Betty and Jill with me, living in a suburb of Gloucester, and the first few hours we had together were anything but serene, as I was unable to conceal my worries about my flying from her; it had become very apparent to her that I was extremely unhappy about something.

The next few lessons I had with Messiter were terrible, but on 19 March I was lucky enough to have Plt Off Smith again. As result, I learnt more in forty-five minutes than I had during the whole of the previous week. Each day I dreaded looking at the notice-board to see whom I would be flying with. The next seven lessons were all with my tormentor. On a nice fine day, it was quite simple to fly around once you were airborne, but the comparatively few seconds of both take-off and landing were another matter. The difficulty was that during take-off one is controlling three quite different attitudes of the aircraft, all at the same time. Only practice finally trains the old brain to compute just what is required. At first, this is somewhat tricky, especially for a pupil aged twenty-six, compared with one of nineteen. However, when you are trying to get it all sorted out at the same time as someone whom you have positively grown to hate is bawling in your ear, then it becomes almost impossible.

My seventh lesson with Messiter was on 26 March, and lasted forty-five minutes. By the end of it I was no nearer to going solo than I had been at the beginning of my first lesson – this after eight hours of instruction. Messiter had been concentrating on my landings, doing all the take-offs in quick succession himself. On one occasion I almost flew the aircraft straight into the ground. I had been expecting him to 'talk me down', as he had been doing earlier. 'What the hell do you think you are doing?' he stormed; 'Why didn't you hold off just before we touched down?' 'I was waiting for you to tell me when to do so', I stammered. 'Well, don't wait next time, you idiot' he yelled. 'Hold off as soon as you think you are at the right height.' Then he grabbed the stick, rammed open the throttle and, having climbed to circuit height, handed the controls back to me for another try.

I flew around the circuit, did a quite nice approach and gliding turn, and when I had judged our height to be about right, I eased back the throttle for the landing. Almost at once I knew I was about ten feet too high. Before I had a chance to put on a bit of throttle for a gentle touch-down, he bellowed in my ear, 'What the bloody hell did you do that for?' 'Well,' I shouted back, 'you told me to hold off when I thought I was right, and I did.'

During this exchange of words, he savagely grabbed the stick once more, and put on full throttle. Doing a steep turn at treetop height around the airfield, he brought the aircraft down until the wheels touched the ground. Instead of completing the landing, he flew at full speed across the grass surface, banging the wheels up and down like a jumping kangaroo, shouting with each bump, 'There's the ground. There's the ground. There's the ground.' At the end of this display, he did another split-arse turn around the field, landed and taxied back to the parking area. He then walked away, shaking his head and muttering, 'I can't go on with this much longer, it's time you were scrubbed.'

A very low-spirited airman travelled home that night, and on the bus back from Worcester. I said little to Betty about the day's events, but I did confide in a fellow pupil. It was not Bill Beck, for he had already gone solo and, convinced I would be wiped off the course, had more or less given me up. My confidant was named Caldwell. He was a big, quietly spoken man who had come over from Buenos Aires to volunteer for the RAF. He knew before he came that at his age he might take some time to pick up flying. So, before leaving Argentina he had taken flying lessons and flown solo. He kept quiet about this, telling everybody that he had never flown before. Of course, his instructor had been very pleased with his progress and quite amazed at the way he had apparently picked it up. He too had just gone solo. He was not really my buddy as Bill had been, but I had got to know him fairly well while we were at ITW, and I think we had established a sort of mutual respect.

Caldwell seemed to take the whole thing very seriously and pondered over it that night for some time. He told me later that he thought it was a damn shame that I was stuck with a man like Messiter, and decided that he would do something about it. Although only an LAC, like the rest of us, he decided to seek an interview with the Chief Flying Instructor (CFI) the next morning. He would tell him quite clearly just what his opinion was of people like Messiter.

It was no easy matter to find time during lectures to go through the necessary procedures required to bait the CFI in his den. Without telling me of his intentions he finally managed to get an interview. I doubt whether there was another cadet on the course who would have got away with it, but Caldwell, with his air of authority, managed to carry it off. I don't know what passed between these two men of such unequal rank, but whatever it was Caldwell came out the undoubted winner. The next day when I looked at the notice-board I was delighted to see that I had not been scrubbed, but had been given a new instructor.

Pilot Officer Perkins was the kindest and most able instructor on the staff. Like Caldwell he was a big man in both stature and character, with an important job in civilian life – Member of Parliament for the constituency of Stroud. Flying had been his pre-war hobby. It is thirty-seven years since that day when, with my parachute slung over my shoulder, I walked out with him to our Tiger Moth. With an easy friendly style, more like a father with a six-year-old son, he turned to me as we walked and said, 'What's the matter Laddie? I gather from the CFI that you have run into some sort of difficulty.' I warmed to him at once and blurted out, 'Everything's the matter. I can't keep the aircraft straight on take-off, and don't seem able to co-ordinate all the controls properly. I'm not much better at landing, either.' He gave me a grin and replied, 'Well, we'll just have to see what we can do. Let's have a go at getting the take-offs cleaned up first, shall we?'

We climbed aboard and did our brief cockpit check. A friendly erk swung the prop, and my new instructor trundled the aircraft around the airfield to the take-off position. He turned the aircraft into wind and, pointing to a tree in the distance, told me to put my feet on the rudder bar and concentrate on keeping the aircraft heading straight towards it. 'Just do that, Laddie,' he said, 'and I will take care of the rest of it.' He opened the throttle and we were away. With only the rudder to think about, it was easy to keep the aircraft pointing in the right direction. As soon we were off the ground he handed the controls back to me to carry out a normal approach and landing. I won't say the landing was a good one, but we did get down in one piece.

'Well now,' he said, 'how about trying it all on your own? I am sure you can do it.' With that remark he clasped his hands on the top of his head, just to show me they were nowhere near the controls. With a last look around for other aircraft, I opened the throttle and we were away. This time I found that my dull old brain had finally got the message, and to our mutual delight the circuit was a complete success. 'That's great,' cried Perkins, 'now taxi over to the flight office and we'll have some well-earned lunch.'

Feeling very pleased with myself, I sought out Caldwell to tell him of my good luck in getting Perkins as my instructor. He was as pleased as I was and, unable to restrain his delight, he told me about his interview with the CFI. I could hardly believe that he had had the nerve to do so, and thanked him profusely. I only wish that at the end of the war I could have told him that my good luck in the RAF had followed me from that day onward. However, at the end of our course we had different postings and I never saw him again. He rose to the rank of squadron leader and became Assistant Air Attaché in Lisbon. I heard later that he had been killed in an air crash while flying on duty as a passenger – a sad end for a fine man. A couple of days later, on 2 April 1941, I was due to get my Pre-Solo Test. It was a fine sunny day, and as I took off with Plt Off Day as my instructor, I felt full of confidence. He gave me a thirty-minute check, going over just about everything that might befall me on my solo flight. More spins and recovery, engine failure after take-off and the procedure for fire in the air. Then we landed and walked back to where Perkins was waiting for us. I stood a little to one side as he chatted to Day. Then with his usual cheery smile he called to me saying, 'Off you go, Laddie: just one circuit, then taxi over, pick me up and we will finish the day with some more dual.'

So, in Tiger Moth R5066 I at last became airborne on my own. Mindful of my instructions I just carried out a normal circuit and finished off with a fairly neat landing. I taxied back to pick up my instructor, whose warm smile was only just eclipsed by my own. Thereafter, I received another forty-six dual instruction flights, learning aerobatics, map reading and a host of other exercises.

On 8 May I had my last flight in a Tiger Moth. I would have liked to fly it with my warm-hearted instructor Plt Off Perkins. Instead, it was with my first instructor, Plt Off Smith. We did forty minutes' low flying, which, as many pilots will agree, is the most exciting flying of all. When high in the air one gets no impression of speed, nor are there any ground contours to follow. Good fun can also be had by flying along the tops of cloud layers with a brilliant blue sky above, or

YEAR 1941		AIRCRAFT		PILOT, OR	2ND PILOT, PUPIL	DUTY
MONTH	DATE	Type	No.	1ST PILOT	OR PASSENGER	(INCLUDING RESULTS AND REMA...
—	—	—	—	—	—	—— TOTALS BROUGHT FORW...
MARCH	26	T-MOTH	R-5200	F/LT. MESSITER	SELF	6. MEDIUM TURNS.
						7. TAKING OFF INTO WIND.
						9. GLIDING APPROACH AND LAN...
MARCH	26	T-MOTH	R-5200	F/LT. MESSITER	SELF.	6. MEDIUM TURNS.
						7. TAKING OFF INTO WIND.
						8. POWERED APPROACH AND LAN...
						9. GLIDING APPROACH AND LAND...
MARCH	28	T-MOTH	R-5066	P/O PERKINS	SELF.	7. TAKING OFF INTO WIND
						9. GLIDING APPROACH AND LAN...
MARCH	28	T-MOTH	R-5066	P/O. PERKINS	SELF.	10. SPINNING (2. 4. 2 R)
MARCH	28	T-MOTH	R-5066	P/O. PERKINS	SELF.	7. TAKING OFF INTO WIND.
						9. GLIDING APPROACH AND LAN...
MARCH	28	T-MOTH	T-5623	P/O. DAY.	SELF.	10. SPINNING. (2 L. 2 R.).
MARCH	29	T-MOTH	R-5066	P/O. PERKINS	SELF.	10. SPINNING. (2 L. 2 R.)
APRIL	2	T-MOTH.	R-5066	P/O DAY.	SELF.	TEST.
						I CERTIFY THAT I UNDERSTA...
						THE PETROL, OIL AND IGNITIO...
						SYSTEMS OF THE TIGER MOT...
						sgn. J.H. Bareystock 2nd April
APRIL	2	T-MOTH	R-5066	SELF	—	11 FIRST SOLO ! 1 LANDING.
APRIL	2.	T-MOTH.	R-5066	P/O. PERKINS	SELF.	7. TAKING OFF INTO WIND.
						8. POWERED APPROACH AND LAN...
						9. GLIDING APPROACH AND LANDI...
APRIL	2.	T-MOTH.	R-5066.	SELF	—	7. TAKING OFF INTO WIND.

GRAND TOTAL [Cols. (1) to (10)]
........11......Hrs.......35......Mins.

TOTALS CARRIED FORW...

The author's log, showing his first solo flight on 2 April 1941.

SINGLE-ENGINE AIRCRAFT				MULTI-ENGINE AIRCRAFT						PASS-ENGER	INSTR/CLOUD FLYING [Incl. in cols. (1) to (10)]	
DAY		NIGHT		DAY			NIGHT					
DUAL	PILOT	DUAL	PILOT	DUAL	1ST PILOT	2ND PILOT	DUAL	1ST PILOT	2ND PILOT		DUAL	PILOT
(1)	(2)	(3)	(4)	(5)	(6)	(7)	(8)	(9)	(10)	(11)	(12)	(13)
·35												
·40												
·45												
·30												
·25												
·15												
·25												
·15												
·30												
·5												
·40												
	:25											
·	·30											
(1)	(2)	(3)	(4)	(5)	(6)	(7)	(8)	(9)	(10)	(11)	(12)	(13)

Summary for MARCH 1941.
Unit NO.2. E.F.T.S. Aircraft
Date 29 March 1941. types
Signature L.H. Baveystock

1 TIGER MOTH 9·50
2
3
4

I certify that I, LH Baveystock, have been instructed in airscrew swinging in accordance with the standard procedure as laid down in A.P. 129. (F.T.M Part I. Chap II Par 24) and Reserve instruction NO.9 Section 2.

signed. LH Baveystock

19

perhaps a full moon. That sort of flying was to come later, and not during my Tiger Moth days.

My stay at No. 2 EFTS came to an end after I had completed just over sixty hours' flying, of which twenty-six hours had been solo. We were given an assessment of Below Average, Average, Above Average or Exceptional. I got an Average, for nobody ever got a Below Average assessment, which would have meant being scrubbed automatically. I never met Perkins or any members of the school staff again, though I did hear from him late in 1944. Another spell of leave followed the Staverton course, but soon I was back at Staverton awaiting my next posting. This turned out to be Wilmslow, near Manchester, a holding station where we were kitted-out with khaki drill uniforms, causing much speculation as to our next destination. Most of us thought it might be to somewhere tropical, but the more experienced chaps shook their heads, pointing out that we had not been given pith helmets. So Canada was the likely place, which proved to be correct.

At last, we set off for Liverpool, where we embarked in a 10,000 ton armed merchant ship and set sail for Canada. Our ship was the sister-

An Airspeed Oxford. *(Philip Jarrett)*

ship of the ill-fated *Jervis Bay*, and our captain was the brother of its commander. The gallantry of the *Jervis Bay*'s crew in giving their convoy a chance to scatter and escape is now part of naval history.

We spent just under a week crossing the Atlantic, and, strange to say, it was a happy week. No storms or enemy ships were encountered. The ship was well run and the Navy chaps kept her spotlessly clean. I believe the crew much preferred making a fast trip across the ocean with just 500 or so aircrew, compared with their usual task of creeping along at slow speed with a straggling convoy to protect. A very good spirit existed between the crew and us airmen, the main reason for which I did not understand until our return journey later in the year. Soon we were in Halifax, where we disembarked and boarded a train to take us to the West. With everybody aboard the train began the five-day journey across Canada. Finally, we arrived at the airbase at Moosejaw in Saskatchewan. Harvard aircraft, used for training fighter pilots, were based there and I stayed only a couple of days. Here all our reports were studied and we were divided into two equal groups. One half remained for training on the Harvards, the rest of us went on to Medicine Hat in Alberta.

Whereas Moosejaw was under the command of the RCAF, No. 34 Service Flying Training School (SFTS) at Medicine Hat was an RAF station, with many RAF personnel. The school was equipped with the Airspeed Oxford, a small twin-engined aircraft, designed especially for us older and more sedate 'multi-engined types'. To make things even easier for us, the days were long and ideal for flying. It was a beautiful new camp, set in desert country a couple of miles from the town.

Our arrival had been on 21 June, and two days later I had my first flight with an instructor named Flt Lt Hunter. The Oxford was a clean, speedy machine, which responded well to the controls; though we did have one problem with them regarding three-point landings. This was because the airfield, which had sealed runways, was over 2,000 feet above sea level; also the temperature on the base was often 106 ° F. The high altitude and the heat made the air very thin, thus reducing aircraft engine-power and lift from the wings.

On my first flight, I did not take the controls, which was fine, for I could enjoy just looking down on this strange new country. The more I looked, the more it became apparent that this part of our training was not going to be at all difficult. On landing, I returned to our quarters, where I met an air of gloom that seemed to have descended on my colleagues, who mostly lay around on their beds. When I asked what was wrong, they pointed to the empty bed next to my own. A married fellow like me had occupied it. I noticed at once that the picture of

LAC Les Baveystock in Canada at No. 34 SFTS, Medicine Hat, waiting for an instructor to give him his first flight in an Airspeed Oxford on 23 June 1941.

his wife that stood on his small locker had gone, and so had every article of his kit. Then I was told that both he and his instructor had 'bought it' that afternoon; but the circumstances of their deaths were unexplained.

The flying itself was enjoyable and posed no great problems for any of us, although we did have to learn to fly on one engine. This, perhaps, was not as simple as one might imagine, as when an engine fails the aircraft quickly goes into a flat spin if corrective action is not taken at once. The other new thing we had to learn was, of course, night flying. Of this I did some six hours forty minutes dual and three hours twenty minutes solo. In reality, only half of this time was, in the air, as duration times were taken from first take-off to last landing. All the time taxiing around the airfield and waiting one's turn to get airborne was included.

I don't think I did more than five or six solo landings at night, and this was around an airfield ablaze with light, as was the town of Medicine Hat alongside. In some ways it was absurd to call it night flying, and it did little to prepare us for flying in blacked-out Britain under wintry conditions and poor visibility.

Although I had lost Bill Beck, who had been one of the few married men selected for fighter training, I soon palled up with two other airmen, named Blake and Brazenor. The three of us would occasionally go into town together and treat ourselves to an enormous T-bone steak. After our wartime diet in England, these were just about as good as a blood transfusion. Later, we would visit the local 'hop', a large wooden building called the Moose Hall, and chat up some of the local talent. I guess my dancing improved a lot while I was in Canada, a fact not lost on Betty when I returned to England. Both the girls and older people of Medicine Hat were very good to us. As the camp had not been opened long, they had had little time to get sick of us.

One of the highlights of the SFTS course was a visit by the Duke of Kent. On the day of his inspection I was attending a navigation class in which we were doing a plotting exercise. During our exercise the door of the classroom suddenly opened, and the Station Warrant Officer (SWO) entered and bellowed, 'Class, atten-shun!' In strode the Duke in full uniform. I was in the front row and the Duke strode straight up to me. I was immediately struck by his friendly manner and youthful charm. He asked me what I thought of flying in Canada, and how I found navigating in the prairie country. I told him I thought it was quite easy, nothing like as difficult as in Britain. Appearing amused, he turned to the members of his staff saying, 'Here is a fellow who thinks it is easy to navigate in the country.' He talked to other fellows in the class; then with a cheery wave he left, followed by his entourage. Even the most sceptical of our cadets agreed what a fine fellow he was, and how much we appreciated his visit. The main feature of the last day of the course was the 'Wings Parade'. We lined up in front of the CO and the school staff. On the table lay a box full of RAF 'wings,' together with separate piles of sergeants' stripes and white armbands. The proceedings began with my name being called out by the SWO. I strode up to the CO and saluted. 'Congratulations', he said, pinning the wings on to my tunic. Then he handed me my stripes and shook my hand. I stepped back, saluted and returned to my place in line. We had completed ten weeks' intensive work with only Sundays off, and yet we did not get any local leave.

We left Halifax and joined a convoy of about forty ships of all varieties. It took two miserable weeks to cross the Atlantic, and I spent each night on one of the staircases. To rub salt into our wounds, some of our course, who had obtained commissions, were also on the ship, but unlike us sergeant pilots, they had cabins to sleep in. They were also given the exclusive use of the first-class facilities.

Looking back, I think that fortnight at sea was my worst experience in the RAF – poor food, little to read and nothing else to do. The weather was lousy and some of the ships so slow that the convoy at times was barely making five knots. However, I did pal up with a fellow from New Zealand a year or two younger than myself. He was a quiet, solid type of farmer who came from the backwoods, and had never before left his home country. His name was Stratford Judd, known as 'Strat'. He too was a sergeant pilot, and very homesick. Like all New Zealand airmen he was a volunteer. I often wondered what made men like him leave their country to fight and perhaps die on the opposite side of the world.

At first light four or five days out from Britain, it was reported that an RAF aircraft had arrived and was patrolling around the convoy. Very soon all eyes were on a Coastal Command Whitley aircraft, which was circling around us. The sight was a tonic for everyone on board, for we believed that no U-boat would now be able to get within torpedo range of us without being spotted. From then on we had continuous air cover provided by the RAF, and I marvelled at my first sight of a Sunderland flying boat when it arrived over us. What an aircraft, I thought, and what more worthwhile job could one possibly have than to guard some forty or so ships with hundreds of crew and passengers all depending on you. 'That's the job I fancy', I thought to myself.

We arrived in Liverpool and were sent down to a holding unit at Bournemouth. Within a couple of days all the British airmen were given leave, but those from the Dominions were not so lucky. For the authorities could not let the many hundreds of them roam freely, as previous experience had shown that almost to a man they would head for London. There they would simply increase the strain on the under-staffed hotels, which were already bursting at the seams. The only exceptions were for men with relatives in England to stay with. So I invited Strat to stay with Betty and me at Raleigh Drive. Armed with this invitation, he was given leave and spent a week with us.

My next posting was to No. 14 Operational Training Unit (OTU) at Cottesmore in Rutland. The summer was now over and the country-side had taken on the bleak look of winter as I journeyed north to Oakham. My mind was on the unknown that lay ahead of me, particu-larly on the type of aircraft I would now fly. It would be the aircraft that I would have to fly on bombing operations, and in which I would either live or die. My wish, if I had one at all, was that it would be the Wellington. This had been found to be a tough reliable aircraft, whose geodetic construction had been able to sustain terrific damage and still get home safely. In the transport on the way to Cottesmore, I heard the drone of an aircraft overhead and I craned my neck around trying to see what it might be. When it came in view my heart sank, for it was a Hampden, an aircraft I knew little or nothing about except its ghastly nickname, 'The Flying Coffin'. It was a product of the Handley Page Aircraft Company, and can only be described as an ugly-looking machine that I never took kindly to. Yet aircrew who had survived a tour of operations on them thought they were marvellous. Later, I was sure it was the pilot who survived his tour who was the marvellous part of the team, not the aircraft. So, in quite a confused state of mind I arrived at Cottesmore where I commenced the most harrowing and nerve-racking few months of my entire Service career.

Avro Ansons. *(Philip Jarrett)*

The course was one of three undergoing operational training. It consisted of sixteen pilots, together with sixteen navigators (or observers as they were then known) and thirty-two WOp/AGs. This provided for a Hampden crew of four airmen. The pilots were broken up into three groups: there were five in my group who later always flew on the same day. We did not team up with any other particular crew members until the final part of our training, when we undertook long night flights. Our training began with a series of lectures, following the standard pattern of ground training.

As I was married, I was given a living-out pass, and managed to find digs on a farm in the village of Market Overton. The conditions were primitive by our standards and the landlady a miserable tyrant who only took us in to avoid having evacuees.

After the first two weeks of lectures we commenced flying. We began on Avro Ansons that were used mainly for instructing navigators. These slow, cumbersome aircraft were just about as different from a Hampden as chalk from cheese. They had absolutely no vices and could be flopped around the sky with absolute safety. Crashes in them were virtually unknown. They certainly gave us a chance to learn our way around the countryside in daytime, and at night to get used to the enormous difference of flying in blacked-out Britain compared with the conditions that existed in Canada.

My first flight in an Anson was with Sergeant Beldam and a couple of gunners. Our instructor was a young pilot officer named Deas. Of course he wasn't really an 'instructor' at all, just another young fellow with scarcely more flying hours than we had ourselves. The instruction was negligible, for he just flew the aircraft around the circuit, made a landing and then handed the controls over, first to me, then to Beldam. After a couple of circuits each, he nodded and said, 'You're okay. Let me off, do a few more circuits each and then come in for lunch.' So, after only one hour and forty minutes between us, Beldam and I were qualified to fly Ansons on our own. Three days later, on 18 November, we flew again as co-pilots on a three-hour trip, taking with us three pupil navigators on a map-reading exercise to RAF Finningley. From then on we made several more trips to train either navigators or wireless operators.

Meanwhile, on the ground we were given instruction to prepare us for the day when we would first fly a Hampden. Not only was it tricky to fly, but it also had the drawback of not being able to provide dual-flying instruction to a new pilot. As the fuselage was no wider than a single-seat fighter, it was impossible to fit two men into the cramped cockpit. Access to the latter was by means of a sliding hatch rather like that of a Spitfire.

To overcome this problem a Hampden had been rigged up on jacks in one of the hangars. Attached to it in the most Heath Robinson manner were all sorts of wires and pipes, by means of which we could simulate flight while remaining safely on the ground. It was in fact a forerunner of one of today's simulators, although one of today's pilots would have died of laughter if he could have seen our efforts then. Considering it had been thought up and built by virtual amateurs, it was a great achievement and the next best thing to actually flying. Of course the engines did not work, but an electric pump fed pressure into the hydraulic system to operate the flaps. As it was supported by jacks, the undercarriage could also be raised and lowered.

During an instruction period the trainee would don his flying gear, get into the pilot's seat and plug into the intercom. He would then go over his cockpit check, calling out each part of the drill so that the instructor could listen and check him. The pupil would then give the signal for the ground crew to start the power booster. An engine start would be simulated, engine sounds being fed into the pilot's earphones. An erk on the ground would wind a little handle under the aircraft fuselage and the appropriate revs would show up on the engines' rev. counters. Having completed his pre-take-off check, the pupil would lower fifteen degrees of flap (which he could check visually), and then call the imaginary Airfield Control for permission to take off.

When this had been granted, the pupil opened the throttles for his imaginary take-off. As he did so, the boys under the fuselage wound their little handles and the appropriate readings came up on the air-speed indicator and the engine boost gauges. Once take-off speed showed up on the dial, the pilot would call out 'Airborne', and pull back on the control column. He then selected 'wheels up' and the undercarriage would retract, the actual engagement of the locking gear being clearly felt in the cockpit. Engine power would be reduced, the airscrew revs cut back and the flaps raised. As the technician wound the handle controlling the altimeter to show 1,000 feet, the pilot would reduce power and revs to normal cruise speed settings. An imaginary circuit would be completed and the normal landing procedure would be carried out. One part of the take-off procedure was the necessity to practise readiness for the very pronounced swing to starboard, which a Hampden displayed when the throttles were opened fully for take-off. This was much more pronounced than on other aircraft, and was caused by the extremely shallow depth of the rear fuselage, which supported the tailplane and rudders. A more usually shaped aircraft, such as the Wellington, had a deep wide body for its entire length. This augmented the vertical fin surface, allowing a more easily controlled take-off, and much more stable flight when airborne.

Another effect of the Hampden's shallow depth of rear fuselage was an extreme tendency to either 'slip in' or 'skid out' during a turn in the air. The pilot had to keep a watchful eye on his turn-and-bank indicator and apply the appropriate rudder pressure. In the event of a really bad turn, which was very easy to achieve, the aircraft was prone to go into what was known as a 'stabilised yaw.' Under these conditions the aircraft would skid outwards, the rudders would slam over owing to the sideways pressure on them, and the aircraft would go into a flat spin. With twin fins and rudders on the tail of the aircraft, the spin would partially blank off the airflow over the elevator surface and the pilot would almost lose control. The most effective way of getting out of this frequently fatal condition was to open up the throttle of the engine on the inside of the turn. However, the procedure absorbed a fair amount of height before recovery could be made, something aircraft did not have when flying round the circuit before a landing.

Strangely enough, although this peculiar and dangerous characteristic was openly discussed among the pupils of the various courses, our instructors never mentioned it to us. Perhaps it was believed we would lose confidence in the Hampden if we knew too much about it. Or

Handley Page Hampdens. *(Philip Jarrett)*

perhaps the many unexplained crashes around the airfield resulted in the pupils making more of this phenomenon than was warranted.

To return to our captive aircraft in the hangar, training was given on the Hampden's swing to starboard on take-off. When we started our imaginary rush down the runway, one of the airmen on the ground pulled a lever, which operated the rudder bar, and the pupil had to push hard with his left leg to overcome it. Thus we practised each single step of our simulated take-off and airfield circuit ready for the day we would fly a Hampden on our own. Although it was not nearly as good as actual dual instruction in the air, it was nevertheless of immense help in preparing us for the real thing.

My first flight was on 9 December. I did not fly solo but went up on a sort of familiarisation flight with Plt Off Bell as my instructor. I must admit that as I walked with him out to the aircraft I did so with considerable apprehension. I had only been at Cottesmore some five or six weeks and already there had been several fatal crashes. On a bright summer's day, perhaps, I might well have felt differently; but the sky was overcast with a low cloud base, and the visibility was down to about three or four miles. However, Bell was a cheerful man, and having picked up another pupil, a Sgt Gittings, we made our way to where our Hampden stood waiting in its sand-bagged dispersal area.

First making sure that the canvas cover on the pitot head had been removed, Bell slid back the cover on the cockpit and climbed inside. Then Gittings and I climbed into the aircraft through a small escape hatch in the top of the fuselage, directly behind the pilot. This was a windowless compartment astride the main spar. Directly behind was the position for the WOp/AG who operated the two upper guns in addition to his wireless duties. In front of the main spar was a short tunnel, which passed under the pilot's seat and led down to the navigator's position in the nose. During take-off the navigator sat in this position astride the main spar, and here Gittings and I took up our position. By craning our necks we were able to peer into the pilot's cockpit, though we were not able to see very much owing to the armour-plate, which shielded the pilot from a rear attack.

Our instructor went through his cockpit check, relaying each step over the intercom system into which we had plugged our flying helmets. The engines were then started and given a preliminary run-up. Bell gave the signal for 'chocks away' and we taxied out to the opposite side of the grass airfield. Having called control for permission to take off, Bell again ran through his pre-flight check. We had been taught to memorise the letters TMPFFG, which stood for 'Trim', 'Mixture', 'Pitch', 'Fuel', 'Flaps' and 'Gyro.' Then he ran up the engines to clear the sparking plugs, tested the individual ignition circuits, and with a last look around the sky for other aircraft, he turned the aircraft into wind and took off.

Back where Gittings and I were, my first impression was of the noisiness of the Hampden compared with the gentle Anson. We took it in turns to peer around the edge of the armour plate to see what was going on, but really we learnt little of any value. We were up for a total of thirty-five minutes, during which Bell did a couple of circuits and landings. Then we returned to the aircraft dispersal point for a final chat with our instructor. There was little he could say except to tell us it was all quite simple and a 'piece of cake', endeavouring to give us confidence. I must confess I did not feel at all confident as I pedalled home to Market Overton. I kept hoping that perhaps tomorrow, when I would most likely go solo, the weather might be a little better and the visibility not so duff as it had been that day.

The next morning I went straight to the flight office to see the flying programme. Sure enough my name was there for a pre-solo test with Flt Lt Petty and a young WOp named Sgt Tabbutt. Petty went through much the same procedure as followed on the previous day's flight, and after flying around for about thirty minutes he landed and taxied back to the flight office. With a cheery nod he climbed out of the pilot's seat and I took his place. At the take-off position I checked and rechecked my cockpit drill. Having called Flying Control for permission to take off, I turned the aircraft into wind. Then, with a last deep breath to subdue the butterflies in my stomach, I uncaged the gyro, which I had set on zero, and opened the throttles. As the aircraft began to roll forward I found it took almost full port rudder to control the swing; but the condition soon righted itself as the tail lifted clear of the ground and the speed built up. With butterflies now forgotten, we were soon in the air. After completing the take-off and climb drills – undercarriage and flaps up, engine revs and boost reduced – we were at 1,000 feet and already miles from the airfield. Not wishing to get lost on my first circuit, I turned on to a reciprocal course and headed back home. When the airfield came into view I flew around for a while to get the full feel of the aircraft. Then, after contacting Control, I made my first Hampden landing. Happily, it wasn't a bad one, though in those days a good landing was one you could walk away from.

Back at the dispersal point, with the engines turned off, I clambered out of the cockpit and jumped down to the ground. I was followed closely by Sgt Tabbutt excitedly muttering to himself, 'Bloody marvellous, just marvellous.'

'Yes, it wasn't a bad trip, was it?'

'Christ! I wasn't referring to the trip. It's just bloody marvellous to be back on Old Mother Earth again!'

I suppose in most ways that remark just about summed up wartime flying. For it made ordinary life seem wonderful: something to be cherished for each ordinary moment of time that flew so relentlessly by, and frighteningly short for so many of us. At this stage of my writing, I feel that I must put on record the extraordinary fortitude and bravery of the young wireless operators on our course and the many courses before and after us. For it had been the practice of many pupil pilots while flying in poor weather around the airfield itself to get lost. One pilot on an earlier course had got lost while on 'circuits and bumps', and had drifted around in search of his airfield. Much to the consternation of Flying Control, he just disappeared. Four hours later a message was received that he had landed, almost out of fuel, at an airfield in Devon, nearly 200 miles from Cottesmore. From then on, every flight by a pupil pilot, even on first solo, had to carry a wireless operator, together with all his coded 'gen' for the day. If they got lost, they could then call base for a compass course (a QDM) to get them home. In bad visibility, some pilots managed to fly right past their base, causing a repeat of the whole procedure. This may sound unbelievable, but it has to be remembered that all the buildings on airfields were cleverly camouflaged. Also, grass airfields were criss-crossed with spray-painted lines to resemble hedges, making them difficult to recognise.

Two days after my first solo, I flew with another young WOp, Sgt Stait. The exercise was to practise overshooting and landings. Following a couple of normal landings to get my eye in, I came round for an overshoot. If, after a normal approach, a pilot decided he had misjudged his height from the ground, he opened up the throttles to repeat the circuit. For practice, it was normal to just touch the wheels on the ground, then abort the landing and go round again. On this approach I deliberately came in a little too high and made my touchdown about a third of the way across the airfield. As I felt the wheels touch the ground, I opened the throttles fully and eased back on the control column. I fully expected the aircraft to climb straight ahead. Instead, the nose refused to come up, the aircraft swung off to starboard and the starboard wing dipped dangerously close to the ground. I had completely forgotten that my flaps were fully down for landing, instead of the one-third that I needed for take-off. The effect of full power was to pull the nose downwards, and the familiar swing to starboard on take-off made itself felt.

For a few moments I sat in my seat almost petrified. I was afraid that if I pulled back harder on the stick I might well cause the aircraft to stall; if I didn't, I would probably crash. By the time I had regained control and stopped the swing to starboard, we were heading straight towards one of the main hangars, and what to me seemed to be an early exit from life. In those few brief seconds, I must confess I thought nothing of the many airmen working in the hangar ahead, but only of the aircraft and myself.

Happily for me, the Day of Judgement had evidently not arrived. As I pulled back on the stick with all my might, we clawed our way upward, our wheels virtually scraping the hangar roof. As we climbed away I fully expected to hear a bellow on the R/T from the control tower; but all was silent. My WOp/AG said nothing at all, probably because his view to the rear had obscured the danger. For me it was different; I knew only too well that we had come within an ace of death, and the fault was due entirely to my own inability and inexperience. That this state of affairs existed mainly because of the impossibility of getting dual instruction on the Hampden did not enter my head. I saw it only as a measure of my own incompetence, and I wondered if I would be as lucky next time I made such a 'blue'.

The author, navigator and two wireless operators standing in front of a Handley Page Hampden on the last day at Cottesmore OTU.

The next day, the '13th', I flew with Sgt Dotrice, with instructions to climb up high and practise single-engine flying. The cloud base was much higher than usual, and we were able to climb to 7,000 feet before starting the exercise. I knew that with the light load we had, my Hampden should fly quite nicely on one engine, but it was still the easiest thing to get into a stabilised yaw. Though we were only practising, it was quite different from the real thing, as in an emergency I needed only to open up the 'dead' motor to regain control. At our high altitude, there could be practically no risk. In any event we could bale out, as getting out of the pilot's cockpit of a Hampden was quite easy. The one snag was the close proximity of an airscrew on either side of the cabin. I learned later how it should be done from one of the instructors who had actually baled out. This was to slide back the cockpit canopy, undo the seat belt, and thrust the control column sharply forward. The pilot would then shoot straight up and out, well clear of the rotating blades.

Between my first flight as skipper on a Hampden on 10 December and Christmas, I flew a total of ten flights, the last one being on Christmas Eve. As I pedalled home to Market Overton I was thankful that I was still in one piece. I now had two days off, and I would be out of danger for at least that short period.

On 27 December I reported back to the station and, as usual, went straight to the notice board in our flight office. I was scheduled for my first attempt at night-flying in blacked-out Britain. It was to be with Plt Off Linacre, in an Anson, an aircraft which now seemed so friendly and desirable after my recent trips in a Hampden. However, when the flight took place I was, at first, completely shattered. For, unlike Medicine Hat, with its rows of 'gooseneck' flares burning brightly along each side of the long sealed runway, we had only a single line of small cats-eye lights set into the grass airfield.

Cottesmore was in the process of getting a Drem lighting system. This consisted of a circle of lights around the airfield with a radius of about three-quarters of a mile, each light being fixed to the top of a tall pole. At points in line with the flare path there were funnel lights to guide aircraft in. Once in the funnel, the flare-path lights could be picked up, and from then on landing was comparatively easy. There were also glide-path indicators to show the correct angle of approach. The indicator, which stood to one side of the start of the flare path, displayed three beams of light. The top beam was coloured amber, indicating too high an approach. The middle beam was green, which indicated that a correct approach was being made. The lower beam was red, and the signal to increase power to get back into the green beam with all possible haste. This was a simple yet excellent device that in some ways made positioning of the aircraft easier by night than by day. Fortunately for us, the Drem funnel lights were in operation and were a great help in picking out the flare path. We made a normal approach for landing, but as we neared the ground I found the small electric lights a poor substitute for the gooseneck flares we had used in Canada.

During those early days at Cottesmore there were many crashes, as I have already mentioned. Fortunately for our morale, they had all been suffered by courses ahead of our own. Then, as we had come to dread, the day came when a Hampden, flown by one of our group, crashed and burnt out, killing its pilot and WOp. As usual, it was quite near to the airfield and while I was flying locally, also in a Hampden. I did not see the crash occur, but only the ominous cloud of smoke rising from close to one of the nearby farms. I flew over, but it was apparent that nobody could have survived either the crash or the ensuing fire. We never knew what caused the crash, but guessed it must have been our dreaded enemy, the stabilised yaw. Had it been anything else, I felt sure that the pilot, Plt Off Webb, would have had time to call on his R/T and warn Control of any problem. A stabilised yaw at circuit height would have given him only a few seconds before the aircraft hit the ground so disastrously.

Of the thirty-eight airmen killed while I was at Cottesmore, on my own course of sixteen pilots no fewer than five were killed in aircraft crashes, together with their five young WOp/AGs. When I recall those grim winter days, I wonder how we ever managed to overcome our daily fears for survival. I guess there was no alternative, and all the resilience of youth was on our side.

Throughout January the weather was consistently bad, and I managed only some seventeen hours of flying time. Local flying such as circuits and bumps was now behind us and we had moved on to cross-country flying and high- and low-level bombing. This was as much for the navigators' and WOps' benefit as it was for the pilots'. Our bombing training was carried out with 11 lb practice bombs, which exploded with a white puff of smoke to mark their point of impact. Although you would not want to be near one when they went off, they were not dangerous to the aircraft itself. Our exercise on 29 January was to carry 500 lb bombs that we were to drop on the live range at Holbeach. Although there isn't much danger in carrying bombs, taking off with a load of high explosives is rather nerve-racking for a pilot who is comparatively inexperienced. I had Plt Off Williams as my navigator and Sgt Willis as my WOp/AG. I remember that I was as apprehensive as I had been on my first solo. However, all went according to plan and I guess my crew members were as relieved as I was when we landed back safely after an hour and a quarter's flying. I must confess that during those days at Cottesmore I never flew without being somewhat fearful for my life. I never managed to taxi an aircraft out to the take-off point without having butterflies in my stomach, and fear as my constant companion. Once the throttles were wide open and I was committed, it was all right.

In February, the weather was still atrocious and we did very little flying of any sort. During a period while there was still much ice and snow around, our course moved to the satellite airfield at Saltby that was used mainly for our night-flying training. Saltby was one of the many new airfields that had sprung up all over the flat countryside of Lincolnshire. It consisted of a few Nissen huts, quite unlike Cottesmore with its permanent peacetime buildings. Thankfully, it had runways, good long sealed runways, and better still, instead of the piddling little electric lights it had the good old-fashioned gooseneck flares for night flying. But like Cottesmore, there was one really bad snag, and that was the visibility factor. On most winter days it was seldom more than a couple of miles, and frequently much less.

The airfield at Saltby was some twelve miles distant each way from Market Overton. In the winter weather, this was too much to cycle, so on my first free afternoon, I went yet again on a search for digs for the three of us. I had little luck until I tried the next village, Sproxton, where I found accommodation on another farm. This was a delightful place, owned by John and Vi Holmes, who made us so welcome that a friendship sprang up between us that has lasted to this day.

On 4 April 1942, I received my assessment as a heavy bomber pilot: it was 'Above Average'. I began to think that at last I was on my way up and might soon be able to apply for a commission. It was not to be, as I soon found out that most of the course had been given an Above Average assessment. I reckon the CFI must have felt that anyone who survived the course was above average if he remained in one piece.

Chapter 3

50 SQUADRON AND THE MANCHESTER

My posting was to 50 Squadron, whose headquarters was at Swinderby, though all flying was done from the satellite airfield at Skellingthorpe. I had no idea what aircraft they were equipped with, though I knew it would not be Hampdens, as these had just been transferred to Coastal Command for torpedo-bombing. Indeed, I had been told before I left Cottesmore that many of the aircrew on my course had gone to that Command. I very much hoped that my new squadron flew Wellingtons.

On arrival at Swinderby, I found that I had jumped out of the frying-pan into the fire; for the aircraft they were flying over Germany were Manchesters. Big black ugly things they were: the forerunners of the immortal Lancaster. Instead of the four 1,000 hp Rolls-Royce Merlin engines of the Lancaster, they were equipped with two Vultures. The Vulture engine was really two V-12 Kestrels joined one under the other in the form of an 'X', and sharing a common crankcase. Thus, unlike the Merlin with twelve cylinders, it had twenty-four cylinders, yet the horsepower of each engine was only 1,760. This gave a total of 3,520 hp, compared with the Lancaster's more than 4,000 hp. They also had a shorter wing-span. Their all-up weight was 56,000 lbs maximum with 1,116 gallons of fuel, giving a theoretical range of 1,630 miles. With a slightly higher wing-loading than the Lancaster, the overall result was that the aircraft would not fly high enough with a full load. They could 'stagger' up to around 16,000 feet before finally running out of steam. As soon as the power was reduced for cruising speed, the aircraft slowly lost height to around 12,000 feet.

As every aircrew member knew very well, that was no height at all from which to bomb a major target. However, the chief worry was that the engines were unreliable and were prone to overheat very easily, many of them catching fire in the air. What perhaps was even more unsettling was the fact I knew absolutely nothing about them. There

The Avro Manchester

was no OTU training programme; one just had to ask questions and learn as best one could.

I didn't have long to wait before I made my first Manchester flight. The day after I joined the squadron I flew on a forty-minute local flight with Flt Sgt Willet and his crew. That was on 21 April. On the 23rd, I flew with a Sgt Wilkie and we did some practice bombing at Bottesford. As yet, I had not touched the controls, but despite the aircraft's bad name I felt more at ease in it than I had done in the Hampden. It was good to be able to move around and be part of the crew. As second pilot, I had the job of watching the engine instruments that were on a panel on the starboard side of the fuselage. (Flight engineers did not exist then.)

The next day I looked at the flight notice-board to find I was down to fly with a Sgt Gruber on an operation that night. The target was not mentioned, only the crew, aircraft number (Manchester 7521) and the time for briefing. As I had only been on the squadron some four days, I had no idea who Gruber was, or any of his crew. My first job was to find him and make myself known. I suppose an airman's first ops trip is something to be approached with a certain amount of doubt. One naturally wonders how one will react when things get a bit hot. In my case, I guess the main concern was how would I cope if the skipper was wounded or killed, and I had the job of bringing the aircraft back to base, never having actually flown the aircraft or even handled the controls.

When I found Gruber, he seemed a likeable enough chap. The fact that he was still only a sergeant meant that, like myself, he could not have been long out of OTU, and was probably little more qualified than myself. However, there was little to do that day so I returned to my billet and tried to get a few hours' shuteye, as I would obviously get none that particular night. Of course, sleep just wouldn't come. This inability to sleep before an ops trip was to remain with me during the whole of my time in the RAF. There always seemed to be so much to check over in my mind, worry about the weather or how the engines would perform. Silly little worries in fact and nothing to do with the more dangerous part such as flak or fighters. The time soon passed, and after a pre-ops meal I met my new crew in the ops room. The first thing that everyone does on entering the room is to look at the large map of Europe on the wall and follow the white tapes that mark out the path to the target. Rostock on the Baltic looked a devil of a long way off – a long sea crossing but otherwise not too bad at all, seemed to be the consensus. There was a short passage over Denmark, which was not heavily defended; thus, there would be little time for the enemy to vector night-fighters onto us. Our CO, a short tubby man named Wg Cdr Oxley, stood up and the gathering hushed. 'Well, gentlemen,' he began, 'the target for you tonight is the Heinkel aircraft factory at Rostock. Each aircraft will drop one 4,000 lb blockbuster, and I need not tell you it must go down bang in the middle of the main buildings.' He then went on to explain our run-in and how we were to identify the target. The bombing level was to be 4,000 feet. 'Nothing lower, gentlemen,' he said, 'or you will feel the effect of the blast and that could prove slightly unpleasant.' The Intelligence Officer came next, and indicated where to cross the coast and where flak would most likely be met, then a few words from the Armament Officer and lastly, and often most importantly, the Met. Officer. Here things were fine, as was the expected weather. With a full moon and a river down to Rostock itself, the target should be easy to locate. Following a couple of questions, with a final 'Good luck' from the CO the briefing was over.

Immediately, there was a general buzz of conversation while navigators gathered up their equipment bags, and the WOps assembled their 'gen'. As we began to troop out, each aircrew member collected his 'escape money' and emergency gear from the Intelligence Officer's staff. Outside, the WAAF airwomen would be waiting to take us to our aircraft. Arriving at Manchester 7521 (it crashed at Waddington later in the year) I was struck by the grim black appearance of the machine that the seven of us would soon be relying on for our very lives. It was difficult to believe that only six days earlier I had been in our London home, and I had not yet even held the controls of this ominous monster. The crew, whose names I had not yet had time to memorise, seemed entirely at ease. I followed them into the fuselage rather like a new boy on his first day at school.

Soon the engines were running; everything was checked and we took our turn at the end of the main runway. There was no calling on the R/T for take-off clearance, as radio silence was in force until we were on the way home. Instead, we received clearance via a green Aldis lamp signal. With a full load of fuel, but only one 4,000 lb bomb, we soon became airborne and climbing to set course over Lincoln. As we were going to bomb at 4,000 feet, it seemed pointless to waste fuel in climbing too high. So Gruber decided we would cross the North Sea at 6,000 feet, which would give us a bit of spare altitude if we had engine trouble. Crossing the coast, our navigator got a good pinpoint to check his position. Then we settled down for the long sea crossing.

Our intended track was to the northern tip of the island of Sylt, then direct to a point on the Baltic coast north of Rostock. By keeping to this route, we had been told that we would avoid known AA positions. The time passed slowly and little or nothing was spoken over the intercom system, except for an occasional exchange between the skipper and the navigator. During this time, I had little to do except watch the engine gauges, and keep a lookout for fighters through the Perspex blister which protruded from the starboard side of the aircraft. The mid-upper gunner watched the port side and the rear gunner concentrated on our tail area. At last, we got a glimpse of the coastline ahead showing up quite well in the moonlight. We could not see our landfall on the tip of the island, and guessed that we must have arrived at its centre. We then turned due north to run parallel to the coast to our next turning point. After flying north for some while, we realised that we must be well off course and had actually arrived off the mainland well to the north of Sylt. Turning south, we arrived over the northern tip of the island, where we turned onto our course for the target.

Gradually losing height to 4,000 feet, we crossed Denmark, leaving Esbjerg behind us. The sky was now clear, and with the full moon we had no difficulty in arriving at the German coast dead on course, where we could see some flak going up from Warnemunde. We skirted round to the east of it, and headed down the river to Rostock and the Heinkel works that lay to the north of the city. It was a very easy target to identify; with the moon ahead of us, the main building showed up very clearly, giving our navigator a good long run-in to the target. With only a few corrections to make, his report, 'Bombs gone', came almost as an anticlimax. Seconds later the rear gunner excitedly came on the intercom to report that he had seen a huge explosion right in the middle of the works area. A photograph taken later by a recce aircraft showed a direct hit on the main building, which of course we were quite sure had been done by us. There had been only a little light flak in the target area, and none of it had come particularly close to our aircraft.

In a jubilant mood, we set course for home. As the main danger from then on would be from night-fighters, we descended to 800 feet to make it difficult for one of them to come up under us, where he could not be seen.

We crossed the Danish mainland just north of Flensburg. Then, all of a sudden, the inside of the aircraft was lit up as bright as day by a searchlight that caught us in its beam. At once, a stream of flak opened up on us. The coloured tracer shells seemed to leave the ground very slowly then accelerate rapidly as they shot past us. Our rear gunner was ready for such an attack; aiming his four Browning guns, he fired straight down the beam of the searchlight. The guns, set to give a good pattern at 600 yards, must have been very concentrated at our height of 800 feet. A few seconds' burst succeeded in shooting out the searchlight (and maybe its crew), and we went on our way unscathed.

We re-crossed the coast and settled down to our long flight over the North Sea. The navigator was now able to work out a good ETA (estimated time of arrival) at base, which was much later than we had anticipated. A reading of the fuel gauges indicated that we would be lucky to reach base without running out of fuel. We cursed the error in our original landfall on Sylt, and decided that as soon as we reached the English coast we would land at the first airfield whose beacon light showed up. The skipper now flew at the slowest possible speed to conserve fuel; while the navigator repeatedly checked our course taking star shots with his sextant. Our flight across the sea was without incident, and with our shortage of fuel many eyes peered anxiously for the coastline long before it was due to appear.

The excitement of the raid itself had now passed, and I became conscious of extreme tiredness in my legs after having to stand more or less in one position for over seven hours. With so little to do, for me the return trip was long and wearisome. At last, way ahead we could see tiny red flashing lights of airfield beacons, and then the coast itself appeared out of the gloom. We headed for the nearest beacon, which we identified as Hemswell. Flying directly overhead, we fired off the allotted identification signal. Almost immediately, the white 'T' sign was illuminated alongside the beacon. Following the direction in which the long arm of the 'T' was pointing, the runway lights were now visible. Our skipper wasted no time in flying round the circuit. After permission to land had been given, he went straight in. Our fuel gauges were now knocking on the empty stops, and, half expecting to hear our engines cough and die, we made our approach perhaps a little too high. We hit the runway halfway along, but fortunately were able to stop just short of the end.

Other aircraft had not been so lucky. By the grey light of dawn that was beginning to break, we could see a gap in the hedge through which a Wellington had ploughed before coming to rest. Later, after debriefing, we heard that it belonged to a Polish squadron and had been shot up and had lost its hydraulics and brakes. We did not see any of the crew, but two months later I was to meet one of them in the most unforeseen circumstances.

After a meal and a few hours' sleep, we returned to Skellingthorpe. It was a marvellous feeling to just crawl into bed and drop off to sleep, back in dear old England. I had done my first trip, had seen a bit of flak, and had got home safely. In just a few short hours, I had gained every confidence in my skipper. Later I was to find that once a crew had made a few successful trips with their own particular pilot, they seemed to build up an enormous feeling of trust and confidence in him. I do not remember ever hearing any crew member criticise the skill or behaviour of their skipper. I wondered if a crew would ever feel the same way about me, and guessed it would not be long before I found out. My guess proved to be very wrong, for instead of becoming an operational skipper in a few more weeks, circumstances were to deny me that privilege until more than a year later, and it would not be in Bomber Command. The following day saw us off on another night operation. Again, the target was the aircraft works at Rostock. This time the thought of the trip did not fill me with the apprehension the first one had done. I had still not had any dual instruction on the Manchester, but I felt confident I could land one if I had to. On 26 April, with a nearly full moon to help us, we set off again. This time, instead of one 4,000-pounder, our load, including full tanks, was six 1,000 lb bombs. On this occasion, we were to attack at 1,000 feet, a very low height indeed, though quite appropriate for the particular target.

Not repeating the error of the previous trip, we crossed the Danish coast on time and on course, and set off for Warnemunde. Arriving as before a little to the north, we could see considerably more flak than on the previous occasion. It was of light calibre and from a distance very pretty to watch. We had a very easy run-in to the target, releasing our stick of bombs across the works from approximately 1,500 feet. We broke away to starboard and dived to clear the area quickly.

A feeling of excitement and exuberance now seemed to come over the crew, with quite a bit of chatter over the intercom. Then gradually the noise subsided and we mentally girded ourselves for the long trip home. We made base just as dawn was breaking after a trip of over seven and a half hours. Our previous raid had taken us over eight hours. During both of them, Sgt Gruber never once left the pilot's seat. After the last landing, we still had fuel to spare, but by modern safety standards it was precious little indeed.

I was now beginning to feel like an old hand and had more or less been accepted as a member of the crew. The meal that we had together after debriefing was quite a jolly affair, despite the lack of a night's sleep. With the sun now fully up, we returned to our billets and piled into bed until the late afternoon. That evening I joined up with the crew for a few beers in the mess. One great advantage of being in an all-NCO crew was that we spent our leisure hours together. Later on

I was to find it a great disadvantage to be in a crew with mixed ranks, as we automatically split up into two groups for everything, except while flying. The next day, 28 April, I flew with Sqn Ldr Jeffs for an hour's local flying; but again I did not get a chance to fly the aircraft. Later that same day I flew with Fg Off Stone on a night cross-country flight lasting over four hours. I liked Stone very much, but for all the good the trip did me I might just as well have spent the time shut up in a tin box. Nevertheless, I guess I was as necessary as any other member of the crew, excluding the skipper and the navigator. I got to bed in the small hours of the morning. When I finally surfaced at lunchtime, I was surprised to find that I was to fly with Gruber again that night. We didn't usually fly on two successive nights, but I suppose my flight with Stone did not count, as it was non-operational. We arrived for briefing and found we were on a 'Gardening' trip to the Baltic, very close to Rostock. Gardening was the nickname for minelaying. Our task was to drop four mines across one of the shipping channels between Germany and Norway.

Most crews felt that mining was an easy job, compared with hitting a major target. Yet the number of aircraft shot down while mining was surprisingly high. There were several reasons for this. First, the mines had to be dropped at low level and at low speed. Next, they had to be dropped in narrow channels where ships had to pass. These channels were few in number and were all defended by flak ships. Then, of course, we had to mine on nights when there was a moon, when we could be seen as well as being able to see. Few aircraft were used for the job, and what flak there was did not have to be shared around so much. Lastly, in case of trouble we had barely enough height to allow baling out or to permit any margin of error.

Nevertheless, the crew seemed happy, for our trip did not involve deep penetration into enemy territory. Furthermore, if our aircraft got shot up during the actual minelaying we were close enough to the Danish coast to have a chance of baling out, and perhaps even escaping. Setting off for Sylt again, we arrived there right on track. Crossing the island we descended to 800 feet, and soon were able to pick out the channel between two islands where we were to lay our mines. With almost a full moon, Gruber flew around until he got in the correct position for the drop. With the bomb doors open, he began a slow run-in to the target area, while the navigator, crouching over the bombsight, gave minor corrections to the course. It all seemed too simple, but we had not seen a small ship lying close to the coast just where our mines had to be sown. With our low run-in now committed, the ship suddenly opened fire. In seconds, streams of coloured tracer shells surrounded us. I just held my breath, certain that we would be hit; for we were now down to 400 feet and flying in a dead straight line. Miraculously, nothing did hit us, though several hundred shells must have been fired at us in those few moments.

After what seemed an age, the navigator reported, 'Bombs gone', and our skipper turned away towards the land. I now knew why laying mines was called gardening and the mines called vegetables; for you might sow them all right, but you never knew what you might later reap. Of course, the flak ship would report our operation and, no doubt, minesweepers would be out next day. According to our briefing, the mines would not explode on the first sweep. Their internal mechanism was set so that perhaps up to a dozen ships might pass harmlessly over, until the fateful setting was reached and the mine would explode under the next ship. All that was out of our hands. Our job had been done and we were on the way home. As before, we crossed Denmark at an altitude of 800 feet. Leaving the threat from night-fighters behind us, our only worry was the somewhat temperamental nature of our Vulture engines. Again they did not let us down, and some two and a quarter hours later we landed back at base.

On 1 May 1942, I did a couple of local trips to Abingdon and back with Fg Off Stone, who was a very solid unruffled type and, like Gruber, inspired confidence. The next day when I found my name down for an ops trip with him that night, I felt quite relaxed at the prospect. Our task was to fly to Rennes in France, and after dropping leaflets, to take photographs of the railway system with the aid of parachute flares. We were to fly at 8,000 feet and commence our leaflet drop several miles to the west of the city. Calculations had been made to ascertain the rate of fall of the pamphlets and the effect of the wind strength on their ultimate arrival point. Our dropping point had to be precise if the pamphlets were not to be scattered wastefully over the empty countryside. We were instructed to fly on a special course, crossing the coast at a particular point and time. We had to arrive at the target on time, then depart on another set course, re-crossing the coast at a precise time. We did not know why it was necessary to adhere to these particular instructions, and I don't think our Intelligence Officer did either. Certainly the crew, if we bothered to think about it at all, believed it was to help us avoid enemy flak and night-fighters.

We took off with our harmless load, and climbing to 8,000 feet we skirted the sprawling suburbs of London. Getting a good pinpoint as we crossed the south coast enabled our navigator to check the wind speed and direction against the Met. Officer's forecast. Out over the Channel our gunners kept an especially good lookout, as I also did from the starboard blister in the cockpit. Northern France was liber-ally covered with fighter airfields and our every movement would be reported to them once we had crossed the coast. However, in 1942, the German night-fighter defences had not reached the high state of efficiency that they attained later in the war.

Crossing the French coast on time, we altered course for Rennes. Arriving at the outskirts, we dropped our leaflets in a long stick, across wind at the required distance from the town. Then we approached the town to drop our flares and photograph the railway yards. I didn't expect any opposition from flak at Rennes, for it was not an important city from the military point of view, and not one that we would bomb under normal conditions. However, I was quite concerned when we suddenly became the target of heavy-calibre flak. Probably no more than one battery was firing at us, but it was my first taste of heavy flak and I found it very frightening.

The rest of the crew seemed quite unperturbed as we flew on and dropped the flares. Fg Off Stone's evasive action, if any at all, was measured and unhurried; just as it should have been. For the pilot who threw his aircraft around in a series of corkscrews, though it might reassure his crew, in fact made his aircraft more vulnerable. Since, in spite of the corkscrewing around, the aircraft more or less covered a straight average course. The heavy guns could fire along this average course and the aircraft was just as liable to fly into a shell burst as away from one. Once the gun-predictor crew picked up the aircraft, and the point of interception had been transferred to the guns, the shells had to be fused for the correct height, then loaded and fired. This took some twelve to fifteen seconds before the shell and the aircraft arrived at the predicted point. So the correct thing to do was to stay on one heading for at least ten or twelve seconds until the gun crew were ready to fire; then turn some twenty degrees either to the left or right, getting well away from the predicted point of interception.

If not on a bombing run, it also paid to push down the nose of the aircraft and lose some height. This not only increased speed but also put the aircraft below the bursting point of the flak. When a shell exploded, the fragments bursting upwards had the velocity of the shell to add to their speed. While those exploding downwards had the speed of the shell to counteract their movement.

In spite of this knowledge, it still seemed odd to be flying in more or less a straight line as our skipper was doing. Thankfully, his steady and seemingly unhurried approach paid off; for although we could see and hear the near shell-bursts, we suffered no damage. We dropped our flares and obtained the photographs as ordered. Then it was just a case of getting to hell out of it and setting course for home.

I now began to feel very settled in with my new squadron and had become friendly with several aircrew in the mess. As yet, I did not really belong, since I had not become a full-time member of any particular crew. Like all squadrons equipped with aircraft having several crew members, most friendships formed between the men in their own particular crew, which of course, was understandable. The greatest hardship I had to endure was missing Betty and Jill. As I have mentioned, operational aircrew in Bomber Command were not allowed to live out, as having wives around just did not work out. The strain on both husband and wife had been found too difficult to endure. What the wife did not know she could not worry about, and the husband did not have the almost impossible task of melding his home and operational lives together.

Luckily, I seemed to be kept pretty busy. In just two weeks, I had crewed on eight local and four operational trips, but had not even had a feel of the controls. I did another night cross-country trip with a young pilot officer named Calvert. Then Fg Off Stone took me up for fifty minutes and gave me some dual instruction. I did not attempt a landing, but at least I was able to fly around for a while and get the feel of the aircraft. Though I enjoyed the flight very much, I found the Manchester much heavier on the controls compared to the Hampden.

On 9 May, I did a four-hour night cross-country flight with a Plt Off 'Mickey' Martin. Little did I guess then that, following his part in the Dambusters Raid, he would climb to the top of the Service promotion ladder to become Air Marshal Sir Harold Martin, KCB, DSO, DFC, AFC, Commander-in-Chief RAF Germany and Commander 2nd Allied Tactical Air Force. Two more local trips followed, the second one being with Sgt Crossley. He gave me forty-five minutes' dual, and I was able to do a couple of landings. I use the word somewhat loosely when I say 'dual'; for like the rest of the pilots, he had never been on a flying instructor's course and his instruction was quite basic. Later that same day I went up with him again. During this flight he demonstrated a glide landing, then let me try one myself. I will always remember his introduction: 'Guess I had better show you a glide landing,' he said, 'just in case you ever come home on one engine and have to glide in; and don't let flying Hampdens fool you either. Make bloody sure you are almost over the end of the runway before you shut off your good engine.'

'Why? Do these Manchesters go down steeply in a glide?'

'Christ, they don't glide at all, they go down just like a brick with a feather up its arse', he replied.

46

After two glide landings, the second of which I did myself, he pronounced me ready to go solo.

Normally, there was a prior requirement for a flight test by a senior pilot. However, we taxied to the end of the runway and turned on to the perimeter track, where Crossley handed the aircraft over to me. 'Just do one circuit and then come in', he remarked. With a cheery wave, he then disappeared down the fuselage to the rear door. A few seconds later one of the crew came on the intercom to report that he had gone and the rear door had been secured.

As I taxied to the take-off end of the runway, I wondered how the rest of the crew would be feeling. I had had only two hours and twenty-five minutes of dual flying on a new and utterly different machine from the one on which I had been trained; much of that time would have been spent on the ground between take-offs and landings. Yet nobody seemed unduly worried at the thought of it being my first solo in a Manchester.

Arriving at the intersection of the runway and the perimeter track, I did my cockpit check. Then, having obtained permission to take off, I turned the aircraft into wind and opened the throttles. With a nice wide runway and without the starboard swing of the old Hampden I felt no qualms at all.

Having no bomb-load and less than a full fuel load, the aircraft came unstuck when only halfway along the runway. As we climbed away, I experienced a most exhilarating feeling. At 1,000 feet I throttled back and flew around the airfield thoroughly enjoying myself. This was what I wanted, to be in command, as few pilots like flying with some-one else. It's too much like being the back-seat driver in a car.

I had been told to do only one quick circuit, and it was now quite late in the day. I knew the crew would be impatient to get down and get cleaned up well before it was time for dinner. So I brought the aircraft round and made quite a good landing. I felt that at least one of the crew might make some sort of remark on my successful first solo, if only as an expression of their inward relief; but they seemed completely unimpressed. 'His first time up? Oh well, we all have to have a first time at whatever we do.' I looked at my watch as we taxied back to our dispersal area: just ten minutes' flying, that's all. Now I would be qualified as first pilot – just one more milestone along the path of my Service life.

After going solo I did three more local trips as 'second dicky', and was then sent off to No. 1506 BAT (Blind Approach Training) Flight at Waddington. I stayed there for just one week, flying twice every day. The aircraft were Oxfords, the same as I had flown in Canada. I got through the course all right, though I never felt completely at home during a blind approach. Strangely enough, I never used the system at any time during the next three and a half years.

Back at Skellingthorpe, I did two more local trips as second pilot, the first being with Sgt Roy. Like me, he had only recently gone solo on Manchesters, and this flight was his first solo at night. We did an hour and a half of dusk and dark landings. For the first time I knew the feeling that aircrew must have when they accompany a pilot up at night for the first time. So far, I had flown with eleven pilots since joining 50 Squadron; all were different in some way or other, and so were the crews. The quiet steady skipper seemed to have a quiet steady crew; while the more exuberant pilot seemed to have a noisier one. With many, there seemed to be too much trivial chatter on the intercom. I think I learned a lot during my time as a second pilot, which stood me in good stead and helped me to establish a good pattern of crew-drill in later years.

Some ten days before the end of May 1942, the station ran into a period of little or no flying. At the same time, the ground crews were especially active in getting all unserviceable aircraft ready for use. It soon became apparent from conversations amongst aircrew from the many different bases around Lincoln that the same state of affairs existed on all of them. Rumours were flying around, some suggesting that we were standing by for an invasion attempt: whether by the Germans or ourselves we could never agree. It was obvious even to the NCO aircrew that our senior officers were just as much in the dark as we were.

The days passed with little to do except attend a few lectures concerning the new four-engined version of the Manchester now coming from the aircraft factories, named the Lancaster. Two of them were at Skellingthorpe and they generated enormous interest. They had four V-12 Merlin engines, like those in the Spitfire and Hurricane. These gave a total of over 4,000 hp, against the Manchester's 3,520. They had a wingspan of 102 feet, against the Manchester's 90 feet. The power-to-weight ratio was better, together with a slightly lower wing loading. They carried 2,154 gallons of fuel and an enormous bomb load. More importantly, they could carry their load to a height of over 20,000 feet, which was a great advantage. I looked forward eagerly to the day when I would skipper one of them, chiefly perhaps because of the extra margin of safety which four engines gave.

During this period of flying inactivity most of the crews would go off to Lincoln after the evening meal and spend the time in some pub or other. This did not appeal to me particularly, especially as I was not a full-time member of any crew. So, I usually spent the evening in my billet, a Nissen hut I shared with another airman, writing to Betty. I wrote her several letters every week, and in return received one back at least every other day. I destroyed each letter when the next one arrived. I believe most aircrew did likewise, not wishing to leave letters from loved ones lying around in case they did not return from a trip.

As I had not seen Betty for some six weeks, I decided to ask my Flight Commander if I could have the following weekend off. He was not too sure about it, but as nothing seemed to be coming up such as we had all expected, he finally agreed. Since it would mean a terrific rush to get down to London and back in two days, I hit upon the idea of booking in at a hotel in Lincoln and getting Betty up by train. I phoned her and soon had the whole thing arranged. She was still staying with her parents in Wembley; so there would be no problem with Jill as Betty's mother was devoted to her.

I had booked in at the Station Hotel and arranged to meet Betty at the railway station at midday on Saturday, 30 May 1942. Rising early on the Saturday, I allowed plenty of time to catch the bus into Lincoln, but I was in for a rude shock. One of the fellows who knew me hailed me and said, 'Hey Bav, the Flight Commander wants you over in his office.' Quite unaware of what was going on, I wandered over to the Admin building and was surprised to see a large and excited crowd around the notice-board. Joining the group, I heard one fellow say, 'Seventeen crews on ops? Christ man, we haven't got that many aircraft, what are we going on, bloody bicycles?'

Elbowing my way to the board, I scanned the long list of crews going on ops that night. Somehow, I knew that in spite of my 48-hour pass I would be on it. Sure enough, I was, and I had been allocated to yet another different crew. I looked at the names and knew none of them, especially, of course, the three officers; the skipper was Plt Off Leslie Manser. Even more disconcerting was the instruction that we were to go over to Coningsby during the day to collect the aircraft that we would be flying that night.

Wearing a very worried look I walked across to the Flight Commander's office, knowing very well what he wanted me for. God, what the hell could I do? I had no way of stopping Betty from coming, for she would already have left Wembley and there would be nobody to meet her at the railway station. The Flight Commander told me that my leave was cancelled. I explained my predicament but to no avail. 'I am sorry, Old Man,' he said; 'I don't know what it's all about any more than you do; but tonight there is going to be a really major effort and we need every pilot we can lay hands on.'

I walked over to the officers' mess and got one of the orderlies to find Manser for me. When he appeared, I told him I was to fly with him that night as his co-pilot. I didn't know how long he had been on the squadron, but somehow I had not seen him around before. He was tall and good-looking, and appeared to be very young. My guess was that he had come straight out of college and joined the RAF. He seemed to be a friendly sort of fellow, so I explained my predicament to him. He was very understanding, and told me I need not fly over to Coningsby with him, as he would take only a skeleton crew. 'So you just get off to town and meet your wife, and I will see you at briefing tonight', he said.

I returned to my billet extremely relieved, and in due course caught the bus into Lincoln. On the way my thoughts were all on the forthcoming raid and where and what it might be. I wondered how this young officer would cope if we got into serious trouble. At least I had flown solo since my last ops trip, so I felt no qualms about the possibility of having to bring the aircraft home myself. As I sat and fretted, I wondered how Betty would take it when she heard the news. I need not have worried, for Betty, as usual, unselfishly understood. The next twenty-four hours, though perilous indeed, would prove that, in placing my life in the hands of Leslie Manser, destiny had once more dealt me an ace.

With such thoughts I arrived in Lincoln and in due course met Betty off the London train. I took her to the hotel and broke the news to her. Naturally, she was disappointed, and worried about the flight that night. I explained that we never did ops trips on consecutive nights, and she could therefore stay over till Monday before returning home. I would come straight to the hotel first thing on Sunday morning. As I still had my old bicycle from my days at Cottesmore, I would cycle into Lincoln before the first bus. We could have a quiet day in the countryside, where, perhaps, I could snatch a few hours' sleep.

After chatting for an hour or so in our hotel room, I arranged for her to catch the bus out to Skellingthorpe and meet me outside the guardroom as soon as our early briefing was over. There would be time for us to have a walk in the surrounding lanes before I had to return to the base, as briefing was a long time before our actual take-off time. Then I left her and returned to the base.

Arriving back in my billet, I packed my few personal belongings, as was the usual custom. I then found another aircrew colleague I knew who wasn't flying that night and explained the situation to him. I asked him if he would go to the ops room first thing the next morning and find out if our aircraft had returned safely. If we had been diverted to another airfield, then he was to phone Betty and tell her. In the event of our aircraft being posted missing, or having crashed, he was to go to the Flight Commander and tell him where Betty was staying. Later, I was to realise how well I had done this.

Chapter 4

COLOGNE – THE THOUSAND-BOMBER RAID

S oon the time for briefing arrived and I joined the throng of aircrew in the ops room. It was already jam-packed, as over a hundred aircrew were due off that night. My eyes went straight to the map on the operations board to discover our target for the night. I was surprised to see it was Cologne. Why on earth did we need to scrape the bottom of the barrel in order to send seventeen aircraft to a target like Cologne, when our normal number was only seven or eight? We soon found out, for shortly afterwards the Station Commander walked in followed by our Squadron Commander, Wg Cdr Oxley, and some 'Top Brass' from Group HQ. Maybe the presence of the Top Brass was the reason for the unusually early briefing, as they were going on to other RAF stations after visiting ours. Amid much noise and confusion I found Manser and his crew and managed to get a seat with them. The Station Commander held up his hand and the general buzz of conversation died down. 'Gentlemen,' he said, 'tonight you are taking part in what will probably be the most important raid of the entire war. In fact, it may well finish the war. For tonight we are hitting Cologne with over 1,000 aircraft.' Immediately a murmur went through the assembled aircrew. A thousand aircraft, good God, what on earth would they do to a single target?

The senior Brass Hat then took over:

'We aim to tell the German population what they can expect if they choose to continue the war in the face of our ever-expanding aircraft production. We sincerely believe that we will so saturate the city defences that our percentage of losses will be far lower than usual.

The first 800 aircraft will carry nothing but standard 4 lb incendiary bombs. This means somewhere around three-quarters of a million incendiaries will rain down in the first half-hour of the raid. We must not waste bombs indiscriminately, but must aim at our specified area of the target. If that area already seemed well alight, then we must aim between that and the next area on fire, so as to spread it to the entire city.

By that time, we imagine that the entire male population of the city will be out fighting the fires that will ensue. At this point we will send in the final 200 aircraft, each equipped with one 4,000 lb "block-buster", in addition to more incendiaries. This we believe, will seriously discourage the efforts of the fire-fighters.'

At this last statement a gasp went round the assembled aircrew – three-quarters of a million incendiaries, and then 200 block-busters. Good God, no wonder the Top Brass thought it might well finish the war. Looking back today, after so many years have passed, the mind boggles at the filthiness and futility of war; but in those days we thought little of this. Our job was to bring the war to an end, an end in which all Europe would be free from the yoke of tyranny.

The ops room staff then continued the briefing. The weather was good with a full moon over the target and little or no cloud. We had to go in on specific courses, and out the same way so as to minimise the risk of collision. We had to maintain our allotted height, which was to be 12,000 feet. Hell, I thought, just out of reach of the light flak, but too damned low down for the heavy stuff. Still, with that number of aircraft to fire at, we might get away unnoticed. What wishful thinking that was!

After the briefing was over we returned to our respective messes for the evening meal. As soon as I could I nipped out to meet Betty. She arrived on the next bus from town and together we walked along the lane adjoining the base. Excitedly, I told her a little of the raid that I would be going on. There was nobody in the world whom I would rather trust with such a secret; but the very magnitude of it made me keep her entirely in the dark as to where we were going and anything about it. Telling her that it was an inland target, if we got shot down I would have plenty of time to bale out over land.

If our aircraft did not return and I had been taken prisoner, she would be notified by the Red Cross within a couple of weeks. Should she not hear from me for anything up to six months, she must not give up hope. I fully expected to be able to escape by way of Spain and Gibraltar, in the same way that Flt Lt Rennie had done the previous year.

On no account must she phone the squadron if I did not arrive in time for breakfast; as I had made arrangements for her to be told when any news was available. She asked me who the captain was, and what sort of fellow he appeared to be. I told her he was an officer and seemed very pleasant; but I avoided telling her how young he was. Soon the bus appeared; I kissed her goodbye, with a final comment not to worry and that I would see her next morning. She stood at the rear of the bus as it receded into the distance, and I watched and waved till she was no longer in sight.

With a feeling of considerable apprehension about what lay ahead, I returned to the mess, where I met up with Manser's NCO crew members and did my best to mix in with them. I particularly liked Sgt Mills, the rear gunner. He was a most happy and friendly individual, and it was apparent that all the crew liked him. Our front gunner was a Scot named Sgt Naylor, a very solid unshakeable type, though perhaps, like many Scots, appearing somewhat dour. The other NCO was Sgt Stanley King, a quiet, anxious type of individual. He was second WOp/AG on the crew and normally would have occupied the mid-upper gun turret. I met the rest of the crew at the flight office, where we boarded the transport to take us out to our aircraft. In addition to Manser, there was our navigator, Plt Off Barnes. He wore pilot's wings, having been trained as a pilot, but for some reason I never fully understood had become Manser's navigator. The final member of the crew was a newly commissioned pilot officer named Bob Horsley, also a WOp/AG. He was young, boyish, and very handsome. With his cap set at a jaunty angle he looked the epitome of what every young boy would fancy himself to be.

Arriving at our aircraft we were met by a young corporal armourer. He pointed out that our aircraft did not have a mid-upper gun turret. Manser interrupted, saying that the aircraft was an old one that had been relegated to flying circuits and bumps at Coningsby; in consequence the turret had been removed. 'Don't worry,' the corporal went on to say, 'I have put a couple of machine-guns in the fuselage, together with a few pans of ammunition, in case you are attacked. Perhaps you could poke a hole in the side of the aircraft to fire the guns through.' This well-meaning but utterly stupid idea completely appalled me. I would have demanded that he take the guns off the aircraft and not saddle us with so much useless weight. But Manser just nodded and said nothing. At this stage I would have sent Stan King back to the mess, as I saw no point in carrying a spare man if there was no job for him. However, again nothing was said. So we piled into the aircraft and found that, in addition to being filthy, it had no automatic pilot. Also, the rear escape hatch in the floor of the fuselage was evidently faulty, since it had been permanently secured with small metal plates.

Another thing that irked me was the fact that I did not have the usual escape pack or escape money safely tucked away in my battledress. Apparently, with seventeen aircraft taking off from our base that night, there had been insufficient of these items for every crew. As a result, our navigator was given only three packs and money wallets; Barnes, reluctant to decide who should have them, had simply avoided the issue and had kept them in his navigator's equipment bag.

I was still irritated by the sight of the two heavy useless guns and their ammo lying on the floor of the fuselage. It seemed so utterly pathetic to think we could poke a hole in the sides of an aircraft completely covered with wiring, hydraulic pipelines, control lines, oxygen bottles and a dozen or more such things. If we did manage it, how could the gun be held without a mount, and how could a fighter be seen coming up from the rear?

Somehow I managed to put these things out of my mind, as everyone was ready for take-off, the engines having been started and run up. As we taxied out to join the long line of aircraft awaiting the green light at the end of the runway, I got one more jolt to my composure. Barnes had been talking to the skipper, giving him his first course to fly after setting course over Lincoln. Manser then announced his intention of carrying out the entire flight at 7,000 feet. We had been briefed to go in at 12,000 feet, which was about normal for a Manchester, though still too damned low for a well-defended target. Seven thousand feet was not only just great for heavy flak to get us, but was in range of the medium and light stuff as well. Immediately, I questioned him about it and he answered saying, 'They will be banging away at all the aircraft higher up, and with a bit of luck we could get away without any trouble.' I swallowed hard and hoped to hell his assessment was right, but, good grief, with three-quarters of a million incendiaries going down we might well catch one from our own aircraft. (A bomb did hit one aircraft; though it killed one of the crew, the aircraft returned safely.)

In a rather troubled state of mind, I sat on my small jump seat awaiting the moment to go. There were four aircraft in front of us, the rest of the seventeen trundling up behind. They looked terribly impressive with their huge propellers (sixteen feet in diameter) turning lazily round on fast tickover. Then one by one the aircraft ahead of us got a 'green,' turned on to the runway and took off.

At last our turn came. The wind was light from the west, and we were on the longest runway. Having carried out his final cockpit check, Manser turned straight onto the runway and uncaged his gyro. Then he gave me a 'thumbs up' and opened the throttles. We gathered speed down the runway towards a row of trees in the distance. Holding on tightly, I watched the airspeed indicator creep slowly towards take-off speed. We were carrying 1,260 4 lb incendiaries, held in fourteen containers, a full fuel load and seven crew. Looking at the end of the runway, I tried to gauge when we would come unstuck. At last the aircraft rose slightly, gently touched the deck once more, and we were off. As I watched the trees pass harmlessly below, we had made it with plenty of room to spare. Climbing slowly and turning we headed back towards Lincoln Cathedral, from where we would set course. How strange it seemed knowing that Betty was down there and would hear our engines, without knowing it was us. As we flew towards the coast we could see dozens of other aircraft going in the same direction. By the time we had climbed to 7,000 feet and were out over the sea, the last light had gone and was replaced by a beautiful full moon. Normally, I regarded the moon as my best friend, for it made night-flying so very much easier; not that one didn't have to fly entirely by instruments whether there was a moon or not. However, I had found that on a moonless night staring continuously at the dimmed instruments in an almost completely blacked-out cabin had a strange mesmeric effect. This made it extremely easy to get slightly disorientated, and imagine the aircraft was behaving strangely. However, an occasional glance at the moon, plus a mental check that it was in the correct quarter of the sky, would reassure me that we were still on our right course.

Tonight was different, for there were many miles to fly over enemy territory during which we could be intercepted by night-fighters. The moon would be almost entirely in their favour, not ours. So, perhaps for the very first time I viewed its smiling face with inward hostility. After crossing the coast, I kept watch from the starboard blister, bearing in mind the fact that without a mid-upper turret we would have no lookout to port. I gave an occasional glance at the engineer's panel, but apart from checking engine temperatures and oil pressures there was little else to do. As our fuel was carried in just two tanks, these were simply turned on before the flight. Unlike later aircraft with more tanks, we did not have any complicated system of switching from one to another.

We crossed the Dutch coast and shortly afterwards saw one of our aircraft crash. Although there was no flak, we suddenly noticed an aircraft on fire in the air some miles ahead of us. I watched as it crashed and burnt. An enemy fighter must have caught it. Later we saw two more crashes. Seeing their load of incendiaries burning on the ground in a rough circle indicated that an aircraft in trouble had jettisoned them. Bombs dropped on a target always fell in a long stick. A few moments later we saw the aircraft hit the ground quite close to the jetti-soned incendiaries. We could only hope that the crews had baled out, but there was no sign of parachutes.

The flight across Holland was uneventful. Then at last a dull red glow in the distance began to show up; Cologne was already on fire. As we flew in from the north, the Rhine shone clearly in the moon-light. The target lay dead ahead and was well alight, with long bright carpets of fire lying in rows across the city. There was a lot of flak, which, as Manser had predicted, was bursting a considerable distance above us. For a few moments, as Barnes began to call out corrections to our course, I thought we were going to get away unscathed. Then suddenly, while we were still some miles from our dropping point, one lone searchlight flicked on, catching us directly in its beam. Within seconds the whole sky lit up, as some twenty or thirty searchlights came on and caught us in their cone of light. Immediately, the AA guns opened up. The heavy stuff exploded around us, with the light tracer flak flying rapidly past, exploding some way above. I must confess that it was all very frightening, but I was amazed at the way Manser held the aircraft dead steady while responding to Barnes's corrections.

It seemed an age before Barnes shouted 'Bombs Gone' over the inter-com. At once Manser thrust the stick forward and put the Manchester into a steep dive to increase speed in an effort to get clear of the blinding searchlights; but twist and turn as he did, he could not escape from their beams. As our altimeter rapidly unwound, we came more into the range of the light flak. It seemed a miracle that, with so many shells exploding around us, we were not shot down. At one stage our angle of dive was so steep that there appeared to be more searchlights shining through our roof than there were under us. I was so disorientated that I had no idea whether Manser still had control of the aircraft or whether we were in our final death dive.

The situation became more fantastic as we got lower and lower, with the sight of the thousands of incendiaries burning in long rectangular areas as stick after stick of bombs rained from high above us. We still could not escape the searchlight beams, until at last Manser pulled out of the dive at some 800 feet and all but a few beams had failed to keep contact with us. During these few hectic minutes I didn't have time to feel unduly frightened, as I needed all my strength to keep my feet on the cockpit floor.

As we pulled out of the dive and started to climb again, cold fear gripped me as the aircraft began to fill with smoke, and a voice on the intercom shouted that we were on fire. Immediately, I thought that we must have had a 'hang-up' with some of our bomb load, and that the fire was in the bomb bay, as no sign of fire was apparent in the aircraft itself. Hastily, I opened a small hatch in the floor that led to the bomb bay. I looked through but all was normal, with no sign of fire. I called to one of the crew to do likewise at the rear of the fuselage. He also found that there was no fire. However, as he could see the ground below, the rear of the bomb doors appeared to have been blown off. While this was going on, Mills in the rear turret came on the intercom asking for help. His turret was damaged and inoperative, and shell splinters had hit him. One had cut across his nose, another had gone through a flying boot and nicked his foot, while the third had gone through the flesh of his shoulder and blood was running down his sleeve and filling his glove. The skipper shouted at him to stay put till we had located the fire and then he would send down help.

Meanwhile, we had managed to climb up to about 2,000 feet, but were still uncertain of the cause of the smoke that was now all but choking us. Suddenly, there was a 'whoomph', and the port engine burst into flames. At once Manser closed the throttle and instructed me to feather the port airscrew. This I did, watching the blades slowing down until they had feathered and come to a stop. Then I operated the fire-extinguisher button, hoping desperately that it would put out the fire; but, of course, it made no difference to the flames that now poured back across the wing surface. I knew only too well that the extinguisher would only deal with petrol fires around the area of the carburettor.

It was now apparent that the engine had been damaged by flak and had lost either its coolant or its lubricating oil. It was the engine components themselves that were now on fire, and not the petrol. At once I realised that I should have gone to the engineer's panel and looked at the gauges when the smoke first appeared. But in the few minutes of turmoil, I had not thought to do so. However, I do not think the outcome would have been any different; for although we might have prevented the fire breaking out, we would still have had to shut off the engine. We might have done this while we were still climbing, and at a lower altitude than we were now flying.

Now, as I watched the flames pouring from the engine, I knew real fear. For the effect of the slipstream on the fire was similar to that of an oxy-acetylene cutter, and Manser and I could both see the panels around the engine nacelle burning away. I felt sure that the fire would heat up the petrol in the main tank, causing the vapour to erupt from the fuel-tank breather. If this happened, I knew that it would be the end for all of us.

For a few seconds I was filled with panic, and my one thought was to get out while we still had time. I turned to Manser, hoping that he would give the order to bale out; but he was made of sterner stuff than I was. Calmly he announced over the intercom that we would hold on and see if the fire would burn itself out. Perhaps he was influenced by the fact that Mills was still in the rear turret and unable to get out on his own. Manser then ordered someone to assist Mills. I rather expected Stanley King to do this, as he was completely free of other duties, but it was Bob Horsley who left his radio and went aft to help.

Meanwhile, I turned off the fuel supply from the starboard tank, having first opened up the balance valve between the two tanks, leaving our live engine to run off the port tank. This was normal practice, for by lightening the load in the wing behind the dead engine, the aircraft would become progressively easier to fly, requiring less opposite rudder to keep the port wing up and the aircraft on course.

As there was nothing more I could do to assist Manser, I left the cockpit and went back into the almost dark fuselage to jettison unwanted equipment. The flares, the two useless machine-guns, the pans of ammunition and boxes of spare 303 ammo all went overboard. With considerable difficulty, I started to rip off the oxygen bottles from the side of the fuselage. Long before I had finished, Bob Horsley came up alongside me and shouted that the skipper had given the order to abandon aircraft.

Horsley had been dressing Mills's shoulder. Fortunately, Mills was plugged into the intercom as he lay on the emergency seat just behind the main spar. Although he had been given a shot of morphine, he heard the order to bale out and relayed it to Horsley. Promptly, I went forward to the cockpit where I could see that Naylor, our front gunner, had already left his turret and was opening the forward escape hatch. Barnes was standing in the centre of the walkway behind the navigation table attaching his parachute pack. As I made to brush past him he grabbed my hand, gave it a quick shake and shouted 'Good luck!' Then he went forward and jumped. By this time, I had plugged into the intercom again and I asked Manser if I could help him. He shouted, 'No, get out quick!'

Taking a hurried look at the blind-flying panel, I strained my eyes to read the dimly lit dials. The altimeter reading was 700 feet, and our speed down to 110 knots. This was just about our 'critical speed,' less than which would result in complete loss of control while flying on one engine. The aircraft had now started to shake quite violently, and I knew that the buffeting was a sure sign that the aircraft had begun to stall.

Quickly I took my parachute pack from its stowage behind the

YEAR 1942		AIRCRAFT		PILOT, OR	2ND PILOT, PUPIL	DUTY
MONTH	DATE	Type	No.	1ST PILOT	OR PASSENGER	(INCLUDING RESULTS AND REMARKS
-	-	—	-	—	—	—— TOTALS BROUGHT FORWARD
MAY.	24.	MANCHESTER	7490	SGT. ROY.	SELF & CREW	DUSK & DARK.
MAY.	25.	MANCHESTER	5786.	SGT. TAYLOR.	SELF & CREW.	LOCAL.
MAY	30	MANCHESTER	D	P/O MANSER	SELF.	OPERATIONS - COLOGNE.
			L 7301		P/O BARNES	14 S.B.C. 90 × 4 lbs incd
					" HORSLEY	PORT ENGINE ON FIRE OVER TA
					SGT. MILLS	BALED OUT 700' 0200 HRS.
					" NAYLOR.	CAPTAIN KILLED. NAVIGATOR CAPT
					" KING.	REACHED GIBRALTER JULY 1
				SUMMARY FOR AUGUST	1942.	MANCHESTER
				UNIT. 50 SQUADRON	AIRCRAFT.	OXFORD.
				DATE 1·8·42·		
				SIGNATURE.	J H Banystock.	
				F/O LESLIE MANSER.	POSTHUMOUSLY AWARDED	VICTORIA CROSS.
				P/O BARNES AWARDED	D.F.C. —	(PRISONER OF WAR).
				P/O HORSLEY AWARDED	D.F.C.	
				SGT. MILLS AWARDED	DF.M.	
				SGT. NAYLOR AWARDED	D.F.M.	
				SELF. AWARDED	D.F.M.	J. H. Banystock.

GRAND TOTAL [Cols. (1) to (10)]
308 Hrs 35 Mins.   TOTALS CARRIED FORWARD

The author's log on the day of the fateful 1,000-bomber raid to Cologne,
30 May 1942.

SINGLE-ENGINE AIRCRAFT			MULTI-ENGINE AIRCRAFT							PASS-ENGER	INSTR/CLOUD FLYING [Incl. in cols. (1) to (10)]	
DAY	NIGHT		DAY			NIGHT						
PILOT	DUAL	PILOT	DUAL	1ST PILOT	2ND PILOT	DUAL	1ST PILOT	2ND PILOT			DUAL	PILOT
(2)	(3)	(4)	(5)	(6)	(7)	(8)	(9)	(10)		(11)	(12)	(13)
26·35			49·00	99·45	12·30	8·45	29·45	41·50		24·45	29·40	1·40
								1·25				
					1·00							
								3·10				
			2·25	·10	6·25			20·25				
			11·20									

SPECIAL G.R. COURSE COMPLETED. 10/8/42 – 19/9/42.

AVERAGE MARKS OBTAINED. 80.9 %   PASS

ASSESSMENT --   ~~Exceptional~~
                 Above average
                 ~~Average~~
                 ~~Below average~~

.... Wing Commander
21/9/42   Chief Instructor
                 No. 7 P.R.C.

| (2) | (3) | (4) | (5) | (6) | (7) | (8) | (9) | (10) | (11) | (12) | (13) |

pilot's seat and clipped it on to my harness. Then I took Manser's pack and, leaning across him, I attempted to clip it to his harness, to hurry his escape after I had gone. This, of course, is the normal duty of the second pilot when an aircraft is abandoned. But Manser knew very well that, with no automatic pilot to fly the aircraft, once he let go of the controls the aircraft would drop its 'dead' wing and roll over into a spin. At such a low height, all hope of his getting out would have gone. So, with no thought of himself, he half turned in his seat and roughly knocked the parachute pack from my hands, screaming at me as loud as he could, 'For Christ's sake get out!! We're going in!!'

I needed no second bidding, and as fast as I could I clambered down to the forward escape hatch. Placing my feet on each side of the hatch and doubling up my body, I dropped through. A split second previously, before closing my eyes, I could roughly make out lines of hedges and trees rushing past below. So as soon as I cleared the hatch, I pulled my ripcord handle. It was obvious that counting to three was definitely not the thing to do at my height. The slipstream from the aircraft turned me on to my back, and when I opened my eyes a half second later, the belly of the aircraft was about ten feet above my head; whilst the ripcord handle was free in my hand. For one awful moment, I was sure that the handle had come adrift from the pack without opening the chute. Then almost at once a gentle tug on my harness told me that my chute had already opened.

The aircraft continued its downward plunge, and within seconds hit the ground about a hundred yards in front of me. It blew up on impact, showering the area with blazing petrol. A few seconds later there was an almighty splash and I too was down. By a stroke of luck, I had fallen into a small stream that completely broke my fall. I struggled to the bank, enveloped in a tangled mass of shroud lines and silk, and stood with water up to my chest spitting out what I had inadvertently swallowed. For a few moments I just stood there, thankful to be alive and uninjured. Then I operated the quick release that held me to my parachute. At the same time, I tried to gather in the canopy and hide it under a small bush that overhung the side of the stream. However, the mass of air bubbles trapped under its folds kept it afloat and finally I gave up the attempt.

With all the pressures that had been on me during the previous twenty minutes or so, plus the shock of the cold water, my bladder was now at bursting point. Unable to unzip my flying suit, I thought that my water could hardly be any more unpleasant than the water I now stood in. So I let my muscles relax and enjoyed the sense of release and the warmth that flowed around my loins. Marvellous, I thought,

The wreckage of the crashed Avro Manchester in which Les Manser, VC, died after his valiant efforts to keep the doomed aircraft flying to allow his crew to escape.

Flying Officer
Les Manser,
VC.

'I'll never have another one like that!' Then I got rid of my Mae West and crawled up onto the bank.

While I was in the water, the banks and foliage alongside had prevented me seeing across to where our aircraft had crashed. Now, though the many trees prevented me from being able to see the aircraft itself, I saw quite a big fire in the wooded area where it had crashed. For a moment I hesitated as to what I should do. Already the ammunition in the gun turrets had begun to explode and bullets were flying through the trees. I was certain that Manser had not even attempted to follow me from the aircraft, and that there was not the slightest chance that he could have survived the crash or the holocaust that followed. Also, in the distance I could hear the voices of people calling out and I did not want to been seen by anyone.

As I had no idea whether I had landed in Germany, or just inside Holland or Belgium, already my one thought was to evade capture and to escape back to Britain. Now perhaps, this seems utterly callous, but my one thought at the time was my own survival and my own skin. Thoughts of the fate of the rest of the crew and the unselfish sacrifice that had cost Manser his life were thrust from my mind. My one thought was to get as far from the crash as possible before dawn. Fortunately, the night sky was almost cloudless and the full moon still high in the sky. This enabled me to pick out the constellation of the Plough and the Pole Star. By keeping it on my right, I could follow a rough course to the west, and hoped-for freedom. So, off I struck on my long journey homeward.

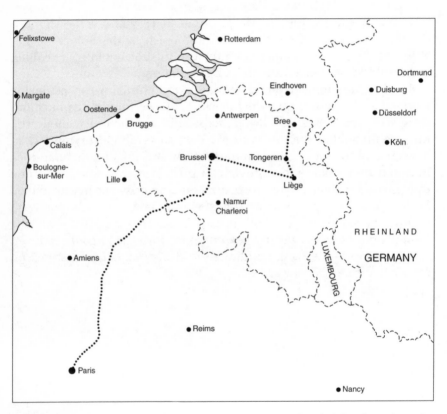

The escape route taken by the author from Bree to Paris after the Manchester's crash-landing.

Chapter 5

ESCAPE –
THE NIJSKENS FAMILY

The stream I had fallen into, though it had broken my fall, had, of course, soaked me through completely. My battledress and the regulation thick and heavy underclothing I wore to keep me warm in the aircraft, plus thick socks and fleece-lined flying boots, were saturated with water. It weighed a ton, with the water squelching through my toes at every step I took. My state of mind was one of utter confusion, and as I trudged on into the unknown I tried to take stock of my position. Apart from my clothes, I had nothing at all except a soggy handkerchief and my knife, that miraculously had stayed tucked

The stream that the author parachuted into on the night of 30 May 1942.

into a flying boot. Bitterly, I thought of the three escape packs and the escape money that were lost in the aircraft fire, and without which my escape would be that much more difficult. My only hope of reaching home was via Spain and Gibraltar, which lay fully a thousand miles away. Yet in some strange way, I was convinced that I would get away and emulate Flt Lt Rennie who had escaped the previous year. I did not contemplate for one moment the possibility of spending the rest of the war in a German POW camp.

On I trudged, avoiding houses whenever one showed up in the moonlight, continuing to head in a westerly direction. Almost at once I passed through a line of small concrete 'dragon's teeth,' that could only mean I was over a national border, somewhere or other. I now redoubled my vigilance in case I ran into a German soldier who might be stationed on the frontier. A short time later I came into a small clearing lit brightly by the moon. Suddenly, I was aware of a man standing some thirty or forty yards away from me on the opposite side of the clearing. We both seemed to spot each other at the same moment and immediately froze. He stood unobscured by shadows from the surrounding trees and appeared to be wearing a dark grey uniform. I felt sure I had encountered a German soldier. I could not see well enough to know if he was armed and thought it unwise to run in case he was. So I just stood quite still and left the first move to him. I certainly did not fancy getting into a fight, and perhaps a killing, as Rennie had done.

Feeling so unprotected, I slowly slid my hand down my side and took my knife from my flying-boot. The blade was still open and its rough handle soon nestled snugly in my hand. After what seemed like an age, the man made a slight movement and called out in unmistakable English, 'Who's there?'

'It's me, Les Baveystock', I stupidly replied.

He ran, or rather hobbled towards me, and with utter relief I saw it was Stanley King, our second WOp. Overjoyed at finding a friend instead of an enemy, we embraced each other and danced around in the moonlight like a couple of demented pixies. The utter relief after our moments of terror in the aircraft and our subsequent 'jump' was terrific. For some moments we babbled away to each other with complete disregard for our present predicament. Then just as suddenly, our position dawned on us and we quietened down and looked around.

At the time, I did not realise how I could have met Stan at all. He was the first to jump from the rear door, followed by Horsley and Mills. In landing, he had hurt his ankle and had barely moved from where he had landed. I knew that I was the last to leave the aircraft, yet here was Stan, some way to the west of where I had landed. Many years later, I came to the conclusion that, when Manser gave the order to bale out, he had already begun to lose control of the aircraft. It would have turned towards the left as the dead wing dropped lower and lower. Indeed, Mills later told me that the aircraft was banking over to port when he jumped from the rear door. By the time it finally crashed it must have been heading back towards the east. At the time, neither Stan nor I was interested in what had happened. So we quickly took to the shadows and set off once more towards the west. I helped Stan as best as I could, but our progress was painfully slow. I explained to him how I intended to escape to Gibraltar, and that well before dawn we must find a cornfield and hide up for the day. My main concern was about my saturated clothing, and I intended to strip off when the sun came up, hoping to get myself dry. We would have to lie doggo all day without food or water, and then push on at nightfall to get further away from the crashed aircraft before seeking help. Stan was not too happy at the prospect because of his damaged ankle, but he agreed to stay with me and see how things panned out.

Shortly before dawn we found a field of green corn and gingerly made our way out to the middle of it. We lay down some ten or twelve feet away from each other so as not to make too big a hole in the corn in one place. As I curled myself into a ball to try and keep warm, the wetness of the ground and the way the moisture oozed up around me caused me some concern. To make matters worse, the sky had now clouded over and it looked likely to rain. Barely an hour passed before the rain arrived in a steady soaking drizzle. I was now desperately cold and as wet as I had been when I first landed in the stream. After lying miserably in the rain for another hour or so, I started to suffer from cramp. At first, it was only in my legs, but later I felt it in my arms and shoulders and I knew it would be impossible to lie there all day. I called out to Stan and told him I would have to find shelter, adding, 'I might as well die in a prison camp as lie here and die of pneumonia.'

I was now pretty sure that we were in Holland. For just after dawn we heard church bells ringing in the distance, which I guessed was for early Mass (it was Sunday), and I remembered the dragon's teeth I had passed earlier. Looking cautiously around, a little way to the west I saw some farm buildings, and a couple of fields away I could see a young lad herding some cows. Keeping low, I scurried across to where Stan was lying to tell him my plan. 'Look,' I said, 'let's go over to the young fellow with the cows. If we are still in Germany, the look on his face when he sees our uniforms will be a sure enough sign for us, and he will obviously double back to the farm to report our presence. That will give us time to hightail it out of here.' Stan nodded agreement, as he was now almost as wet as I was.

We stood up, and after trying to straighten out our aching limbs, walked over to the boy. Seeing us approach, he turned and waited for us, seemingly unconcerned. Trying some of my schoolboy French I said, '*Je suis Anglais*', but it was obvious that he did not understand. I pointed to the wings on my tunic, and then to the sky, while at the same time making a noise like an aircraft. Then I mimed an aircraft in flight and a parachute dropping from the sky. Finally, I pointed to Stan and myself. He caught on at once and gave us a friendly grin. After muttering a few words that we could not understand, he turned back to his cows, just as though seeing a couple of airmen from another country was a routine occurrence. Amazed, we stood and watched him as he returned to herding his cows. I grinned at Stan, 'If he's a German, then I'm a flaming Dutchman. Come on, let's go across to the back of the farm he has just come from.'

Crossing the intervening land, we came round the back of the farmhouse where we could not be seen from the road. Even if we were in Holland or Belgium, we knew that the Germans who would be scouring the countryside for us occupied the whole territory. We entered the farm through an iron gate that led into a large yard enclosed by the farm and its many outbuildings. Then a woman of about thirty years of age came out from the main house and saw us immediately. A look of utter amazement came over her face at the sight of the two dishevelled figures that confronted her.

For a second, I think she took us for Germans, but then, excitedly, she spotted the wings on my battledress. Pointing at them, she said 'RAF,' as one word. I nodded and gave her the friendliest grin I could muster. At once she crossed to a little green door in the nearest outbuilding and motioned us to enter. Inside she indicated that we should stay there then closed the door and disappeared. I turned to Stan reassuringly. 'We're okay!' I said, 'I am sure she is Dutch and we have reached Holland.' Then we flopped down on some sacks, thankful indeed that for a while at least we had found sanctuary.

We did not have long to wait before the door opened and the woman reappeared, followed by a stocky man of about fifty-three years of age. Neither of them could speak any English and I guessed they were Flemish. It mattered little, for the man was a most jovial fellow. He danced around us like a huge elf, obviously glad to see us in spite of the danger our presence would be to them if the Germans discovered us. Soon a slightly older man who could speak a little

English joined us. We learnt that the men were brothers, and somehow got the idea that the woman was the wife of the older man. Years later we were to find that she was their sister. They brought us some darkish bread, spread with a layer of sour cheese, and some very black coffee. We thanked them profusely, for we knew they would be on very tight rations in spite of being farmers. As we ate, we listened to a discussion among our kind hosts, not understanding a single word. Then I explained by mime how I had fallen into water and was still very wet. One of them fetched an electric fire, and brought me an old raincoat. I stripped off my clothes and, donning the coat, commenced the job of drying off. It took over an hour to dry my underclothes and shirt, and practically the whole day to get my uniform dry enough to wear again. I hurried too much over my flying boots, as the right one had so shrivelled up that I was unable to get my foot into it.

During this time, the elder brother made it plain that although they were happy to help us, they feared for their lives lest the Germans should discover us with them. This fear was very real, as they could not be entirely sure of the boy who had been herding the cows. Accordingly, it was agreed that we would move on at nightfall. While drying my clothes I remembered that during my time at Cottesmore, I had fortuitously got hold of a secret file from the corporal in charge of the Intelligence Library on the subject of escaping. In it was the name of a Belgian patriot involved with the 'Escape Line.' This made me think that Liège would be a good place to make for, as it was where this Belgian lived.

I now gathered that we were not in Holland, but just inside Belgium. So I asked the older brother if he had a map, and could show me exactly where their farm was located. He indicated a spot a few kilometres east of a town called Bree. I then said that I wanted to get to Liège, and would set out for it at nightfall. I told him about the contact in Liège, and that if I got there safely I would go into the smallest café I could find and throw myself on the mercy of the owners.

My host then showed me the line of a canal that crossed the road between the farmhouse and the town of Bree. This led straight into Liège, about forty miles away to the south. It would be easy to follow on a moonlit night and I explained my idea to Stan, but he seemed very ill at ease with the proposal and not at all confident of its success. He told me he did not think he could go along with the plan, as his ankle was not up to it. Finally, we agreed that we should part company at nightfall, and after I had set off he would walk to Bree and give himself up to the Germans.

Our new friends, whose name was Nijskens, fitted me out with some wooden clogs, and agreed I could keep the old raincoat to cover my uniform. I remember clearly how excited I felt at the prospect of starting my journey, though I must have been pretty irrational to fancy my chances. I had already missed a complete night's sleep, yet here I was looking forward to spending the coming night walking in a pair of ill-fitting clogs. I would have to trek some forty miles through countryside where every German on duty would be watching for members of our crew.

I explained my plan to the older of the brothers, and while I was still drying my battledress trousers, he sat beside me and asked if I was quite sure that I intended attempting to escape. 'Yes,' I replied, 'I will make for Gibraltar, as a friend of mine did last year.' He pondered for a while, then said, 'If you are determined to escape, then I believe we can help you.' He spread his hands, and in stumbling English began, 'We believe Doctor Groenen, who lives near here, is in touch with an organisation that is working for the British Intelligence. This afternoon, I will send my sister to him. She can pretend she requires medical aid and no one will be suspicious. She will tell him you are both here and are determined to escape. Meanwhile, you must stay hidden until after the boy you saw has left, for we are not sure of his loyalty. We have

The Nijskens house and farm seen from the air in the late 1970s.

Mr Nijskens's house.

already told him that we could not help you and that you had gone away.'

This was exciting indeed, and I could hardly contain myself until late afternoon. At last, I finished the job of drying my clothes and, standing up, I felt ready for anything. Funnily enough, I did not feel at all tired, which was probably because the situation was so unreal that my nerves were on edge.

The two brothers and the woman returned, and one glance at the younger man told me that the visit had a met with success. First, the woman told her story to the brothers. Then the older man began, 'The doctor has said that one of your crew was killed in the crash. Another has been captured and taken away from here. A third is hiding in a nearby wood and a young girl is taking him some food. The other two members of your crew have been picked up by local people and are already on their way to Liège. We are to hide you somewhere safe on the farm and arrangements will be made to pick you up, probably tomorrow night.'

Stan and I were overjoyed at this good news and amazed that the local people had got the complete story so quickly. Now we had to remain where we were, as the men had work to do on the farm. Late in the evening the younger brother appeared and took us across the small courtyard into the parlour in the main house. The room was not very large and had an old pot-bellied stove against one wall. Seated at a table in the centre were two elderly people who were the parents of the brothers. Also present was a younger woman who they said was their niece.

We sat down and joined them all at their evening meal. We could not understand a word of what was being said, except when they turned on a radio. Grinning hugely, they tuned into the BBC news in English and we heard all about the big raid on Cologne the night before. It seemed rather strange when we heard that forty-four bombers were missing, knowing that one of them was ours. I kept feeling that it was not real, and soon I would wake up. I could not but wonder at how these people were helping us in utter disregard for their own safety. For we were sitting in their parlour with no blinds drawn, still in our uniforms. Any German coming into the courtyard would have seen us immediately. When the news had finished, they prepared to retire for the night. We rose from the table and the younger brother beckoned us to follow him. He took us over to a peculiar-looking haystack and pointed to a small gap under what appeared to be a

A typical haystack of the type in which the author was hidden.

thatched roof over the stack. Motioning us to stay silent, he then helped us up into the space beneath the roof.

In spite of the full moon that had made it easy to follow our guide to the haystack, the small space between the roof and the hay itself was quite dark. Making a small burrow in the hay, I covered myself over while Stan did likewise. After the excitement of the previous twenty-four hours, I now felt safe and relaxed.

For the first time I was able to think about what must have happened to Betty. To be alone in a strange hotel, in a strange city where she knew nobody was bad enough. Then to be confronted with the news that our aircraft was missing, and with no one to console her, was appalling; if only she knew that I was alive, or that we had sent out an SOS call before abandoning our aircraft. Then at least she would have known that we were over land and might not have met a sudden end. I also thought of Manser and how he had died in waiting to get us all safely out. Thank God his death must have been instantaneous. My musing soon ended, for within minutes I fell fast asleep.

Meanwhile, back in England, Betty had suffered the most miserable day of her life. She had gone to sleep the night before, lulled by the noise of the many aircraft setting course over Lincoln cathedral. Then, at about 4 o'clock in the morning, she had been wakened by the first of a stream of aircraft returning to their bases. She had listened to each and every one wondering if it was Manser's aircraft. She did not sleep any more until about 7 o'clock, when she fully expected me to come bouncing into her room. When I did not arrive, she got dressed and went down to breakfast.

The 8 o'clock news came on and she heard the report of the big raid on Cologne with more than usual interest. The news that forty-four aircraft were missing filled her with apprehension, but she still kept a watchful eye on the door for me to appear. Breakfast over, she retired to the lounge and read the Sunday paper. She knew that I had told her not to phone the station, but when 11 o'clock came she could contain herself no longer. She was put through to the Squadron Adjutant and asked if there was any news of us. Of course, he already knew that our aircraft was missing, and had most likely told the CO that she was waiting for me in Lincoln. Obviously, they had delegated the awful task of telling her to the Padre, overlooking the fact that he would have the Sunday Service to attend to and would not be able to see her until later. So the Adjutant told Betty to stay where she was and they would call her when there was any definite news.

She had lunch, and towards the end of the meal the manageress looked into the dining-room a couple of times to see if she was still there. So it was no surprise that when she rose to leave the manageress met her and told her a gentleman wanted to see her. She was led to a small sitting-room that had been cleared of visitors. An officer in RAF uniform rose to greet her, and as he turned towards her she noticed his Padre's 'dog collar.' She knew at once that I was either dead or missing, and her heart sank. But at that moment the full implication did not register with her and she could only feel sorry about the ghastly job the Padre had been given to break the news. He was kind and consoling, but of course could tell her virtually nothing. We had taken off and obviously cleared the shores of England, but that was all. Nor had Group HQ heard any signal from us. So they could only surmise that either our wireless transmitter had been put out of action, or that we had gone down in too much of a hurry to use the radio.

Betty was utterly bewildered, and when the Padre left she returned to her room to try and compose herself. Her one thought now was to get home to London as quickly as possible. She walked to the nearby railway station to find the time of the next train. Being Sunday, it did not leave till 6.30 p.m. So she phoned her stepfather and asked him to meet her at the station. Then, not knowing what to do, she walked aimlessly around the city in an effort to kill time. In spite of its history and charm, she found herself hating every part of it. Even today she would never visit Lincoln again by choice.

After returning to the hotel and paying her bill, she caught the train to London. Not able to afford first-class travel, she found herself in a compartment that was full of servicemen, all of whom were discussing the big raid of the night before. One ground staff airman, little realising Betty's plight, thoughtlessly said, 'Oh yes, another big raid, then the next day we usually get air-gunner pie for dinner.'

She returned to Wembley and the long weeks waiting desperately for any glimmer of news. Pop also had the rotten job of telling my father that I had been 'posted missing'. I think my father took the news as hard as Betty had done, in fact much more than did my mother. She had had the misfortune to be knocked down by a bicycle. Being a bit of a hypochondriac, she tended to wallow in self-pity more than she did about my possible fate. Consequently I do not think she was of much comfort to my father.

It was 1 June when Stan and I awoke. The sun was already high in the sky; it was obvious we had slept like logs for the best part of ten hours. We peered out from our haystack to discover that it was a beautiful summer's day, and the work of the countryside was in full swing. We were surprised to find that we were very close to the road that ran past the farm, so close indeed, that we hoped the Germans would not think that we had either the cheek or the stupidity to be hiding there. The road was quite busy, and by making spy-holes in the hay we could watch what was going on without fear of being seen. At one stage we were a trifle alarmed when we saw two German soldiers approaching on a motorcycle and sidecar. We held our breath as they approached in case they slowed down and entered the driveway to the farm. Fortunately, they drove straight on, looking only ahead of them.

A little while later there was a rustling in the hay at the rear of the stack and the smiling face of the younger brother came into view. He handed us some food wrapped in paper and a flask of black coffee. Then, although we could not understand anything that he said, he made it clear that we must remain well hidden all day. A cheery wave and he was gone. We were both pretty hungry and consumed all that we had been given, not stopping to think that it would be nightfall before our benefactor would return to us. Then we settled down to pass the day as best we could. Needless to say, time dragged with leaden feet, but I consoled myself by thinking that every hour that passed would probably mean that the Germans would be searching farther afield for us.

We chatted together, wondering which two of the crew were already on their way to Liège, not knowing then that it was Mills and Naylor. They must have linked-up together rather like King and I had done, in spite of the fact that one of them dropped from the front escape hatch and the other from the rear door.

Time passed slowly. Time we could only guess at, as neither of us had been wearing a watch when we left Skellingthorpe. At about six o'clock our good friend appeared at the side of the haystack. Beckoning us to follow him, he moved quickly to a washhouse at the far end of the farm building. He gave us a razor and some soap, and after a good wash and a shave, we both felt really on top of the world.

We joined the family for the evening meal, and again listened to the BBC nine o'clock news that was still reporting the raid on Cologne. At about 9.30 p.m., there was a knock at the back door and a young man about twenty-five years old entered, followed by a young woman. Lastly, came our young gunner, Bob Horsley. He had been the crew member hiding in the wood.

We never knew the names of the young couple who were to be our guides for the next, most dangerous part of our journey. Thirty-three years later I was to learn that the young man was named Jean Bruels. He lived at the grain mill at Dilsen, which was to be the first staging post of our journey. The girl accompanying him was Antoinette

Verheyen who came from Ophoven. She later married a Dutch Army officer and was last heard of in Weert in Holland. Bob Horsley was of course delighted to see us, and amused at some old clothing he had been given to hide his uniform. We all talked excitedly for some minutes. Then Stan King and I had to garb ourselves in some more clothes that the young couple had brought with them. I put an old pair of trousers on over my uniform, together with the raincoat and clogs that had been given me by the Nijskens family. Stan dressed up as best as he could and the three of us stood around laughing at each other, as if we had been playing charades at a Christmas party.

The young couple chatted to the Nijskenses, explaining their plan to get us out of the area and how they were intending to evade the Germans. They mentioned that our parachutes had been found and that the Germans were now trying to find us before we got clear of the district. The three of them had arrived on bicycles, with the man pushing an extra bike alongside him. On departure, the girl would ride on the crossbar of the man's bike, so that there would be a bike for each of the three of us. Their bike was equipped with a small red rear lamp powered by a dynamo, which, if at any time they were stopped, would obviously go out. We were to follow them, without lights, keeping about two hundred yards behind them. Should the red light

Mr Nijskens and his sister photographed in 1979. He hid Bav and Sergeant Stanley King in the haystack and brought food during the day.

78

go out, we were to dismount from our machines and hide in a ditch or hedgerow until our guides returned for us. The elder Nijskens brother relayed these instructions to us with some difficulty.

At about 10 o'clock they prepared to leave, and now it was time for us to say goodbye to these wonderful people who had risked their lives to help us evade capture. I grasped the hand of each one of the Nijskens family and shook it warmly; though it was impossible to convey adequately my feeling of gratitude. Not only had they helped us so unstintingly, but they were also the link that had put us in touch with the first section of the Escape Line that would lead us to freedom.

Chapter 6

TO LIÈGE WITH ARMAND LEVITICUS

We filed out into the courtyard where our bicycles awaited us, and pushed them down a track that led to the nearby road. After our guides had departed, King, Horsley and I set off behind them. Pedalling silently through the countryside, we were grateful that the moon was still bright, as we had no lights on our bikes. We passed through a small hamlet, not far from where we had first set out, that I later found out was Tongerloo, and soon we were heading south.

Twice the red light went out, and we quickly hid ourselves in the hedgerow. After a while our guides returned, the first time to say all was safe. The second time, they told us we must make a detour through fields to avoid crossroads guarded by soldiers. This necessitated pushing our bikes, and progress was very slow. Although we seemed to have covered a good distance, we had gone only about twenty kilometres when we arrived at a building that appeared to be a grain mill. It was on the outskirts of a place named Dilsen. In some ways I was sorry we had arrived so quickly, as I enjoyed cycling so much more than walking. I would have been quite content if our guides had told us we were to cycle all the way to Spain. However, the first and probably the most dangerous part of our journey was now over, and we were out of the area where the Germans would most expect to find us.

On arrival at the mill, we were shown into some living quarters on the ground floor. Soon we were all sitting round a large table. In addition to our party, there was a young woman aged about twenty-eight, who a long time later I learnt to be the sister of Jean Bruels; her name was Gertrude, and she was later arrested by the Gestapo in May 1943 and died in Ravensbrück Concentration Camp. There was also a man named Armand Leviticus. The babble of conversation was quite lively, and as usual, not understood by the RAF party; so we sat in complete ignorance of what was now being planned for us.

We stayed there for some three hours, and were provided with black coffee. I sat next to Armand Leviticus, who spoke a little English, and got along with him very well. He told me that he was a Dutch Jew, and was on the run from the Germans. Like us, he was hoping to reach England. He was carrying false papers in the name of von Statton, as his own name would have caused trouble with the Germans. He had a spare suit with him, and offered to fit me out in his clothing, provided I promised to keep things for him after I reached England. Agreeing willingly, I was soon wearing a quite respectable-looking suit, a smart shirt and tie, and a pair of shoes that unfortunately were at least one size too small for me. However, they went better with the suit than the clogs had done. The suit was far too

The mill at Dilsen.

short, even after I had dropped the braces to their full extent. To complete the outfit, Armand gave me a silver cigarette case and a couple of handkerchiefs, again asking me to keep them safe for him when I got home. He also made me promise to keep them until the war was over, should he be unlucky enough to be captured by the Germans. Although I willingly agreed, I was not over-impressed by the actual value of the clothes; and the final outcome of the war appeared so uncertain and many years away. We stayed at the mill until just after 5 o'clock, when Armand explained that we had to leave, as we were to catch a train on the outskirts of Dilsen to take us to Tongres and on to Liège. There we would make contact with the Resistance organisation which would plan our final escape. He did not know the people who were to meet us; but had been instructed that we must enter a certain church in the centre of the city at exactly 10 a.m. It was arranged that Jean Bruels's sister Gertrude would act as the guide for Bob and Stan. They were to follow her at a discreet distance as she headed for the station where we would catch the train to Tongres. Armand and I would follow behind them.

Just after dawn, we set off from the mill, leaving Jean Bruels behind. There were several people waiting for the train by the time it arrived. So that we would not attract any special attention, we stood separately from each other. We knew of course that if any of us was stopped and questioned, we must act as though we were entirely on our own, and in no way incriminate our guides. At last, the train arrived and I followed Armand onto it, though I did not sit next to him. I had been given the exact fare for the journey, so I said nothing when the conductor came round for the fares. I settled down in my seat and pretended to sleep to avoid the possibility of conversation. Not that I could have spoken to anybody, but I dare not risk being discovered to be English. Although the vast majority of Belgians were anti-German, one could never be quite sure.

The journey took some considerable time, and after many intervening stops, we arrived in Liège. I waited until Armand had left the train and then followed at a safe distance. When we were well clear of the station and obviously not being followed, I caught up and walked alongside him. He explained that we must kill some time before going to the church, and decided we would go to some friends of his who would probably give us breakfast. I did not see what happened to Bob and Stan, for they had followed their guide and lost touch with us once we left the train.

Armand hailed a taxi and directed the driver to an address a little way into the suburbs. When we stopped, he left the taxi and walked a short distance down the street to where his friends lived. Meanwhile, the taxi-driver turned to me and apparently asked me something. Of course, I did not understand and said nothing. He spoke again, and when I still made no reply, he got quite annoyed. Fortunately, by the time he next spoke to me, Armand's friend appeared at the front door of the house. So, pretending I had just recognised an old friend, I jumped out of the taxi and hurried over to Armand. Thankfully, his friend welcomed me into the house, leaving Armand to placate the taxi-driver.

To my amazement, this new friend spoke perfect English. In conversation, I learnt that he had spent some time in London, and that he was an experienced peacetime pilot. A magnificent breakfast of bacon and eggs was served, which in view of rationing and the shortage of food was surprising. We sat and talked until it was time to leave. Armand went with his friend, while I was accompanied by a young man about twenty years of age who had just come into the house. I did not know the names of these people until after the war, when I was to learn that the young man was Lucian Gaumier, while Armand's friends were Guus and Mies Oderkerken.

We arrived at our destination well before time, so we sat on a seat in the square that fronted onto our church. It was a beautiful day and people were everywhere, among them quite a few German soldiers. I think I was still in a bit of a dream, as it was still less than three days since I had been walking through the lanes around Skellingthorpe with Betty. Yet here I was, sitting with my very life dependent on two men unknown to me less than eight hours previously, and waiting to be picked up by members of the Belgian Resistance movement. Where I would be in the next hour, I had not the slightest idea. I sat in the morning sunshine, conversing with this amiable young man in a mixture of French and English.

Our rendezvous time came up, and our friends rose to go. Lucian clasped me by the hand and wished me *bon voyage*. Then, as a further gesture of friendship he removed a silver-plated pencil from his pocket, and bade me keep it for good luck. After more handshaking from Monsieur Oderkerken, they rose and made off into the crowd. It was now just 10 o'clock, and Armand and I strode up the wide steps to the church. Entering through a small side door, we soon spotted Bob Horsley and Stan King, who were seated by an aisle on the left-hand side, together with Jean Gruels and Gertrude. Not wishing to be identified with them, we crossed the nave and sat on the opposite side of the church. There were several people deep in prayer, and Armand and I followed their example.

83

It was apparent that we were in a Catholic church, where it was the custom for people to slip in and pray at odd moments of the day. We fully expected a priest to make contact with us, and waited eagerly for something to happen. Our two colleagues had of course spotted us when we first entered. After some time had elapsed with nothing occurring, they appeared to be getting restless. I whispered to Armand, asking him what he thought our next move should be. He shrugged his shoulders and said, 'My friend, I do not know, but I think something has gone wrong. We will wait a little longer but we can not stay here too long as it will look suspicious.' For a few minutes I sat quietly, then asked him, 'Where do you think we should go?' Again he just shrugged and said, 'We must see, we must see.' Again, I sat quietly, but this time I prayed in earnest that a miracle would happen and set us on our way to France and Spain. For I was as determined as ever that somehow I would get to Gibraltar, even if I had to walk the whole way.

My thoughts were brought to an end when Armand touched me on the sleeve and pointed to the other members of the crew. They had risen from their seats and were making for the door. I nodded and we rose from our pew, and making the customary bow to the altar, we followed them. Emerging from the church, we looked around for the other three of our party. By the time we had spotted Bob and Stan, the woman had disappeared, leaving them on their own. Now very much on the alert, we followed them down to the square. Within a few moments, we saw a man from the crowd go up to one of them, and taking him by the arm he led him away on his own. A few minutes later, our other crew member was similarly picked up. Armand and I looked at each other in amazement, as it had all taken place so quickly and unobtrusively. We did not have much time to speculate about what was happening before another man materialised from the crowd and collected Armand. I was dumbfounded, and wondered when my turn would come. Again, I did not have long to wait. From out of nowhere a man appeared at my elbow and, drawing me into step with him, chatted away like an old friend. As usual, I could not understand a word that was said; but hell, what did it matter? My miracle seemed to be taking place in a quite astonishing manner.

As we walked along together, I felt on top of the world. However, this state of blissful happiness did not last long. While we were walking along the streets of Liège, I became aware that we were following a very tall man, dressed in a long black overcoat and a bowler hat. As he turned each corner and crossed every street, we followed at a respectable distance. Not of course, that this was anything to worry about. What did get me worried was that every time we passed a Belgian policeman this man was given a smart salute, which he returned by raising his hat. On two occasions when he passed a German officer, again he was saluted. I now felt very alarmed, and almost certain that we had walked into a trap. The tall figure in black now looked exactly like I had always imagined a Gestapo agent to look. Furtively, I glanced at the man at my side, wondering if he had guessed that I had caught on to the situation. But he looked as unperturbed as before, and still talked away in spite of my not replying. I walked on wondering what the devil I should do. I hardly dare risk walking into a trap, yet how could I run, and more importantly, where to? Finally, I made up my mind to do nothing, reasoning that if the man at my side was from the Gestapo he would undoubtedly be armed. My running away might end with a bullet in my back. So I continued on with my guide, leaving everything to fate.

We must have gone about a mile from the city centre, when I began to get the idea that I was being deliberately led around to confuse me regarding my location. Then, while walking along a suburban street where houses fronted right up to the pavement, the man in the long black coat stopped at a house and let himself in. A few moments later we also entered the house and went through a narrow passage to a room at the rear, where a babble of voices met my ear. Seated round a large table were about ten people. Among them were Bob Horsley, Stan King and their guide Gertrude, Mills and Naylor, together, of course, with the man in the long black coat.

I did not learn till the end of the European War that this man was the Chief of Police for District IV, Liège, and that he was working for the Allies under the very noses of the Germans. He was later shot by the Gestapo. Also, I understand that he was the man that Doctor Groenen had contacted and who had arranged our pick-up and journey to Dilsen and then Liège.

Full of excitement I shook hands with everyone, being especially happy to see Mills and Naylor. As we talked together it soon became obvious that our new friends were not entirely sure about us. From my training at the OTU, I knew that there had been incidents where German airmen had been dropped into Occupied Territory dressed in RAF uniforms. They had at some time lived in England and spoke perfect English. In certain cases, they had been picked up by the local members of the Resistance and had gone along with a planned escape, only to turn on their benefactors and denounce them. That there were five of us from one crew probably allayed their doubts; but for a while, they kept us all in one room and did not let us out of their sight.

About midday, they brought in another man to question us and decide if we really were RAF airmen. He asked us many questions that only an RAF member could answer, such as: 'What is the official form number of a leave pass? What colour is it? How many sections is it made up of? Are they the same size? If not, which one is the biggest, and is anything written on the back of it?' These and many more were easily answered. After a while, they all nodded together, convinced that we were the genuine article. Our interrogator now took our names and service numbers, and asked us for the number of our squadron. We were then told not to worry, as we might well be back in England by Thursday. Naturally, we were astounded, for today was Tuesday; how could we possibly get home in two days? So, of course, I asked. 'The RAF will send an aircraft over at night. It has been done many times', was the reply. The man who had interrogated us now took his leave, telling us he would return later. Sure enough, at about 4 o'clock that afternoon he reappeared. 'Gentlemen, we have radioed London and sent them your names and numbers. But', he continued, shaking his head, 'you will not be home for some little while, for you must return via Gibraltar. You will remain here for a few days until we get the next part of your journey organised. Obviously, you will not be allowed out of this house for it would be too dangerous.' Far from being upset about the news, we were delighted. At least London knew that we were safe, and our families would be notified that we were alive and well. Gibraltar was as much as I had ever hoped for anyway. Unfortunately, neither our squadron nor our families were told anything at all about us. The message to London had been sent through a secret radio station used for Intelligence work, the existence of which could not be divulged. However, being totally unaware of this, we were content to sit back, happily thinking that our families would not be worrying about us. That night, in spite of overcrowding, we slept peacefully in a bed for the first time since the previous Friday. Oddly enough, none of the crew ever complained of tiredness. I guess it was all the excitement that kept us on the top line.

The next few days passed slowly, and our only exercise was to walk round the small, enclosed garden at the rear of the house. We had little or no conversation with the men who stayed in the house with us. Apart from Armand Leviticus, I never got to know the names of anybody there. However, on the Friday morning after three days of inactivity, we left the house in Liège and journeyed to Brussels by train. I was sorry when Armand did not leave with us, and reluctantly I bade him goodbye. I returned the silver cigarette case that he had given me, telling him I would keep his clothes safely for him if I got back to England. Alas, I did not imagine that I would never see him again.

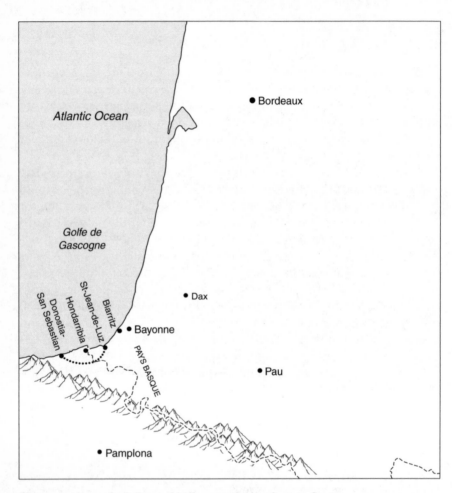

The route along which Bav trekked across the border into Spain.

Chapter 7

BRUSSELS–PARIS–SPAIN

As before, we followed our guides, with Bob Horsley accompanying me. We were given local newspapers to read on the train, to deter strangers from talking to us. Although we could not understand a word of what was printed, we carefully 'read' them through slowly page by page, stopping only for an occasional feigned sleep.

Arriving in Brussels, we were taken to apartments opposite the Palace of Justice in the middle of the city, most of which were occupied by the Germans who had taken over the Palace of Justice building for their Headquarters. Bob and I were to stay with a family named Evrard in a ground-floor flat on one side of the building. Their only daughter, Gisèle, had acted as our guide. Stan King, Ben Mills and Alan Naylor were taken to a similar flat on the other side of the building occupied by the Steenbeck family. Henri Steenbeck had been their guide. Monsieur Evrard was a big and jolly man. His wife was quiet-natured and aged about thirty-five. She cooked for us, washed our shirts and underwear, and generally mothered us both as if we were part of her family. Their daughter, Gisèle, lived at home. To say that she was beautiful was something of an understatement. She was nearly seventeen, and her lovely face and figure were equally matched by her sweet and gentle nature. She got on well with Bob, our handsome crew member, who teased and flirted mildly with her the whole time we were there. Had I been Bob, and not happily married to my Betty, I am sure I would have gone back to find her after the war. Though Bob did go back, he had already married a young WAAF whom he had met on one of the RAF stations.

The Steenbeck family consisted of a husband and wife, a few years older than the Evrards, and their son and daughter. The girl's name I do not remember, but Henri was the son. Later in the war, I met Henri again at my home in Whetstone. I was to learn, then, the whole sad story regarding both families, a story I will never forget, but one that must come later in this chronicle. Bob and I stayed with the Evrards from the Friday until the following Tuesday evening. They looked

Gisèle Evrard in 1942. She guided the author and Bob Horsley from their arrival in Brussels by train to her home in the Palace of Justice apartments.

after us wonderfully well; in spite of inactivity and not being allowed to go out, we had a happy few days.

The sequence of events that had befallen me since I had met Betty just six days earlier had been so extraordinary that in some ways I was just not my normal self. However, the tranquillity of the Evrard home acted like a tonic on me. In those few days, I recovered normality. Nevertheless, our time with the Evrards was far from dull. Every evening we would either go over to the Steenbecks' flat to play cards with our colleagues, or they would come over to us. Fortunately, there was access between the flats through the basement of the building. The somewhat tortuous route made it all seem a bit of a lark at the time. But we would not have thought so had we known that, in May 1943, Monsieur Steenbeck would be lying there in a pool of blood, shot by the Gestapo and allowed to bleed to death.

At the Palace of Justice apartments there was always a steady stream of comings and goings; one man in particular had me puzzled. He spoke perfect English, and in conversation he mentioned that he had seen some of the current shows in the West End of London. When I asked him how this was, he told me he had been in London only ten days earlier. He was married, and his wife lived close by in Brussels but did not know he was there too. He had been unable to contact her in case she was under surveillance. Apparently, he had returned to Belgium from an airfield somewhere in Bedfordshire. The RAF had flown him to a point north of Brussels where he had parachuted to where the Resistance were waiting for him. One day when he arrived, he took from his pocket an automatic pistol that I recognised as a .32 calibre Browning semi-automatic. Intrigued, I asked him if he normally carried a gun. 'No,' he replied, 'I never carry guns in case I am stopped and questioned. Today I must, for if I am stopped, I will have to shoot my way out of it.' Seeing that I did not understand just why, he opened a suitcase and inside was another pistol, much ammunition, and a portable radio-transmitter and receiver. I asked him how he could operate it without the Germans picking up his signal and locating his position. He smiled, 'The answer is easy. I go into a toilet in a hotel or public building; then it takes but a few seconds to plug into an electric light-socket, hang my aerial out of the window and quickly send my message. By the time the Germans have got their bearings plotted on a map and located my approximate position, I will have flown.'

He also mentioned that he had a contact working on a German airfield, reporting aircraft movements. Quite casually, he said that the information he was getting was very limited, as his contact did not have a very good knowledge of German aircraft. 'Well,' I said, 'I can soon fix that for you.' During my initial training I was lectured on the different types of German aircraft, and the fundamental differences, which allow easy recognition. Luckily, I was also quite good at drawing. So I obtained paper and pencil from the Evrards and spent several hours drawing every German aircraft I knew, showing them in plan, frontal and side view. I also made notes on ways to distinguish one from the other easily. Gratefully, he took the drawings away with him. Whether they were of much use I do not know, for I never saw this man again, nor did I know his name. Perhaps I was never meant to, for we were not home yet. The less we knew about people working for the Resistance, the less chance there would be of the Germans getting information from us if we were caught before reaching Spain.

Some years later, however, I found out that he was Joseph Romainville. His code name was Edgard and he had been dropped into Belgium in May 1942, probably by an aircraft from Tempsford. He died about five years after the war ended.

On another evening we had photographs taken for our false identity papers. Bob and I had gone over to the Steenbecks' flat, where they had equipment that they normally used to photograph maps and plans. As film was scarce, they lined us all up against a wall and took one large photo, which was cut up into individual pictures of us. There was one snag: our identity cards would have to be back-dated to when the Germans first occupied Belgium and issued identity cards to everyone. Obviously, it would look strange if we were shown still wearing the same clothes as when the cards were allegedly first issued. The simple solution was to exchange clothes between us before we were photographed.

Mills had quite a different problem. Unfortunately, he had been hit by a piece of shell splinter that had scored a deep furrow across his nose. This had healed up very well, but still left him with a large scab on the centre of his nose. How would he explain still having the scab on his nose and in the photograph supposedly taken over a year earlier? The problem was solved with the use of some stage makeup and wax. A false nose was built up over the scab, and then carefully camouflaged with grease paint. To be true the nose did not look too good when he finally got the photo, but it was good enough.

The following evening we were given our new identities. The photographs looked just perfect, indeed too perfect, for they were meant to look old and worn. So we spent some time wearing away the edges with a nail file, and then dirtying them up by rubbing them on the carpet. I had been given the name of Van Ollebecke, with an address in Limbourg. Like the other crew members we spoke only Flemish, so that when we were in France we would not be expected to speak the language.

On Tuesday 9 June Bob and I were told that we would be off to Paris that evening on the next step of our journey. Monsieur Evrard said that our guide would be a pretty little girl named Dédée. She was the daughter of one of their leaders and very courageous. The other three members of the crew would stay a little longer with the Steenbecks as it would be unwise to move too many of us at one time. We were sorry they would not be coming with us, but we were eager to continue the journey home. Madame Evrard busied herself washing some spare clothes I had been given. Then she made preparations to give us a good meal before we set out.

At about 5.15 p.m. there was a knock at the door of the flat and Monsieur Evrard welcomed our guide. We were introduced to her and I was struck by her youthful appearance. She was not a bit like Gisèle, being much smaller and more demure in appearance. She stood talking to the Evrards, clad in a long black wool cloak that had an attached hood turned back over her shoulders. I stood and watched this young and innocent, almost fragile little girl who was about to risk her life escorting us over the border into France. I was most impressed, and a feeling of gratitude welled up in me that I had difficulty in controlling. Though she did not have the same bloom of youthful beauty as Gisèle, she nevertheless had a certain indefinable air that aroused the strongest feelings of protective instinct in me. I was to be with her for only some fourteen hours, and most of those in complete darkness. But I carried a picture of her, standing in her black cloak, in my memory until the war was over, nearly three-and-a-half years later.

It was now time for us to go. With much handshaking and our heart-felt thanks, we said goodbye to the wonderful Evrard family. Parting from such people was very difficult, for it was impossible to thank them enough, or even to convey our true feelings of gratitude. We knew they had risked their lives by helping us, but at the time did not guess at the terrible future that lay ahead of them on our account. I suppose Mr Evrard knew the risks that they faced, and perhaps his wife did as well. But Gisèle, for all her youthful beauty, was still little more than a young girl who had become entangled in a web of activity through no wish or fault of her own. In so doing, she had quite undeservedly sealed for herself a terrible fate. Our goodbyes over, we left this peaceful haven to continue our journey.

Having made sure that all was clear, Dédée left the flat first, followed closely by Bob and me. We walked for some way until Dédée arrived at a tram stop, and we stood a little way from her. We had been told that it would not be safe to go direct to the main railway station to catch the train to Paris, as there would be many German police watching for people like us. The plan was to go to a small station east of Brussels to board the train. It was unlikely that there would be any police activity there. In any case, the impression they might get would be that we were simply taking the train into the city. We boarded the tram and set off through the suburbs of Brussels. Arriving at the station, we went to one end of the platform to avoid being noticed.

When the train arrived, it became apparent that it was only going to stop for a very short time, so we got into the last carriage, that had come to a halt opposite us. It was a corridor train and I was alarmed to find that the carriage was entirely occupied by German soldiers *en route* to Paris. The corridor was not the type that ran down the side of the train, but straight down the centre between the seats. Therefore, we had the unwelcome excitement of having to walk through several carriages full of our enemy, and picking our way through their equipment on the floor. I do not know how Dédée felt about it; perhaps she was used to the sight of German uniforms. For Bob and me, it was quite hair-raising.

Before we reached the front carriage used by civilians, I had the misfortune to bump into one of the soldiers. Had I apologised, I doubt whether this trivial incident would have been noticed. Of course, we had been warned never to speak, in case our ignorance of the language gave us away. So I just acted dumb and continued along the carriage. The soldier I had bumped into took this to be a personal insult and caught hold of my shoulder, pulling me back and shouting angrily in German. I remained silent, but acted menially, bowing and scraping. This display evidently placated him and he let go of me. I made a couple more apologetic gestures, then turned and scurried after Bob and Dédée, who were unaware of the incident. Finally, we reached the front carriage, of the type where the corridor ran alongside the seats that were all in separate compartments. Months before, I had read in the Press that all German troop trains passing through Occupied Territory usually allowed the front carriage to be used by the civilian population. This ensured that the Resistance forces would not sabotage the train. We found a compartment with plenty of room and settled ourselves down with Dédée between us. Not having papers to look at this time, Bob and I pretended to nod off. Arriving at the main station in Brussels, a motley crowd of Belgians appeared along the corridor, filling every vacant seat and every square inch of the corridor with baggage of all shapes and sizes. They all talked to each other, all at the same time, apparently knowing each other. Long before everyone had settled down, the train moved out of the station, and again Bob and I feigned sleep.

Before we had gone many miles, an extraordinary sequence of events began to take place. First of all, the blinds of our compartment were all pulled down, and a man in the corridor was evidently told to keep guard on our sliding door. Two of the men then climbed up and sat hunched up on the luggage racks on each side of the compartment. Their legs hung down to about shoulder level, and as I sat next to the corridor I got the occasional boot in the ear. They then began to unscrew the wooden beading that held the roof panels in place, handing the screws and strips of beading to their companions below. Once the beading from the corridor end of the roof had been removed, the job of taking down the panels was started. Periodically, I would alter my position to avoid the dangling feet, and open my eyes to see what was going on. I was quite at a loss to understand what was intended, and could only guess that they were going to short-circuit the lights so that a proper search could not be carried out at the frontier. Actually, that was not the reason at all, for when the roof lining alongside the corridor had been lifted, the reason became obvious. The roof of the compartment was dome-shaped, as was that in the corridor. Between the outside shell of the carriage and the place where the compartment met the corridor was an empty space, obviously an ideal place to hide anything, but what? We found out when our door into the corridor was partially opened, and dozens of small packages about ten inches long and four inches wide were passed hand-to-hand from outside to the men on the roof racks. The packages were tied together with long lengths of twine, in groups of about a dozen, leaving a gap of a foot between each package. This arrangement allowed them to be retrieved quickly when the time came.

At last the final package was hidden in the roof, and the job of replacing the panels and beading was undertaken. By the time it was finished, darkness had fallen on the countryside and everybody attempted to sleep. Dédée still sat quietly between Bob and me, and from the time we left the Evrards' home she had not spoken one word to us. Occasionally, I could steal a glance at this brave girl who was risking her life to help two strange men she had met only a few hours before; men who would be able to continue the fight for the liberation of her country, if only they could be safely taken to Gibraltar.

As the hours passed by, my thoughts turned to what might lie ahead. I had no idea where we would be going after Paris, or whether we would be handed over to another guide. I could not even understand why we were going to Paris at all, since I knew the usual route taken by escapees was over the eastern end of the Pyrenees to Barcelona. It did not dawn on me that we might be going into Spain via the western end, for I was aware that the whole of the western seaboard of France was a restricted zone, requiring special passes from the German authorities.

My thoughts of the future were soon brought to an end as the train, which had been slowing down, now ground to a halt at a station that I guessed must be on the frontier. When it had stopped, soldiers came along the platform shouting for all the civilians to clear the train. Everyone left the compartment. Clutching my small green case I followed closely behind Dédée and Bob along the dimly lit platform.

Joining the crush of people, we entered a large shedlike building that must have been the pre-war customs post. We lined up in rows, waiting our turn to pass through the barrier where everyone was being questioned and having documents checked. As we got nearer, Dédée took the case from me, 'They may ask you what is in it', she explained; then she went on alone. When I arrived at the barrier, one of the guards began to question me; but, of course, I had no idea what he was saying. So I just nodded and started fumbling in my pocket for my papers. I knew exactly where they were, but I acted dumb and first took out my ticket that I handed over, never looking directly at the man who was examining me, or the soldier standing nearby. I found my identity card and handed it over and then my papers and travel permit. Had we been there individually, I doubt whether Bob or I would have got away with it. However, people were jostling all around us with their bags, and it was in the middle of the night when nothing is quite normal. Everything went as planned, and I breathed a sigh of relief when my identity card and papers were returned to me, and I was allowed through.

By this time, Dédée and Bob had left the building, and I followed the general stream of people back onto the platform. Rejoining the train, we made our way through the tangle of people and luggage in the corridor until we came to our original compartment. Of course, other people joining the train, making it even more tightly packed than before, had already taken our seats. Eventually, we found ourselves wedged in about halfway along the corridor, unable to move either way. The train started on its way again, and I sighed with relief knowing that we were now safely inside France.

We found the corner of a suitcase protruding from a pile of baggage alongside us, and Bob and I took it in turns to sit on the end of the case, with little Dédée sitting on our lap. The next few hours were just about the most tiring that I could imagine, with cramp and aching in every joint. Yet here I was, sitting uncomfortably in the dark with this pretty little Belgian girl, her arm around my shoulder, while I cuddled her close in the only way possible under these strange circumstances. My right hand lay across her lap, as there was just no room for it to go elsewhere. So, quietly I whispered to her, '*Pardonez-moi, mademoiselle.*' She turned and whispered, '*Pourquoi?*' For the life of me I could not remember the meaning of this simple word and this she must have realised, for she said, 'Why?' I shrugged my shoulders and replied, '*J'ai une femme et une petite fille.*' I could not see her face, but the sound in her voice told me that she was smiling when she replied, 'It does not matter'.

Looking back through the years, I suppose this may seem incredibly corny and might well raise a laugh among friends who may read this one day. But at the time it was not so. For the strangeness and unexpected happenings of the ten days since I had walked in Lincoln with my wife still bore the air of dreamland. To find myself sitting and cuddling, albeit in a brotherly manner, a pretty girl whom hours before I had never met, in a darkened train, in an enemy-occupied country, wearing another man's clothes and with another man's fictitious identity, was more like an unimaginable dream: truly a case of 'truth being stranger than fiction'. Slowly, the grey light of dawn crept over the countryside speeding past us. I was now very weary, for it had been impossible to snatch even a moment's sleep. Concerning me most was the 'call of nature' that had been bothering me for some time and was now becoming urgent. So, having once more changed places with Bob, I set off down the corridor to find the toilet. After climbing over mountains of baggage and picking my way carefully past sleeping bodies that sprawled everywhere, at last I located the toilet. There, I was dismayed to find three women inside the open door; one of them was sitting on the seat, while the other two sat on the floor each side of her. By signs, I made it known that I wished to use it, and after a few moments the woman sitting on the toilet rose and stood slightly to the side. The other two women never moved. This wasn't surprising, for there was insufficient room in the corridor for them to vacate the toilet compartment, even had they tried. This was a situation I just could not cope with, and reluctantly I had to abandon my quest and return to Dédée and Bob. After about an hour of my acute discomfort, the train entered the suburbs of Paris and I caught a fleeting glimpse of the Eiffel Tower in the distance. The train drew into the station and we joined the crowd of people on the platform. We had no bother at all going through the barrier, for everybody seemed too tired and uninterested in the people milling around with their baggage.

At 7 a.m. on the dull cold morning of 10 June 1942, we found ourselves on the streets of Paris. Indicating the time, Dédée said that we must wait for two hours until she handed us over to the next contact. As best I could, I explained to Dédée that I still needed a toilet, so she found a small café that was open and we went inside. She ordered coffee for the three of us and at last I was able to use their facilities. The disgusting condition of this typical 'john' (just a hole in the floor, with a couple of foot wells each side so as to not fall over backwards, in a somewhat run-down building) was of no concern to me, as I looked upon it as a thing of beauty. I rejoined Bob and Dédée, and we sat sipping the coffee very slowly in an effort to kill time.

Dédée now explained to us that she would hand us over to another Belgian girl, who originally also came from Brussels. She was Mlle Andrée de Jongh, and she too was better known as Dédée. Later, of course we were to find that she was the person who had created the whole escape route known as the Comet Line. This was a line that helped hundreds of airmen escape back to England, for which Andrée became world-famous, and after the war earned her the award of the George Medal. She was known later by the name of 'The Little Cyclone', and the full story of her exploits was published in a book of that name, written by Colonel Airey Neave, MP.

Having stayed in the small café as long as we thought expedient, we left and walked round the streets until the time for our rendezvous drew close. During this time little was said between us. Despite a sleepless night, I felt keyed up with excitement. Dozens of questions and doubts filled my mind. Would our guide show up tonight? Where would we be taken? Why were we in Paris anyway? Our appointed time was now due, and Dédée took us to a Métro station where we waited unobtrusively a little way inside.

We did not have long to wait, for almost dead on time we were joined by a bright, vivacious girl, who was taller and slimmer than Dédée Dumont. For a few minutes the two girls talked animatedly together. Then Dédée introduced us to the new girl, who spoke to us in excellent English. We chatted together for a few more minutes, and then it was time to be on our way. We said goodbye to Dédée Dumont in what I later felt to be a most ungallant manner. I could only hold her hand briefly in mine and murmur, 'Thank you, Mademoiselle. Thank you.' Bob did likewise, and then with a sad little smile she turned and was gone. Afterwards I cursed my lack of knowledge of her language and also my English reticence. For I should have warmly embraced her and kissed her on both cheeks in the custom of her people.

In the days that followed I thought a lot about this brave little girl who seemed to have stepped out of a storybook to guide Bob and me from Brussels to Paris, and I wondered if I would ever see her again. Little did I know that I would have news of her from a most unexpected source just a year later, and that the news would be terrible indeed, or that, after the war, I would hear from her and meet her again. After she left us that day, she returned home and later obtained my name and address from the Evrard family. She had written it on a piece of paper that she had sealed in a tin and buried at the bottom of her garden. At the time, of course, I could not guess at the cruel fate that would befall this wonderful girl. I could only continue to carry a picture of her in my mind, standing in her long black cloak while I held her hand and uttered my inadequate words of thanks. Bob and I were now following this new Dédée, down into the Métro itself. She obtained the tickets for the three of us and we stood waiting silently for the train, which soon appeared. Inside we sat down some ten seats away from her. To our amusement, we found ourselves directly opposite two Luftwaffe girls who looked very smart and attractive indeed in their grey uniforms and forage caps, worn jauntily over their blonde hair. They took no notice of me but were obviously interested in Bob. As I have mentioned earlier, he was young and good-looking, with a fresh, boyish complexion and hair as fair as that of the two girls who now eyed him with approval. Among the typical French people in our compartment he stood out like a sore thumb and must have convinced them that he too was a German. I looked around at Bob and was half amused and half annoyed to see that he was enjoying himself immensely, smiling away at the two girls and doing his best to get off with them. I could see the funny side of it, but was scared stiff in case they tried to get into conversation with him.

I do not think that Dédée de Jongh had seen what had been going on, and I am sure that at the time Bob did not realise how stupid he was to risk larking about in this way. However, it did not last very long, as a couple of stations further along the line Dédée rose from her seat and we followed her from the train after the exchange of more smiles between Bob and the Luftwaffe blondes.

From the station we found ourselves in the suburbs of the city, but I had no idea where. A short walk and we arrived at some flats where a girl friend of Dédée's lived on the first floor. (The house was No. 10 Rue Dudinot, near the Rue de Babylone.) This girl was a little older than Dédée, but I did not discover her name. We all had breakfast

together and then the girls left us alone for the day. They took our identity cards and papers, and told us we could rest or read but were on no
account to leave the flat or answer the door. Having shown us the bathroom and provided us with a razor, they departed, telling us that they
must now obtain new identities and papers for us.

After a clean-up, Bob and I stretched ourselves out on a couple of
beds. Of course, sleep would not come, as we were still too excited
after all that had happened to us. So we just lazed about and chatted.
About 5 p.m., Dédée returned with a tall good-looking girl whose
name I afterwards found to be Elvire Morelle. She walked with a slight
limp that I took to be some sort of deformity from childhood, but years
later I was to find that this was not the case. She had fallen earlier in
the year while crossing the Pyrenees with a party of escapees, and had
broken her leg. She had been left in the snow while help was sought,
and later had been carried out on the back of their guide. By the time
proper attention had been given to her, things had gone wrong, with
the result that she was left with a limp. But a far worse fate lay ahead
of her in the months and years ahead. Thank God we do not know the
future. The two girls returned full of enthusiasm, complete with our
new identity cards and papers for the next section of our journey to
freedom. Eagerly, I examined my new identity card and was surprised
to see that my photo from the previous card had been cleverly
removed and now lay in a French cover, overprinted with an
embossed German seal. I cannot remember the name they had chosen
for Bob, but my name was now Jean Thomas. Anyone who under-
stands a little French knows that Jean is pronounced more like John,
and John Thomas was a name no Englishman could ever forget! They
had also obtained permits for us to travel though a restricted zone,
together with a letter from the Mayor of Bayonne stating that we were
natives of that city and were required for urgent work.

Now for the first time we learnt that we would be going down the
west coast of France, over the western end of the Pyrenees, and that
we would be going that very night. Our train journey would take us
down through Bordeaux to St Jean de Luz. First, we would meet some
other friends and have dinner with them in the city. Following the two
girls, again we set off via the Métro. Paris was so full of people of all
races that, in the event, we did not follow the girls, but walked openly
with them. They took us to a smart restaurant in the heart of the city
where we met two well-dressed and charming men. Their names I was
unaware of, but I have since learnt that one them was Robert Azlé. We
all sat together at a table in the centre of the restaurant, which, although
it was still early in the evening, was almost full of people, among whom

were several German officers. In spite of their presence our friends sat and talked openly with apparent unconcern. As they spoke almost entirely in French, Bob and I had the usual problem of not understanding what was being said.

When the meal was over, Dédée turned to us and, speaking quietly in English, she told us there was something they required us to do. Shortly, we would go to the railway station to catch our train south. There we would meet two more men, about our age, who were going to come with us. 'One of them is a Belgian boy', she explained. 'We know all about him and he is genuine. The other man is an airman whom we do not trust. He seems to know nothing about the RAF and has been unable to answer many of our questions. We think he may be a German who is excusing his lack of knowledge by saying he is a Canadian and only arrived in England a few days before the raid on which he was shot down. Another reason for suspecting him is that no other members of his crew had been found close to where he landed by parachute.'

Dédée and her friends now faced a terrible decision. Should they take him on the last final lap of the escape line and risk being exposed to the Gestapo, or should they liquidate him? 'So,' continued Dédée, 'we have arranged to have him brought to the railway station, where you must question him yourselves, and decide whether he is genuine or not.' I turned to one of the men in our group and asked, 'What will you do if we think he is an impostor?' He shrugged and replied:

'We will need to dispose of him.'

'But how?' I asked.

'We will suggest that before we board the train we should all use the toilet. Then when he is occupied, we will shoot him', he casually replied.

I marvelled at his coolness, little knowing that in a few months' time, two Germans masquerading as Canadians serving with the RAF would infiltrate the escape organisation. Later they would cause the arrest of many brave people in Brussels. Armed with this knowledge and feeling very uneasy at the decision Bob and I might soon have to make, we left the restaurant and walked to the railway station. There we met our 'doubtful' airman, who told us a remarkable but true story. His name was Harold de Mone and he did indeed come from Canada. He had volunteered to become an air gunner. He had completed a month's air-gunnery course, but had never seen an operational aircraft, nor even sat in a modern gun turret. Neither had he flown at night. Following his month's course, he received his air gunner's brevet and sergeant's stripes. He was then sent across the Atlantic to

101

an OTU at Upper Heyford. Arriving there, he found the same state of affairs that had existed throughout Bomber Command before the Thousand-Bomber Raid on Cologne. He had hung about the station doing little except attend a few lectures. Then, like me, he had looked at the board in the station flight office on the morning of 30 May, to find he was down to fly as a rear gunner on a Wellington aircraft that very night.

His skipper was an ex-operational pilot who was 'on rest' at the OTU, but most of the crew were as inexperienced as he was. Then, on the night of 30/31 May 1942, he had, for the first time, found himself in the rear gun turret of a Wellington, flying through the night to bomb Cologne. They reached the target, but on the way home they were attacked by a night-fighter. Sgt De Mone not only fought off the attack, but also actually destroyed the aircraft. Two nights later he flew with the same crew on a 1,000-bomber raid on Essen. Again, a fighter attacked them and succeeded in setting their port engine on fire. Unable to extinguish the flames and with the wing on fire, the skipper gave the order to bale out. With the flames from the burning wing now spreading aft, to do so from the rear turret was no easy task. After considerable difficulty, he managed to release the turret doors and drop out backwards; but as he fell, his parachute pack caught on the sides of the turret and detached itself from the temporary clips that held it on to the user's chest until the moment it opened.

As he fell headlong through space, he groped for the ripcord handle only to realise that the pack, instead of being on his chest, now swung somewhere above his head. Tumbling over and over, it took him some considerable time to grab the pack, then locate the handle and pull the ripcord. This he finally managed to do, but not before he had fallen many thousands of feet from where he had originally baled out. He landed safely, but was a long way from the rest of the crew, who had been carried many miles downwind.

He had been hidden in a brewery by Belgian patriots, and later brought by the Resistance to Paris. The fact that he had been in England for only a few days accounted for his lack of knowledge of the RAF. The real proof that his story was genuine came from the fact that Bob Horsley had done his OTU course at Upper Heyford where he was then a sergeant. Naturally, having an eye for the girls, Hal de Mone knew the names of the prettiest of the prettiest WAAFs who served in the sergeants' mess. By the time Hal had finished his story, the happy smiles on our faces were more than enough to tell Dédée and her friends that all was well. And I for one breathed a heartfelt sigh of relief that it had not been our job to give the 'thumbs down'.

Meanwhile, our train had been standing in the station, and although it was not yet time to depart, we boarded it and found an empty compartment. Only Dédée came with us, and we said goodbye to Elvire and her two male companions. So now Dédée had four 'children' to guide to safety.

We settled ourselves into our compartment, which, it was comforting to note, was a first-class one, and I relaxed in a corner opposite Dédée. I was now able to take stock of this quite remarkable girl. She was an extremely alert and vital person, whose age I judged to be about twenty-four. Her movements were quick and positive, as was her repartee. She spoke almost entirely in English, which the young Belgian with us, fortunately, could also understand. She always seemed to be smiling and brim-full of enthusiasm. I was not surprised to learn later that she was not only the originator but also the controller of this escape route to Spain. It was 'her baby', born from her enthusiasm and love of her country. Her dynamic personality was the intangible chain that held the whole organisation together and gave the many helpers along the way the courage to risk their very lives in its cause. As for the airmen she helped to regain their country and continue the fight for freedom, as I have already said, we were her children. She called us *Mes enfants*, an appropriate name, as with our lack of knowledge of her country and our inability to speak French we were children indeed.

Thus we sat comfortably in our seats with a feeling of complete trust in this unusual girl. Her abundance of self-confidence made it seem quite a normal thing to be speeding southwards through enemy territory towards England and home. Having been awake throughout the previous night, most of us were asleep when darkness stole over the countryside. When I awoke, we were already in the outskirts of Bordeaux. The next stop was Bayonne, and long before the train drew to a halt, Dédée was leaning out of the carriage window looking for her friends who were to meet us. As the train stopped, two women on the platform spotted Dédée, ran over, and embraced her. One was a fairly young and pretty girl, the other a slightly older person. I never knew their names, but from pictures published after the war in Airey Neave's *The Little Cyclone*, I am fairly sure the older woman was the now famous *Tante Go*. For a few minutes, they spoke earnestly together. Then Dédée turned to us and said, 'Two of you must leave the train now and go with my friends. We will all meet together again later.' It was decided that Hal de Mone and the Belgian lad would be the ones to go. With a cheery nod, they left us and within minutes the train continued its journey.

Dédée now sat back in her seat and took stock of the situation. 'You

103

will be all right', she said to me. 'You look just the part, like a true Basque, in fact.' This was probably right, for I still wore Armand Leviticus's continental-style suit, though I had discarded the tie and wore the shirt open at the neck. I also wore a black beret I had been given before leaving Paris. With my big Roman nose, I really did resemble inhabitants of the region we were entering. Bob was a different kettle of fish. Dédée eyed him for a few minutes and then said, 'I cannot take you through the barrier. You look too suspicious. If they question you and you cannot answer, then perhaps we shall all be caught. So you must leave another way.' She opened her handbag, took out a pencil and paper, sketched a plan of the station at St Jean de Luz and said,

> 'Here is where we arrive, and here at the far end of the platform is a toilet. As soon as the train stops, you must leave and go straight to the toilet. Go inside and wait until everyone has left the platform. When you are sure that nobody has seen you, leave the toilet and walk back up the platform, where you will see a gate about here on the plan. If nobody is around, go through it and you will be in a goods yard. Cross it and you will reach this road. Turn to the left and walk casually along. We will wait for you when we are well away from the station.'

As we travelled on the last few miles I felt terribly excited. The butterflies in my stomach that so often took wing before a take-off again became alive. It wasn't that I was frightened, but simply that I knew that this was the last time that I might be questioned. Everything would depend on how I acted, and on the vigilance or otherwise of the guards at the barrier; but most of all it would depend on Lady Luck. I could only hope that she would not desert me at this crucial time. However, the distance between Bayonne and St Jean de Luz could not have been much more than ten or twelve miles, so we had little time to sit and worry about what lay ahead.

Already the train was slowing down and soon ground to halt at St Jean de Luz. Almost reluctantly, we left the security of our comfortable compartment, and Bob made off in search of the toilet as instructed. Allowing Dédée to get ahead of me, I followed at a discreet distance. I knew that if I was going to be caught, I must in no way involve her but give her plenty of time to get clear. Unfortunately, most of the passengers had left the train at Bayonne, leaving only a handful of us to go through the barrier. Anxiously I watched the people ahead of me to see what was happening. There was a uniformed railway official taking the tickets, while a man in plain clothes was examining papers. Some way behind them were two soldiers with rifles slung over their shoulders. They looked bored to tears and obviously would not bother us unless called upon to do so.

By the time my turn came, Dédée had already left the station. As I had done before, I made a bit of a fuss locating my ticket and papers. I brought the items out one at a time, while they asked me questions none of which I could understand. I merely nodded and fumbled away rather like someone stupid, never daring to utter a single word. The man in plain clothes had a good look at my identity card photo and then at me. Suddenly, I knew that everything was all right, for they returned my papers and stood aside for me to continue. I nodded approval, and was soon out of the station into the roadway. Dédée was walking slowly some way ahead; I followed and soon caught up with her. Having got well away from the station, we waited until Bob had joined us. It all seemed such a huge joke, and we were soon grinning to each other at the sheer relief of getting through okay.

Not far from the railway station we came to a large house where the three of us were admitted. We entered a large bedroom where we were to stay until the following evening. Later in the day, Hal and the Belgian boy who had come over from Bayonne on bicycles joined us. Dédée looked absolutely fit and fresh in spite of the night on the train. She busied herself on a multitude of jobs; one of which I remember well was preparing the salad dressing for the evening meal with meticulous attention to detail. Everything this extraordinary girl did was performed in similar fashion.

Later that evening we were joined by a man aged about thirty-five, who had come over the mountains the previous night. He was going back to Paris with Dédée after she had taken us into Spain. I did not know his name, but he told me he liaised between the British authorities and the organisation in Brussels. He carried an old and battered Gladstone bag that never seemed far from his side. That night he shared the large bedroom with us, five of us managing to sleep together in one bed. The next day, I became curious about the contents of his bag and casually asked him what it contained. He smiled and said, 'Would you like to have a look?' Then, watching my face in anticipation of my surprise, he opened the case for my inspection. It was packed with bundles of crisp new banknotes. 'Well,' I said, 'how much on earth is that lot worth?' Still smiling he replied, 'Somewhere around one million Belgian francs. It is to keep the escape lines going.' I could only shake my head and grin at this seemingly cloak-and-dagger occupation.

The following day was fine and bright, and by the time we rose Dédée had already left. Later in the day, she returned to tell us that we would be going over the mountains that night. She explained how we would first head for a farmhouse that was in the foothills above the village of Urrugne. This we would do in the early evening, when the workers would have returned to the farms. There we would meet our guide. She showed us a map of the district and the rough track we would have to follow into Spain. It looked something like twenty kilometres, but of course this did not take into account the ups and downs, or the winding paths. As none of us had walked more than a few hundred yards during the previous fortnight, I had some misgivings at what lay ahead of us. Nevertheless, I was in high spirits, as indeed we all were. Dédée too was full of enthusiasm, despite the fact that she must have known very well the arduous journey facing her.

Chapter 8

THE PYRENEES
WITH FLORENTINO

From our bedroom window we could clearly see the Pyrenees, and we were eager to be on our way. After a meal, we set off at about 7 o'clock in the evening. Dédée left first, and having given her plenty of time to get well ahead, Bob and I followed, leaving Hal de Mone and the Belgian lad to keep some way behind us. We soon cleared the town and started up the long stony road towards Urrugne. Dédée was now about half a kilometre ahead of us, and we found we had to put on quite a spurt to keep up with her. The road was deserted, though there were still some people in the fields. With every step we took we grew more confident, and I knew that, come what may, I would never give up now that freedom was so near.

With this in mind, I said to Bob, 'What do we do if we get stopped farther along the road, do we give in or make a run for it?' 'Well,' he replied, 'if it's only one soldier or gendarme, then we should make a run for it.' If challenged, we agreed that we would separate and run in opposite directions, making for the nearest hedge. We reasoned that it would take some moments for our challenger to get his rifle off his shoulder, cock it and then open fire. He would not be able to shoot at both of us, and might even be reluctant to fire at all if he was not sure who we were. I reckoned that if we zigzagged away, he would be very lucky to hit one of us when firing from an upright position.

Of what I could remember from Dédée's map, I guessed it was about five kilometres to the farm from St Jean de Luz. At the pace Dédée was walking, I soon found it a bit of an uphill slog, but we dare not slacken our pace for fear of losing her. Glancing behind us, we were relieved to see that we were not being followed, except by Hal and the Belgian, who were about a quarter of a kilometre back.

Steadfastly, we plodded on, heartened by the sight of the hills ahead that drew ever nearer. For a while, we lost touch with Dédée. When we next saw her she had turned off the road and was following a path that led to a farmhouse higher up in the foothills. Losing sight of her again, we assumed she must have arrived there. Redoubling our efforts, we reached the farmhouse to be welcomed inside by the happy smile of our youthful guide.

We found ourselves in a large, sparsely furnished room, typical of the farm kitchens of that area. A kindly faced woman offered us a chair round the table, while her children stood shyly behind her. She was introduced to us as Francia. A huge man, who had been watching from the window when we first arrived, came over and shook hands with us. His name was Florentino Goicoechea.

Bob and I sat at the table and were soon joined by a grinning Hal de Mone and the Belgian. We were given a bowl of milk and some cheese, and sat somewhat bewildered by our surroundings, while we listened to Dédée conversing animatedly with Florentino. Without understanding what they were saying, I recognised that a strong bond existed between them. He was an extraordinary man, probably about five foot eleven tall, broad as an ox, with huge hands and powerful shoulders. His face was tanned by the wind and sun, and had a rugged splendour about it. His nose and mouth had the quiet strength of a man who lived close to nature. With his black beret perched flatly on his head, he looked the very picture of a true Basque.

We were given rope-soled, canvas-topped climbing shoes called espadrilles, and some old trousers. Our shoes and clothes were packed into a huge bundle, which Florentino was to carry on his back through the night. For this small mercy, I was extremely grateful, as the tight shoes Armand Leviticus had given me had all but crippled my feet on the walk up to the farm. We were also given stout sticks to assist us as we traversed the rough tracks in the dark. Dédée then outlined the journey ahead of us, in case we should become separated during the night. We would leave just before dark, and climb to the top of the hills behind the farm. Then for a time would follow the ridges towards the coast, then descend into the valley of the Bidassoa and cross the river, which marked the frontier between France and Spain. We would have to wade across the river, which although fast flowing would present no difficulty at this time of the year, as it was only about four feet deep at the crossing point. There was a manned frontier that we must pass in absolute silence. Once across the river, we would have to climb another ridge at about 1,000 feet. When we reached the top, we would follow the ridges for several more kilometres, until finally descending into the foothills and making for Renteria. We would then be taken by car to San Sebastian.

When Dédée had finished our briefing and answered our many questions, we rose to go, full of confidence and excited at the prospect of the freedom that now seemed so tantalisingly near. We bade good-bye to Francia and her children, little knowing that we would never see her again. To us, it all seemed like a glorious adventure, and our parting with her, like our parting from Dédée Dumont, was brief and undemonstrative. Little could we have guessed that this brave woman would soon be captured with a party of airmen like ourselves. She would have to endure the horrors of a German concentration camp, only to die in the foul stench of Ravensbrück on 12 April 1945. I did not know her full name at the time, but found later that it was Françoise Usandizanga. I also learnt that Andrée de Jongh had been arrested on the same day.

We set out in single file with Florentino in the lead, followed closely by Dédée de Jongh with us four escapees behind her. Darkness came very soon, and we were fortunate that the night sky was not clouded over. For there was no moon, and we had only the dim light of the stars to help us keep sight of each other. Frequently, when we were in shadow, the fleeting clouds temporarily obscuring the light from the stars, it became almost impossible to see the man in front. So we took our handkerchiefs and stuck one corner down the back of our necks. This enabled us to make out the position of the man in front. At first, the path was well trodden and easy to follow, but later, it seemed to peter out, as we followed each other over broken ground. To make it easier to keep in contact, we now held the end of each other's stick, forming a sort of chain down the line.

Trudging on, we were soon able to see the strong beams of the light-house at Fuenterrabia, and then later on, the distant lights of Spain. A few kilometres away lay the frontier town of Irún, where the Bidassoa flowed into the sea. Even farther away, we could dimly make out the lights of San Sebastian. The going was now much easier, for the light from the night sky was sufficient to see by while we traversed the ridges. As we started to descend towards the river, however, the shadows of the hills around us at times made it almost impossible to see the man in front. Our espadrilles were marvellous for grip, but the canvas uppers afforded little protection for our feet when we stumbled against the occasional outcrop of rock. From time to time, the silence was broken by a sharp cry of annoyance or pain, as one of our party would slam his foot into some unseen obstacle.

Another somewhat amusing sound that occasionally shattered the silence was the loud noise that came unashamedly from our huge guide up front. That Dédée was only some three feet behind him mattered little to this man of nature. No doubt, it stemmed from the diet he enjoyed. Soured milk, eggs, and an abundance of farm cheese, well mixed with local wine and copious amounts of his favourite cognac, gave him a digestion that never required the laxatives of city dwellers. I had heard of the Wind in the Willows, but during that night, we heard the Wind in the Mountains blowing quite regularly.

As we moved lower and lower into the valley, it got harder to see the way ahead. Then through the darkness we could hear the sound of the river ahead as it tumbled seawards between its steep banks. Soon we arrived its edge, which we followed for a while until we could make out the lights of the frontier post. Our guide stopped, and Dédée spoke quietly, telling each of us that from now on we must maintain absolute silence. There would be guards on the opposite side of the river who would open fire if they heard the slightest sound. We now moved slower and more cautiously, as we had to pass the frontier post to a point a little further on where the river was easily fordable.

Soon the post was behind us and we stopped at a point where Florentino knew we could cross. One by one we entered the icy-cold river, which though not deep was running swiftly. I thanked my lucky stars that it was in the middle of summer, for I would have hated having to cross during the depths of winter. My feet were already becoming sore, and the muscles of my legs seemed to ache more after our down-hill journey than when we had been climbing; so the cold water was a welcome relief. As we scrambled up the far bank, the steepness of the climb ahead became apparent, and I remembered Dédée's earlier warning that this would be the most arduous part of our journey.

We climbed until we came to the road that ran to the frontier post. While we lay in the bushes in absolute silence, Florentino scanned the road up to the post looking for sentries; but it was quite impossible to see more than a few yards. For all we knew there might a be soldier within easy reach of us. We lay straining our ears for the slightest sound that might indicate the presence of an enemy, but heard nothing. Then suddenly, Florentino rose from the ground, sped quickly across the road and disappeared into the shadows on the opposite side. I held my breath in case a volley of shots rang out, but all was well.

Dédée now crept up to each man in turn and whispered, 'Go.' With a slight pause between each of us, we rose and shot across the road. I leapt at the opposite bank and pulled myself up the slope, my stick now becoming a hindrance. It was so steep that I had to claw my way up, digging my fingernails into the soft earth and clutching at roots and bushes. There was now no way of following each other by keeping the man in front in sight, as the foliage of the trees around us blotted out all light from the sky above. We could only crawl ever upwards on our hands and knees, keeping in touch more by sound than anything else.

It is difficult to convey how arduous the climb was; but I was soon gasping for breath in my efforts to keep close to the man in front.

Thus, we struggled up a steady forty-five-degree gradient, never rising to our feet except for a few moments when, having run into a tree, we clasped it close while we strove to regain our breath. For what seemed like an age, we climbed on until at last the trees started to thin out and the slope eased off. Then we broke out into a small clearing where we could begin to see around us. It was a marvel that we were all still altogether. Florentino was already there waiting for us, with the huge pack containing our clothes still on his back. Dédée was talking quietly with him as he took out a flask from his pocket, and after giving her first go was now having a swig from it himself. The flask was then passed round for everyone to have a drink. It was dynamite, the raw spirit burning my throat as I slowly swallowed it. Fits of coughing from Hal and Bob indicated that they too had found the spirit to be fiery stuff. Once down, it felt good and I was soon ready to go on. Without any further pause, we moved on again. There were still a few more hundred feet to the top of the ridge; but the scrambling on all fours was now over, and again we moved on in single file.

The strong spirit was now coursing through my veins and, but for the aching in my legs, I felt fine. As the aching got steadily worse, I began to worry lest they would let me down. Whether my colleagues felt the same I do not know, but Bob and Hal, like me, had done no walking at all during the last two weeks. As we plodded on, I thought of the map that Dédée had shown us, and realised that we must be nearly halfway through our journey, and the difficult part was now behind us. However, by the time a further hour had passed it was apparent that some of us were feeling the strain and beginning to lag behind. In spite of the huge pack on his shoulder, Florentino still forged ahead, followed closely by an apparently fresh Dédée. To spur the rest of us on, far away to the west we could still see the lights of neutral Spain, and, after blacked-out Britain, it looked wonderful.

Arriving at the bottom of a slight dip, we found a mountain stream, and following the example of our guide, we fell to our knees and eagerly drank the cold clear water. Our pause was short-lived, for in less than a minute Dédée was urging us on again. 'We must go quickly,' she said, 'for dawn will soon be breaking and we cannot risk being seen coming down from the mountains in daylight.' This was one of the few drawbacks to crossing the Pyrenees during the middle of the summer. The hours of darkness were few, and although the going was easier, the crossing had to be done in less time.

Redoubling our efforts, we pressed on as fast as we could. The thought of being caught by the Spanish was even worse than being in the hands of the enemy. For this was 1942, when the feeling in Spain was very pro-German. Great pressure was exerted on the Spanish to intern escaping members of the Allied air forces. Under International Law, a member of the armed services can demand repatriation from a neutral country, provided he has actually escaped from enemy detention. If he has never been in enemy hands and merely reaches, or lands in, a neutral country, then his fate is internment in that country. In places such as Sweden or Switzerland, this was bearable, apart from one's loss of freedom. In Spain, it was a fate worse than being in a German POW camp, internees being sent to the dreaded concentration camp at Miranda in north-west Spain where the conditions were appalling. As the Spanish people themselves were very short of food, they had no wish to waste any of it on the flotsam and jetsam that ended up in Miranda. The chances of surviving until the end of the war were no better there than in the concentration camps in Germany.

So we strained ourselves to the utmost, and after about another hour we arrived at the highest part of our journey. The Montagne des Trois Couronnes lay to the left and slightly behind us; in front of us was Spain, with the lights of San Sebastian now clearly visible in the cold crisp air. Our journey now was all down hill, which was a tonic to us all, and again we redoubled our efforts to keep up with Dédée and Florentino. Lucky for us, the night was fine and dry, for had it been wet then undoubtedly we would have had many slips and falls. As it was, we had to put up with much stumbling, and none of us went through the night without the occasional fall. I now understood how Elvire Morelle fell and broke her leg, and endured untold agony as she lay in the cold winter conditions awaiting rescue. Steadily we pressed on, with the cold light of dawn now breaking in the east. My legs were aching most painfully, but this was no longer my main cause for concern, for I was now getting a sharp pain deep in my hips that was making it almost impossible to lift my feet. Often, I had heard of the phrase 'dragging one's feet', and this was the only way I could describe my progress.

After about another half-hour dawn broke, bathing the countryside in its pale light. We had come to the final stage of our journey, that lay through the open country of the foothills. Here, Dédée stopped and conversed with Florentino. We gathered around, anxious to know what they were discussing. 'We cannot go farther now,' she explained, 'for there in the distance is where we are heading. You can just see the little township of Renteria, but long before we get there it will be broad daylight, and many people will see us coming down from the mountains. So we must go to another place and wait until later in the day. Then perhaps, when I have made sure everything is safe, we can proceed.' So, abandoning our original direction, we set off behind her. After a while, we came to an empty farmhouse, and Florentino went ahead to reconnoitre. When he found it to be entirely deserted, we entered, climbing the stairs to a room above. It was bare and empty, and we sank down on the wooden floor to rest. Hard as the floor was, it nevertheless was wonderful to relax. Apart from our short stay in the farmhouse above Urrugne, we had been walking almost continuously for some twelve hours. Dédée then told us that in about another hour's time she and Florentino would set off on their own for Renteria, where she would phone for a car to come to the village for us. When it had all been arranged, she would return to the farmhouse to collect us.

By now most of us were pretty hungry, though this did not worry me as much as the pain in my hips that had now become acute. Thankfully, I stretched out on the floor and slept, grateful for this brief respite and the shelter of a roof above us. When I awoke Dédée had gone, and the time was now well after 10 o'clock. An hour later, she returned with Florentino. 'All is well', she hastened to tell us. 'A car will be waiting for us by the time we get down to the road. The distance is about four or five kilometres, so it will not take us long.' As I struggled to my feet I was barely able to stand, and I marvelled at the stamina and sheer guts of this remarkable girl who, while we had slept, had completed the journey both ways. Now she was ready to start out again.

Full of hope and eager to get going, we began the final leg of our journey. Florentino went first, with Dédée waiting some while before setting out so that they would not be seen together. Then, having instructed us to wait until each person in front was about half a kilometre away, we set off one by one. Not wishing to hold anyone up, I elected to go last, for I knew I would be lucky to make the journey at all, much less be able to keep up. I cheated a little by setting off shortly after the last of our party, as I knew I would soon trail behind. The day was perfect, and the path we now took was smooth and almost level as it dropped gently towards the sea. Alas, I was in no mood to enjoy the scenery for my hips were now killing me. Had I been asked to raise my leg and kick a football I could never have done so. Deep inside me I felt ashamed at the way my hips had let me down. Only sheer willpower kept me going; for I knew I could not give up and jeopardise the rest of the party, who were now almost out of sight. Then, almost before I was aware of it, I came to the outskirts of the small town and there was the car with the others waiting for me. They helped me in, and I slumped into the rear seat. Without a word the driver set off. Happy as I was, I could not even trouble to look out of the window but just sat quietly, thankful that my journey was over.

As we entered San Sebastian, Dédée explained that it would be ill advised for us to arrive together outside the British Consulate. So the car stopped a little way short, and we finished the last part on foot. Ten minutes later we were safe inside the building, which to me at least was Shangri-La. For the diplomatic immunity of the Consulate meant we were on the equivalent of British soil. Dédée spent a little time with the Consul, and then it was time for her to leave. Once more she must return over the mountains with Florentino, as it was dangerous for her to stay in Spain too long. We said goodbye to this remarkable girl, to whom more than anyone else we now owed our freedom. Many people had helped us and risked their lives doing so. But she was the power, the force and the inspiration that had brought us from Belgium to Spain. Yet, she made light of her help to us, waving away our thanks with a cheery nod as if it were of no concern. Then with a final handshake all round, she turned and was gone. Of course, we did not know at the time that she had already made many such journeys, and that she would continue to do so until, finally, she would be caught. So, rather like the parting with Dédée Dumont, we had not truly expressed the gratitude that each of us felt in our hearts.

After Dédée had left, Bob, Hal and I had a brief interview with the Consul. He told us we must speak to no one concerning our experiences since baling out, until we had been interviewed, in Gibraltar, by a man named Donald Darling. This man, and only this man, must hear our story. Our next step would be to go to Madrid where we would be taken care of in the Embassy. Meanwhile, we must stay in the Consulate and wait until our journey to Madrid had been arranged.

Chapter 9

BRITISH EMBASSY
MADRID AND GIBRALTAR

I t was now the afternoon of 13 June, just two weeks, apart from a few hours, since I had said farewell to Betty in Skellingthorpe. Yet it seemed almost a lifetime. Somehow, I didn't even feel that I was the same man. For here I was, sitting in a strange room in a strange house, wearing the clothes of Armand Leviticus and his tight-fitting shoes, with only Bob's familiar face to remind me who I was. Even Bob I had not known a fortnight ago. But most significant of all was the knowledge that I was now in Spain and that I had crossed the best part of half the Continent under the very noses of the Germans. What an extraordinary thing to have happened to a young married man who before the war had never been out of England, apart from one short holiday in Belgium.

Sitting back in a large comfortable chair, I reflected on all that had happened. My thoughts went back to the many good people who had risked their all to help us; the Nijskens family, especially the younger of the two brothers who was so jovial and so happy to help us; the young couple who had taken us at night from the farmhouse to the grain mill at Dilsen, whose names I did not even know. And who was the woman who had taken the 'boys' to Liège, while I had gone with Armand? The tall man who had walked in front of us in Liège; what part in the scheme of things did he play? The kind and gentle Evrard family, and their lovely daughter Gisèle, would I ever see any of them again? Also little Dédée Dumont, to whom I somehow felt the closest, in spite of being with her for less than a complete day. Finally, Dédée de Jongh: what an amazing girl she was. Surely, there would be few that could equal her for sheer tenacity and sense of purpose. How many girls were there in England who would have done such things for people we only thought of as 'foreigners'? Not many, I fear. That night, as I crawled into a clean bed, I fell asleep thinking of them all. Yet the picture I carried uppermost in my mind was that of Dédée Dumont standing in the Métro just seconds before she turned and was gone. Who really was she, and how was she mixed up in this risky enterprise? I only hoped that I would survive the war and would be able to meet her one day to thank her more appropriately than I had done when we parted.

The next morning was Sunday and I awoke refreshed and content. When I went to get out of bed, I found I was unable to lift my legs, for such was the pain in my hips. I had to drag myself on to the edge of the bed, where I had the greatest difficulty in getting dressed. Although

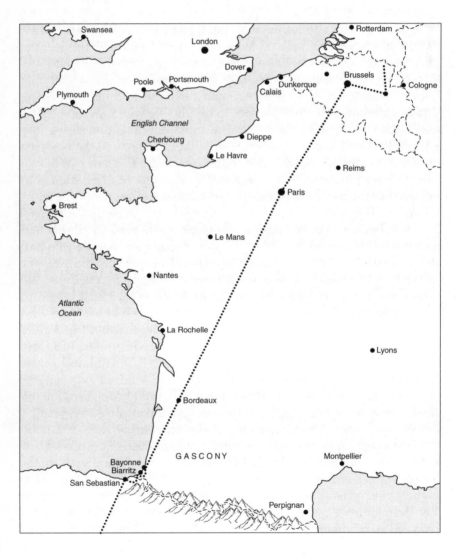

we could not go out, I was more than content to sit in a chair all day, or rest on my bed. My three friends were also terribly fatigued, though without the same hip trouble. We all had blisters on our feet, having almost worn out our Spanish espadrilles.

After another comfortable night in the Consulate, we were told that we would be going by car that day to the Embassy in Madrid. Following an early lunch, we were delighted when a black Talbot car arrived for us, driven by an Englishman who worked at the Embassy. At the time I did not know his name, but he is mentioned in Darling's book, *Secret Sunday*, his code name being 'Monday'.

We bundled into the Talbot, full of excitement and keen to have a look at the countryside, for none of our party had ever visited Spain in peacetime. The car had left Madrid soon after dawn and had driven up on the direct route, but as our driver now explained to us, we must return by an alternative way. This was because the car might well attract the attention of a vigilant policeman on duty in any of the small towns we might pass through. It was a large distinctive car and bore a Diplomatic Corps plate at the rear. If it had been seen heading back from San Sebastian on the same day with five men in it, while earlier it had been empty except for the driver, then it wouldn't take a genius to guess at what was going on if it were reported. The car set off at a cracking pace, travelling at speeds of between sixty and seventy miles per hour, in spite of the generally poor state of the roads. We chatted to the driver, a very interesting man indeed. We asked if they had much difficulty in obtaining petrol for such a journey. Apparently, petrol was not as much of a problem as were the tyres. As they used retreads made of poor-quality rubber, the journey from Madrid to San Sebastian and return usually wore out a complete set of tyres. Of course, the high speed caused some of the wear, but this could not be avoided, as it was necessary to return if possible before dark. The countryside we passed through was quite different from anything I had ever seen before. The towns and villages were squalid and it was obvious that poverty abounded everywhere. Our journey took about six hours and we were soon inside the British Embassy, on British soil once again. The Union Jack that fluttered from its flagpole was indeed a welcome sight. We were taken to our quarters in a large basement room that had been turned into a dormitory containing over a dozen beds of the regulation Service type. I picked one and Hal chose the one alongside. A young Polish chap occupied the bed on the opposite side to mine. Later I found out that he was an airman serving in the RAF and had been flying on Wellingtons from Hemswell. I told him that we had landed there after our first raid on Rostock. They too had been on that raid and had been shot up while over the target, losing their hydraulic control system. On landing without the use of either brakes or flaps, they had overshot the runway. 'Yes,' I said laughingly, 'you went clean through a hedge into a ploughed field, didn't you? I know because we landed right behind you.'

The next day we had an interview with the Air Attaché, who apart from asking us for our names and numbers and particulars of our squadron, had little to say. Indeed, he repeated almost word for word what we had been told by the Consul at San Sebastian, about speaking only to the mysterious Mr Darling in Gibraltar. He issued us with some Spanish money, just enough to buy fruit or a few sweets, as once again we would not be allowed to go beyond the Embassy grounds. We were also told that it might be some little while before we would be on our way to Gibraltar, as it all had to be arranged through the Spanish authorities. From then on, we spent most of the day lying on our beds reading, or writing home. However, there was little we could say then, except that we were alive and well and would soon be home. These letters, which were sent back to England with the diplomatic mail, did not reach our families until after we had arrived back in England. Of course, we all still imagined that our families had been told that we were safe and well, after the radio message that had been sent to England when we were first questioned in Liège. But this had never been done.

After the excitement of the previous two weeks, the time spent in Madrid was a complete anticlimax. The days seemed to be endless, with nothing to do except take an occasional walk round the small Embassy grounds. Access to the Embassy itself was limited to our basement dormitory. We were referred to, by the Embassy staff, as 'the prisoners', and our food was cooked by an elderly Spanish woman separately from that of the staff. It was good wholesome food but very plain and monotonous, with boiled rice every day for dessert. Our Belgian colleague seemed to enjoy it. Being keen to learn our language, of which he knew little, he used to ask us the names of anything unknown to him. So we told him that the name of our dessert was 'bloody rice', with the result that when there was a surplus of rice, he would take his plate to the elderly lady and ask for more, rather like Oliver Twist. With his plate outstretched, he would say in halting English, 'More bloody rice, please'. Our Spanish lady, knowing even less English than he did, would smile and dole him out another huge helping. A week dragged slowly by, with no further contact with any Embassy official or advice of when we would be moving on. On the last evening of the week, excitement arose with the reappearance of

Mills, Naylor and Stan King. They had waited with the Steenbeck family in Brussels for a further week, and had then followed the same journey that we had. Like ours, it had been uneventful except for one episode in which Mills had nearly been caught. He had been walking along a station platform at a discreet distance from his guide, carrying a small bag similar to the one Gisèle had given me. Suddenly, a man in plain clothes had stopped him, clearly a member of the police force or the Gestapo, who demanded that he should open his bag for inspection. Mills could not understand a word of what was being asked of him, and mistakenly thought that the man was offering to carry his bag. So he said the only word he knew in French, which was '*Non*', and then quickly walked on. Again the man stopped him and demanded that he open the bag. Again Mills said '*Non*', and made to walk on. The man was now quite angry and swung Mills round by the shoulder, grabbing the bag from his grasp. Suddenly, Mills caught on as to what was required of him. Apologetically, he opened the bag and then took out his Identity Card for the man to inspect. Noting that Mills was a Belgian from a Flemish part of the country, and not being a Flemish speaker himself, the man now gathered why Mills had not been able to understand his demands. Having looked through the bag and finding nothing except clothes, he returned it to Mills and waved him on his way.

Back in England, our families were having a worrying time. Each day they eagerly awaited the postman, praying that they would receive an official letter from the Red Cross saying that we were POWs. As each day went past without news, they became increasingly certain that we had all gone for good, probably down in the sea. My father took it very hard indeed, as much as, if not more than, Betty did. But their grief and anxiety brought them closer together and Betty gained tremendous comfort from him. Not that my father was able to put his feelings into words, for such was his upbringing and nature, but he let Betty know that she could rely on him to help her and Jill in the future. They agreed that they would sell our car, which had been laid up in its garage, and which we had paid £119 for in 1939. It was sold for £190, and with the money they paid off part of the mortgage on our house. My father also continued to make up my wages above my Service pay.

Earlier in my story, I told how before leaving for Canada I had written two 'last letters', one to my father and one to Betty. These I had given to Betty's stepfather to keep in his safe, against my possible demise. These letters now proved a bit of a problem for Betty's stepfather, as he did not know whether to hand them over or not. Perhaps he was a bit quick off the mark, but when nothing had been heard about me after a week or two, he handed them over. My original idea when I wrote these letters was that I did not want them to sell our house during early moments of distress and that later, possession of the letters might bring them some measure of comfort. At the time, they only served to make them feel more certain that I had been killed, doing little to comfort them in any way.

Meanwhile, Betty continued to live in Wembley with her mother and Pop. Among the most heartbreaking of her tasks was the job of replying to the letters of condolence she received from our many friends. Apart from one letter that she received from Denis Halisey, an old school friend, who was a flying instructor in the RAF in Canada, all the letters she received referred to me in the 'past tense'. Even the letter from the CO of 50 Squadron said, 'Your husband was the best second pilot on the station, and his loss is a blow to us all.'

Later, came the official notification from the Air Ministry, including a list of my personal effects that had been sent to a holding unit at Colnbrook. There were also letters from the Pensions Department to say how my pay would continue until Betty's allotment book ran out in September, and how she would then receive a permanent pension. At that time, she was receiving an allotment from my pay, plus family allowance, that totalled £3 19s 0d per week. In September, if I was still missing, she would receive a grand total sum, for both herself and Jill, of only £1 12s 0d per week. This would be just enough to pay for the weekly outgoings on our house – mortgage repayments, rates and fire insurance. There would be nothing remaining for food, clothing or things such as electricity, gas, winter fuel and the myriad expenses in running a home. When I think back, it did not create much of an entice-ment to go and be killed, however patriotic one felt for one's country.

Considering that there were five aircraft missing from our airfield alone, the squadron were very good indeed. For the COs of both the squadron and the station would have had thirty-five letters to write on one day alone. Betty also received a very nice letter from Wg Cdr Oxley when he sent her the 'wings' from my tunic that she had asked for. Later, Oxley wrote to the families of all the crew when he heard first that Horsley had reached Gibraltar. In fact, Horsley was still in Madrid with the rest of us when the CO received his letter. Since Horsley was a commissioned officer, he had been invited one evening into the Embassy itself, and while there had met a man on the staff who was going to Gibraltar ahead of us. Horsley had prevailed on him to send a telegram to his parents, and arranged that the man would sign it in Horsley's name. This was the first good news to reach the squadron.

One other strange coincidence occurred, concerning a Polish Air Force officer who was staying for a few days at a boarding house in Farnborough owned by Betty's Aunt Ivy. She of course told this officer that her niece had lost her husband on a raid on Cologne. Quite unknown to Ivy, the officer worked in the RAF Intelligence Branch, MI9. At his office, he looked up the records of messages regarding RAF personnel received on clandestine radio by Army Intelligence MI5. Of course, he found out that I was listed as one of five airmen picked up by the Belgian Resistance and being held in Liège. He dare not divulge such a secret to anybody outside MI9, though he did send comforting thoughts to Ivy, pointing out that we had attacked an inland target and that there was a good chance we had baled out over land and were alive. He also said that Betty should not give up hope for several weeks. Meanwhile, like hundreds of other wives and families, who had airmen missing from other raids, Betty listened each night to Lord Haw Haw on German radio. He revealed a few names of airmen safe in enemy hands as bait to get people in Britain to listen to his propaganda programmes. In spite of pleas by the British government to do otherwise, many families listened to his broadcasts in the hope of hearing the names of their loved ones. Of course, our names were never mentioned, as we had not been captured.

With no news, time for Betty and my parents dragged slowly by, and they began to give up hope. Then one night Betty had a vivid dream in which, in her state of despondency, she was certain she had seen a vision. Waking up during the night, she saw me standing at the foot of her bed in my RAF uniform, with my forage cap set at a jaunty angle. She had sat up in bed and listened while I gently told her that I was not coming back, that she must adjust herself to that fact and get on with the job of living and devoting herself to Jill. It all sounded so like what I might well have told her that, in the morning, the dream was still so vivid that she was quite certain that I had actually appeared before her. However, it seemed so ridiculous to tell her mother, who would only disbelieve it, that she told no one. From then on, she felt sure that she would never see me again.

After about four and a half weeks, MI9 received news through the diplomatic mail reporting that we had arrived in Madrid. The Polish officer had been watching out for news of me, and when he found out that I was safe in the Madrid Embassy, he decided to ring Betty and tell her. He came on the phone, and without telling her who he was or anything about himself, he said, 'I have a message for you which is secret and which you must promise to keep entirely to yourself.' This

Betty readily agreed to; then he simply said, 'The person you are interested in is alive and well.' Then quickly rang off. Of course Betty did not know what to make of such a short message and confided in nobody except her mother and Pop. They were of the opinion that the message was genuine; but Betty, still so sure that her dream was truly a vision, could not bring herself to even hope that it might be true. She went through days of ever-changing mood, one day still hoping, and the next down in despair. To the unknown Polish officer, who must have been torn between a sense of humanity and his duty not to give away secret information, I gave my heartfelt thanks. For he risked his commission, or even a court martial, to bring a little comfort to a young wife he had never met. Perhaps it was because as an airman he felt a kind of brotherhood towards Betty and me.

Meanwhile we were all in Madrid with absolutely nothing to do, little to read, and nowhere to go, the days seemed endless and we chafed to get moving. Then, after nearly a fortnight, we heard that we would be leaving the next day. I was told that should the Spanish question me, I must state my name as Captain Michael Standish, the name that had been given to the Spanish authorities on my repatriation papers. I still had my French identity card in the name of Jean Thomas, and I would dearly have loved to keep it as a souvenir. I wondered if I dare hide it in my shoe, but finally decided it was not worth the risk of fouling everything up. Reluctantly, I tore it up and flushed it down the toilet. Later I regretted this, as we were never questioned or searched when we were handed over to the Spanish.

It must have been just about this time that Betty first heard the advance news that Bob Horsley had reached Gibraltar. This news not only brought her fresh hope, but also told her that she would soon know exactly what had happened to our crew. Then, on the afternoon of 30 June 1942, a large open-backed van, of the type used in England for furniture removals, arrived at the Embassy to take us away. We had a Spanish driver and an armed Spanish police escort. About a dozen of us left altogether, including the five of our crew, Hal de Mone, the Belgian and the Polish airman. We all sat in the back of the lorry on a pile of old sacks, thrilled to be heading homewards again. We drove until about 6 p.m., when we stopped at a delightful hotel. There we were able to wash and shower, and enjoy a night of comparative luxury.

Continuing the next morning, we arrived at La Linea soon after midday. The sight of the 'Rock' was marvellous, particularly as none of us had visited Gib before; seeing the Union Jack once again filled us with pride and relief. After a brief exchange of papers between our

Spanish escort and the NCO at the British guardroom, the gates were opened and we entered Gibraltar. A phone call brought out an RAF truck and we were driven to the RAF HQ. There we met our 'Mr Darling', who asked us many questions regarding events leading to our crash and relating to all aspects of our escape. He was a big kindly man and obviously of some importance, though he wore no uniform. He told us that we must not disclose anything regarding our escape until we were questioned further in London.

At the RAF stores depot, we were issued with a new battledress, and returning to the billet we had been given, we spent the next hour or so sewing on our stripes and aircrew brevets. I still had my own pair of 'wings', as when I discarded my old uniform in favour of Armand Leviticus's suit, I kept them, sewn to my under-vest, in case I would ever have to establish my real identity. It was a great feeling to be back in uniform, but even better was the feeling of a new pair of shoes that were of the correct size. Remembering my promise to Armand, I carefully packed his clothes to take back to England with me.

The following day we all rose bright and early convinced that the RAF would find a seat or spare corner in one of the many aircraft flying between Gib and the UK. However, this did not materialise, and we had to wait another three days before setting off by sea. On the day after our arrival we drew some advance pay and set off for the shopping area on the Rock. My first job was to go to the Telegraph Office and send a cable to Betty. I did not know if the office could accept it from a serviceman, so I worded it in a way they could not possibly object to. I had always told Betty that I would make for Gibraltar if I was shot down and not captured. So I simply said in my cable: 'Arrived destination safely. Coming home. Wire me any special news. Love Baveystock.'

A few hours later, while Betty was alone in the house in Wembley, the doorbell rang and a messenger-boy handed her my telegram. She had no idea what it contained, as unlike telegrams from the Air Ministry it was in a plain Post Office envelope. She opened it and could scarcely believe the news. Her mother was out shopping, so she picked up the telephone and asked the operator for her Pop's business number. The operator told her that the line was engaged, but Betty was so excited that she had to tell someone. 'Please don't go,' she begged the operator, 'for if I don't tell someone I think I will burst.' So she poured out her story to this unknown operator who listened sympathetically and was then able to connect her. After telling Pop, she thought of my father, and said to Pop. 'You had the rotten job of telling him the bad news when Bavey was missing, so you can be the one to tell him the good news.' Without waiting to clean up, Pop put on his jacket and walked the quarter-mile to my father's factory. My father was overjoyed for it was now just on five weeks since I had first gone missing. I found out later that he had grieved terribly, and had just about given up all hope of ever seeing me again.

Meanwhile, back on the Rock the weather was perfect and we spent our time either sunning ourselves or swimming in the Mediterranean. Then three days after our arrival we embarked on a ship bound for England. The voyage was without incident, but it took some time, as we had to go well out into the Atlantic before heading northwards to avoid the attention of the Luftwaffe based in western France.

Chapter 10

HOME AGAIN

We disembarked in Greenock on the evening of 9 July. A train was waiting for us, and in no time we were speeding south for London. Our first stop was at Carlisle, where we expected to phone our folks to tell them we were home, but much to our surprise, we found a detachment of 'Red Caps' (Military Police) had been posted at each end of our carriage. They politely but firmly told us that we could not leave the train. We could not understand why until we arrived next morning in London. Here another detachment of 'Red Caps' escorted us to an Army coach that had all its windows blacked out. Unable to see where we were going, we headed off into the London traffic. A few miles farther on we were taken off and marched into what had been a peacetime hotel. The outside was sandbagged against bombs, and we were unable to identify it.

We were taken into a large hall where we sat waiting to be interviewed, unable to leave. At the end of the hall was a telephone booth, and now at last we thought we could phone our families. But again we had no luck, as the phone was not connected to the switchboard. We all now complained loud and long to an official, and I told him that we had been missing for six weeks and that my wife was only as far away as a local telephone call. She was unaware that I was back in England, so for God's sake would he do something. It was then agreed that we could write out a message to our next-of-kin, and after they had been vetted they would be sent by telegram. On no account could we use the phone until we had been cleared satisfactorily.

At about 9 a.m. our crew of five was ushered into an upstairs room to be interviewed by an Army officer whose name we were not given. He had the rank of major, and later I felt sure that he was the legendary Airey Neave who had escaped from Colditz prison. He knew all about us and had a file in front of him that had been sent through the diplomatic mail. Another officer joined him and they questioned us lengthily on numerous things. He was particularly interested in Dédée de Jongh and the members of the Escape Line. It was apparent that the British authorities held her in high esteem and were very grateful for her work. Yet they seemed to have one little niggle of doubt, for originally she had come from nowhere, arriving one afternoon at the British Consulate at Bilbao. She told the Consul that she had travelled from Brussels escorting two Belgians and a Scottish soldier. Now she wanted to start an escape line to bring back airmen who had been shot down.

In due course the escape line was established and was later to become the famous Comet Line (*La Ligne Comète*). Already many men had been brought back to England along it. However, our interviewer was still looking at us with amazement. That airmen like us had started to arrive back was not unusual, but to have five airmen arrive from the one aircraft crew had never happened before, or even been contemplated. Yet here we were, sitting before him; less than six weeks earlier we had been on 50 Squadron at Skellingthorpe. In that short time we had made a quicker return from enemy territory than had ever been done before. So started our lengthy interrogation that lasted until lunchtime. In turn, each member of our crew told his story, answering many questions pertaining to our helpers and the methods they had used to get us from one place to another. Anything that might be useful to the future war effort was of particular interest and duly noted. For instance, while I had been in St Jean de Luz I had asked many questions about the place. The man who had shared our bed and had been carrying the bag with the large sum of money had drawn for me a rough map of the small harbour and the coastline around the town. On the map, he had marked the positions of the defences and gun positions. After I had memorised it, it was destroyed, but now I was able to sketch it again in case it might prove helpful to a raiding force.

When the questions had been asked and answered, we were finally asked one particularly pertinent question. Our interviewer said, 'Please think very carefully before you answer, and when you are quite sure, give me your own individual opinions. My question is this: at any time during your journey through Belgium and France, did you ever think that you should have been arrested, but that the Germans were letting you through knowing full well that you were escaping airmen?' For a moment or two, we did not grasp the full implication of his query. Then one of the crew asked, 'Do you mean that Andrée (Dédée) de Jongh might well be some sort of double agent?' He nodded and replied, 'It is always possible. We think she is a wonderful girl and doing courageous work. But the Germans might have imprisoned one of her family and be putting enormous pressure on her.'

'But why?' we asked, 'What good would that do them?'

'Well,' he replied, 'she is bringing back other men besides airmen. Some have volunteered to be trained by us, then returning to join the Underground Forces.'

He turned to Bob and me and reminded us that we had come from Paris with our young Belgian friend.

'But,' he continued, 'we know little about him except what we have been told by Dédée. It is just possible that the Germans are willing to let quite a few airmen escape in order to plant spies in our Intelligence organisation. They might even know about the whole Escape Line and let it exist just for this purpose. Dédée might not even be aware of their knowledge.'

For some moments we all sat deep in thought, reliving the highlights of our escape. The only episodes that troubled me were, first, 'the man in the long black overcoat' whom I had followed through the streets of Liège. That both the Belgian police and the Germans knew him was obvious. At the time, I had been almost certain that he was from the Gestapo. I never learnt just who he was or what part he had played in our meeting with our guides. Secondly, was the ease and rapidity with which Bob and I had been given new identity cards during our brief stay in Paris; also the papers that allowed us to travel through a prohibited zone of the west coast of France. Then I remembered that the Comet Line with Dédée only began in Brussels, and therefore I should discount what had occurred earlier in Liège. So I must think mainly of the time I had spent in Brussels and afterwards.

It did not take me long to feel certain that Dédée and her many followers were genuine patriots, and in no way constituted any danger to our Intelligence Service, for I could not forget the extraordinary kindness of the Evrard family who had looked after Bob and me as if we were their sons, and the Steenbeck family, who had sheltered the other three boys. I thought too of Dédée Dumont and her sad little angelic face. But my main thoughts were of Andrée de Jongh herself. If only our interviewer had come over the Pyrenees with us and known of its arduous nature, he would never doubt the patriotic fervour that enabled her to carry out this double journey over and over again. Surely, she would never have continued to escort each one of her charges over the mountains if she had not been driven by the highest of patriotic motives. No, it was impossible to believe anything doubtful about her. I could think of no circumstance in which the frontier guards had let us through deliberately. So, one by one, each crew member gave his answer, and all were the same. We were convinced that the British authorities would never experience treachery from these wonderful people. At last, the interview came to an end and we were taken off to lunch.

After our first ordeal, we were interviewed by RAF Intelligence, MI9. They were more interested in the Cologne raid itself, and the manner in which we had been shot down. Also, what had happened to our skipper Leslie Manser and to Plt Off Barnes, our navigator. Here we were at great pains to convey to our interviewer our gratitude to our gallant skipper. While the crew were together in Madrid and then on the ship coming home, we had discussed the manner in which Flg Off Manser had kept us all together in the aircraft when it was first on fire over Cologne. Later, when all hope of getting home had vanished, he had held on long enough while we got safely out of the aircraft, and in so doing had lost his own life. Together we asked our interviewer if some sort of recognition could be given to honour his bravery. He said he would do his best to make sure the authorities knew about it.

When our interrogation was over, we went to RAF Uxbridge to be issued with new kit, ration cards and travel warrants. We were also given a sealed envelope to hand to the department at the Air Ministry dealing with our next posting, as we would not be returning to 50 Squadron. Then we left on our various ways.

I met Bob Horsley during my leave and again after the war. He had become a squadron leader with a DFC and AFC. Later, as a Wing Commander, he was an Air Attaché in the Middle East. Sadly, I never met Mills, King, Barnes or Naylor again; but many years later I saw a picture of Mills at a ceremony at 50 Squadron, so I knew he survived the war. Stepping out into the freedom of the streets of London, my first job was to ring Betty and my father, before catching the train out to Wembley Park. I was still clutching the little green case that had belonged to Gisèle, and I had Armand's suit bundled up under my arm. I felt wonderfully elated, rather like a man who had just finished a six weeks' gaol sentence, for it was six weeks since I had walked freely through the lanes of Skellingthorpe.

It was a perfect day in the middle of summer, and although I felt on top of the world, somehow I seemed detached from the everyday life around me. Arriving at Wembley Park, I ran up the stairs and joined the throng of passengers waiting to go past the ticket collector. There, standing expectantly behind him stood my Betty. Within seconds, I had joined her, and after a quick hug and a kiss we strode hand-in-hand from the station. Not bothering to wait for a bus, we walked the half-mile or so up Park Lane, talking nonstop with questions about Jill and my parents. When we arrived at Betty's mother's house, the excitement was terrific and quite overwhelming. Though many airmen had escaped from the Continent before, for obvious security reasons this fact was never published. So, to many of my friends and relatives my return was unbelievable, as if I had returned from another world, or even from the dead. Wherever I went during the next few weeks, I was the centre of interest. Everybody wanted to know where I had landed and what had happened to our aircraft. Of course, I was unable to tell them anything except the bare bones of the story: that we had crashed on our way back from the target and had finally reached Gibraltar. The man in MI5 had made it plain that a court martial would be the outcome if we disobeyed. The most important thing was never to give away the fact that our route to Spain had been down the defended coastline of France, and over the western end of the Pyrenees, since most of the people who had escaped through Spain earlier had gone over the eastern end of the mountains.

Consequently, our friends became even more puzzled and their interest increased accordingly. Thus, the slightly detached feeling that I had felt when I first walked free in London grew more intense, instead of lessening. I don't think I got back on to a completely even keel for several days, but it was wonderful to be home again. On my second day home, Betty and I went over to see my mother and father. Dad was overjoyed to see me and followed me around as if he did not want to let me out of his sight. He was such a quiet and undemonstrative person by nature that I was very moved by his obvious affection for me. Alas, my mother was quite different. A month or so earlier she had been knocked down by a boy on a bicycle and had suffered a bang on the head. No doubt she had received a bit of a shaking, but knowing her only too well, I felt she was trading on the incident and had adopted the life of an invalid.

Much to my amazement, she did not appear to be the slightest bit excited to see me. When I went into her bedroom, her first words were 'Hello Les, how are you? Have they told you about my poor head?' All she wanted from me was to go upstairs and see how the moths had attacked one of the carpets. Sorry as I felt for her because of her accident, I nevertheless felt much more sorry for my father. Obviously, she had been of little comfort to him during the weeks he had been concerned about me. In addition, he had my brother to worry about, for Sidney was still serving in the Navy in the cruiser *Penelope*. He also had all the problems of running the business on his own. However, it did not really matter, for it was a happy day indeed for my father and me.

The following day, Betty, Jill and I returned to our own home in

Whetstone. There we had a quiet time that allowed me slowly to regain normality. We spent many pleasant hours with our next-door neighbours, Joan and Charles Hotten, who were still carrying on with their normal life, as Charles was in a reserved occupation. The weather was beautiful and, mercifully, we were spared any air raids.

One afternoon we were delighted to receive a visit from Hal de Mone. He told us that the Canadian Air Force in Britain were treating him like a hero, and that he was flying home to Canada the following week. That he was enjoying the limelight was obvious, as was the fact that he was going home. Later, I learnt that he had been credited with the destruction of the enemy night-fighter while on the Cologne raid. This was his first time up at night and in a strange aircraft. Taking account of his subsequent escape after being shot down during the raid on Essen, he was awarded an immediate DFM. He returned to Canada having been assessed as completing his tour of operations in what must surely have been an all-time record for its brevity. I never met him again, though Bob Horsley did so when they both became gunnery instructors.

Now that I look back, it seems strange that I did not visit my old squadron at Skellingthorpe. No doubt, they would have been delighted to see me. However, as we had been told that we would not be returning to the squadron, no railway warrants were issued to enable us to do so. Although I could have gone at my own expense, I might have been stopped by the Military Police at the railway station. To help relieve the general congestion on the railways, non-commissioned ranks were not allowed to travel freely.

However, with Manser dead, I felt it was my responsibility to inform the CO of 50 Squadron exactly what had happened to our aircraft prior to the crash. So, I wrote him a detailed account up to the time that I landed after jumping from the aircraft. I described how Manser had refused to panic when we were on fire over Cologne, and how he had struggled to get the aircraft out of German airspace. Then, when he knew he could not keep the aircraft in the air, he had waited until all the crew had cleared the aircraft. I put particular stress on how Manser had knocked the parachute from my hand when he knew he had lost all hope of saving himself, and how he had shouted at me to 'Get out!' I posted it off to Wg Cdr Oxley, little knowing what it would lead to.

About halfway through my leave, Bob Horsley came to visit us. He lived quite near to Lincoln, and had been to the squadron to see Oxley. He told me that the CO had shown him my report, and asked him to read it through and then comment on it. This Bob had done, telling him that it was an accurate account of what had happened and that he was sure the rest of the crew would agree with it completely. Bob too was full of praise for Manser. The CO told him that the squadron would try to ensure that Manser's courage did not go unrecognised. I did not see Bob again until after the war, when he visited us with his new wife whom he had met while she was serving with the WAAF.

During my leave, I went along to the RAF station at Uxbridge, where escapees reported after having been posted as 'Non-effective'. Many LMF (Lack of Moral Fibre) cases were there as well. This was the official term used for aircrew who had lost their nerve or displayed cowardice. Regrettably, the term was applied to many good men who could not adjust to the peculiar mix of operational flying and almost normal life, like that enjoyed by the great majority of the ground crew. While at Uxbridge, I got my pay sorted out, and drew two new uniforms and kit, but no flying gear. I was then restored to full General Duties (GD) status. Later, I visited the Air Ministry. The sealed envelope I had been given by the officer in MI9 was addressed to the officer who would give me my new posting. In due course, I found myself standing in front of him while he read the letter. Having got some way through it, he pointed to the chair in front of his desk and said, 'Sit down, Sergeant. Make yourself at home.' When I first entered his office, he must have assumed that I was another sergeant pilot, of which there were hundreds in London. The Canadian Training Scheme was churning them out in droves, but the mounting losses of operational aircraft had resulted in a bottleneck at the Operational Training Units and restricted the flow of pilots to the squadrons. Having finished reading the letter, he became very affable. 'H'mm,' he murmured, 'and how long have you been back?'

'About two weeks,' I replied, now feeling more at ease.

'And just what would you like to do in the future?' he asked.

'Well,' I replied, 'what do you suggest?'

Again looking at the letter he replied, 'You can't go back on a bomber squadron, but perhaps we could make an instructor out of you, or put you on something like flying control work.'

For a moment or two I sat back and thought. I did not really want to become an instructor. That would most likely mean I would spend the rest of the war flying around with a bunch of pupil navigators or wireless operators in something like an old Avro Anson. I certainly did not want to go as an instructor at an Elementary Flying School, which would most likely mean a posting to Canada, leaving Betty and Jill in

Britain. Then suddenly I had a brainwave, and one I never later regretted. I remembered that Brazenor had been posted on to Sunderland flying-boats, and I had heard it rumoured that there was a squadron based somewhere on the south coast of England. Without another thought I said, 'How about posting me to a Coastal Command squadron flying Sunderlands?' And with a grin, I continued, 'Somewhere on the south coast will do me very nicely.' My interviewing officer looked a little surprised and replied, 'Lord, that would mean a transfer from my Command. I guess I will have to see what my counterpart in Coastal has to say about it.'

Getting up from his desk, he left me alone in his office. Almost at once, I had a desire to read just what was in the letter that I had given him. So with one eye watching the door, I picked up the letter and read. The first part was an outline of my service in the RAF so far, but the end of the letter was much more interesting and gave me every hope that my request would be granted. 'This non-commissioned officer has recently escaped from Enemy Occupied Territory and must not be posted to an operational bomber squadron. Every consideration must be shown to him in his future posting.' Great, I thought, that should do the trick, and I hastily replaced the letter on the desk. A few moments later the officer poked his head round the door and beckoned me to follow him. 'I think I may have managed to pull it off for you, but it is not all plain sailing.'

He took me to see the Coastal Command colleague, and soon I was being interviewed all over again. He too, looked me over for a moment and then said, 'We'd be happy to have you into Coastal Command, but Sunderlands may be a bit tricky to arrange. For one thing, you would need to take a GR (General Reconnaissance) course and obtain a navigator's ticket if you wanted to become a Sunderland skipper.'

'Well, that's all right by me. When do I start?'

Looking through a mass of 'bumph', he said, 'There is a course starting at Harrogate in a week or so; how about having a stab at that? I can't promise you Sunderlands, but let's see what sort of a pass you get from your exams there and then we will decide. Meanwhile, go home, enjoy your leave, and we will send you your posting notice and railway warrant in a few days.'

Jubilantly, I left and was soon out in the summer sunshine.

The last few days of leave went all too quickly, but I did have a couple of enjoyable days with Dad at our factory. Sidney had also managed to get some leave and the three of us went out to lunch at a rather nice restaurant in Dalston where Dad used to go every day, and he was obviously so proud to be with us. Sidney had had a hectic time at sea, first on destroyers and then on the famous light cruiser *Penelope* (nicknamed HMS *Pepperpot*, because of its hundreds of holes sustained by near bomb misses in the Mediterranean). Having been taken off sea service because of his persistent seasickness, he was given a direct commission and transferred to the Admiralty.

Chapter 11

MY INTRODUCTION TO THE SUNDERLAND

The leave over, I set course for Harrogate. I had arranged with Betty that I would search for some digs, so that she could come up with Jill during the weeks I would be allowed to live out. Yet again, I was based in a large requisitioned hotel with a bunch of fellows entirely unknown to me. The course was composed of about sixty young sergeant pilots, fresh from Canada where they had been mostly together for some time, and had therefore formed firm friendships. Again, I found myself a bit of a 'loner'.

My nature is such that I need companionship, and I soon struck up a friendship with a fellow named Stewart. He had been a bank clerk before his call-up, was married and about my age. What was extraordinary about him was the fact that before the war he had inherited £10,000 from his father's estate. Apart from a house he had bought with cash and where his wife now lived, he had spent the whole of this inheritance in two short years. To me this seemed totally unbelievable, for in those days it represented the amount I would have earned after forty years work at my pre-war job. One could get a night on the town, including a meal at a restaurant and two theatre tickets, and still have enough left out of £2 10s 0d for a taxi home. Nevertheless, he was a gentlemanly fellow and I liked him very much, in spite of his profligate past.

Happily, I found the GR course quite enjoyable. Having obtained some digs, I now had Betty and Jill to return to each day. It was good to be together on a non-flying station, as Betty could relax completely in the knowledge that for a while at least, I was quite safe. After an unfortunate spot of bother in the first digs (not of our making), we moved in with a kindly old soul whose only vice was an addiction to the bottle. One day, after one of her boozing bouts, she retired to sleep it off. She had left the door of her bedroom slightly ajar, and Betty had peeped in to see that she was all right. Much to her amusement, she noticed that Jill's Teddy bear was cradled in the old lady's arms. Hardly daring to breathe, Betty crept in and gently removed it.

Meanwhile, the course was proving very interesting, most of our time being spent on navigational exercises. We also practised Morse on the Aldis lamp, as our future work would be in co-operation with the Navy. Instead of aircraft recognition, we spent much time learning to recognise the many ships in both our own and the enemy navies. This took a while to master, but by the end of the course I felt quite competent at it. Our last four days were spent at exams and collecting our flying kit. Sent on leave, the three of us returned to Whetstone.

While home, I had a phone call from Bob Horsley. He had met Sgt Dampier Crossley, with whom I had flown on 50 Squadron. He told Bob that a notice had appeared on the flight office notice-board at Skellingthorpe stating that several of our crew had been awarded either the Distinguished Flying Cross or the Distinguished Flying Medal. He said he was sure that Bob had got a DFC and that I had collected a DFM. At the time this rather puzzled me, as I knew that, in the past, some escapees had been awarded either Military Crosses or Military Medals. Flight Lieutenant Rennie had been awarded an MC following his escape the year before. Later, I heard that Plt Off Barnes, our navigator, had also received a DFC, in spite of the fact that he had been unfortunate enough to be captured. It was apparent therefore, that the escape itself was not the main reason for our 'gongs'. At the time, I could not really believe that Crossley's report was correct; but the next day, Betty rang the Squadron Adjutant to enquire about it. Much to our astonishment, she was told the report was correct. I must admit that I would be an absolute liar if I did not own up to feeling tremendously pleased by the award. In my heart, I felt that I had not genuinely earned it as I had simply carried out orders while on the aircraft. As for the escape, I had done this as much for my own sake and Betty's as for the RAF or my country. My DFM really belonged to the people of Belgium who had risked their lives on our behalf.

Two days later I received a telegram from 'Bomber' Harris himself, saying, 'My warmest congratulations on your award of the Distinguished Flying Medal.' Then on 6 October 1942, the *London Evening News* carried on its back page a headline and text which read:

'RAF Awards Mystery. Five members of an aircraft crew have been decorated, but only they and the RAF authorities know why. The official citations for their awards say that "In hazardous

135

circumstances they displayed courage, determination and devotion to duty in keeping with the highest traditions of the RAF".'

After my leave I returned to Harrogate with my ribbon, with its narrow blue and white diagonal stripes, sitting proudly beneath my 'wings'. Our postings had not yet come through, so we sat around for a couple of days. Nearly the entire course had asked for postings to a Sunderland squadron, the Sunderland being renowned as a formidable aircraft. When at last the postings came through, I found I was the only lucky one amongst them. The results of our exams were also published, and I had done quite well, getting an assessment of 'Above Average'. Presumably, this must have been good enough for my man at the Air Ministry; for my posting was not to an OTU but direct to 461 Squadron at RAF Mount Batten, Plymouth. I was now off on my own to an altogether different life.

I had to go via London, so I was able to break my journey and sneak another night with Betty and Jill. The next day I was on the train to Plymouth, a journey I had done frequently as a youngster. I felt happier than at any previous time in the RAF, for the stations *en route* were old familiar names to me. The red soils of Dorset, and the run along the coastline around Dawlish, were like old friends. Mount Batten was only a stone's throw from where my Uncle Alfred lived out his retirement at Plymstock.

When I arrived at the RAF station, I got a bit of a surprise. True there were Sunderlands everywhere, but the squadron was not 461, but 10 Squadron, Royal Australian Air Force. Presenting myself to their CO, I learnt that my postings officer had got hold of 'duff gen', for 461 Squadron, which had only recently been formed, was up at Poole, near Bournemouth. Happily, the CO was a friendly chap, and told me to wait while he rang the ops room to see if there was an aircraft going up that way. Luckily, there was one the next day, and the CO said I could hitch a lift on it if I wished. 'The skipper's name is Plt Off Stely, so keep in touch with the ops room to find out the time of take-off and tell young Stely you are going up with him', he said.

I wandered around the station admiring the Sunderlands that were up on the 'hard' (concrete apron above the slipway) for maintenance. After flying Hampdens, and even Manchesters, they looked huge. They had a wingspan of over 112 feet, while the top of the tail fin rose over 32 feet from the ground and the bottom of the keel was only some six inches off the ground. After a meal in the sergeants' mess, and leaving my kit in the transit hut, I set off for Under Lane. Here my Uncle Alfred lived with his lifelong companion, Mrs Johnson, who kept house for him until the day he died. They gave me a great welcome and my uncle was delighted to see my DFM ribbon. Back at the station, I spent the night in the cheerless Nissen hut reserved for visiting aircrew.

The next day was 1 October 1942. Having found out the time of take-off, I went down to the quayside and met the all-Australian crew I was going with. Later I learnt that 461 Squadron had only a few RAF airmen in it and was destined to become an 'all-Aussie' unit like 10 Squadron. As with all the Australians I met, the aircrew were a great bunch of fellows, their only difference in appearance from us being their dark blue uniforms with 'Australia' shoulder flashes. Maybe they were more direct than RAF men, with little 'bullshit' in their everyday life; but when they went for 'ceremonial', they laid it on thick with a trowel. Nevertheless, I liked them, and always felt at ease with them during the five months I spent on 461. Also, I was delighted to be accepted as one of them, with no reserve at all.

A dinghy, actually a motorboat some eighteen feet long with a motor amidships, took us out to a Sunderland moored in the Cattewater. There were already two crew members on board. At that time Sunderlands were never left unattended, and two members of the crew always remained on board as boat guards, doing watches of

The Short Sunderland. *(Philip Jarrett)*

twenty-four hours. However, officers did not do these duties, which was hard luck on the crew that had few NCOs. Perhaps that is why I was popular among the fellows, for I was to find that I was the only sergeant pilot on the squadron, and later the only RAF pilot.

Although I enjoyed this first ride, later I was to hate the sight of a dinghy, as did all flying-boat crews. We seemed to spend most of our time either waiting for one to take us out to an aircraft, or waiting for one to take us ashore. On a wet and choppy night we often got soaked through before we ever reached our Sunderland. Of course I did not realise this as I waited my turn to board. A tradition on 'boats' that I was soon to learn, was that the skipper always went on board first and after a flight came off last. It must have been some sort of archaic custom handed down from HMS *Victory* via the Royal Naval Air Service. Nevertheless, it was the only item of 'bullshit' that any of us ever indulged in, for the most democratic team in the world is an operational aircrew, whatever Command they belong to. Many a large aircraft might have a sergeant or flight sergeant as captain, while the rear gunner could be a flight lieutenant. The flight lieutenant would always address the captain as 'Skipper', who might well reply, 'Okay Joe, thanks.' In the air, discipline never suffered as a result: the skipper was always the skipper, or Skip, regardless of rank.

Like a new boy at school, I went on board a Sunderland for the first time and marvelled at its roomy interior. Entering the front door, one found oneself in a low compartment, forward of which was the front gun turret. Immediately behind the turret was the winch gear for mooring up or anchoring, and in the early days there was also an anchor large enough to hold a battleship. In the centre of this compartment was a staircase, companionway I should say, which had a sliding hatch leading directly to a position between the two pilots' seats. On the far side of the compartment was a door leading into a neat little toilet compartment (the heads), with a tank above it into which water was pumped for flushing purposes. At the entrance to the aircraft, a doorway to the right led into the wardroom. It had a table in the centre, and bunks on each side with underneath stowage.

The next door led into the galley that had a bench and a cooker with a couple of Primus stoves. On each side was a hatch, which could be opened, allowing canvas drogues to be streamed to slow the aircraft when approaching its mooring buoy in adverse conditions of wind or tide. These hatches were also opened for photography purposes. A central ladder led up to the upper deck, immediately behind the main spar and the flight engineer's position. Aft of the galley was the bomb room with overhead powered racks carrying bombs or depth charges. At the sides were two more bunks, above which on each side of the hull was a large door. These were opened by remote control from the pilot's position, allowing the bomb-load to be run out under the wings on recessed rails.

Aft of the bomb room the hull was about twelve feet in height. Up a couple of steps was a workbench where the turret guns were cleaned after every flight. A ladder led to the upper deck and the mid-upper turret. Flares and additional life-rafts were also kept in this area. Going forward, a further door led past the engineer's position to the aircraft's bridge. The navigator's table was on the starboard side, with the wireless operator and his equipment on the port side opposite. Forward of the navigator's position was a curtained-off position where the radar operator had his set. Forward again were the two pilots' seats. My first impression was of the tremendous space inside the aircraft, together with a general feeling of robustness and strength. That the Sunderland was a tough old aircraft I was never in doubt. Another impression was one of frenzied activity going on throughout the entire aircraft. The aircraft rigger and one other member of the crew were up front, with the gun turret wound back from its usual position, grappling with the complicated set of strops that kept us attached to our mooring buoy. Gunners were fitting guns into the turrets, while the flight engineers were up on the main wing, turning over each of the four Bristol Pegasus engines (identical to those in the Hampden) with the aid of handles inserted through holes in the side panels. This was to make sure that oil or fuel was not trapped in the cylinder heads of the lower cylinders, which might cause hydraulic locking when the engines started. The second pilot was also outside the aircraft looking over the control surfaces, including the rudder and elevators.

What intrigued me most was the little twin-cylinder engine (known as the auxiliary power unit) that was situated in the inboard leading edge of the starboard wing. An access section was let down when the engine was required. It was buzzing away merrily while one member of the crew went to each watertight compartment and operated a valve to pump out any water that might have leaked into the bilges under the floor. It also ran a generator to charge the 24-volt battery system supplying the aircraft's electrical power.

It soon became apparent that what looked like chaos to a 'new boy' was, in fact, a well-run and systematic effort of teamwork. Soon, each member of the crew came on the intercom to report to the skipper that his particular job was done and that the aircraft was ready to leave the mooring. The final report was,

'All hatches and bulkheads closed, Skipper.'
'Skipper to moorings; you fellows all ready up front?'
'Okay Skipper; ready to slip moorings.'
'Starting port outer engine, engineer.'
'Okay Skipper, ready to prime port outer.'

The engine sprang into life, and the same procedure was followed to start the starboard outer engine. When both were running, the skipper called the rigger to slip moorings. This was done, and from my position behind the first pilot's seat I watched the front turret being wound forward over the mooring compartment.

The aircraft was then taxied out to the take-off area in Plymouth Sound. As soon as we were clear of other aircraft, the inner engines were started. Leaving the sheltered water of the Cattewater, we ran into quite a chop, but this did not disturb the Sunderland, now moving comfortably at a speed of about ten knots. When the engines reached their correct temperature, each one was run up to 1,200 revs and the separate ignition systems (magnetos) were checked. Then with the wind coming in from the west, we were all ready for take-off. The skipper did his final check, which first entailed checking with the flight engineer that engine temperatures and pressures were normal. This was followed by running out one-third flap; ensuring that the propellers were in fully fine pitch; setting the Direction Indicator to 'zero'; turning the aircraft into wind; uncaging the gyro; and finally warning the crew to stand by for take-off.

The skipper opened up the outer engines first, at the same time hauling the control column back into his stomach. This allowed the nose of the aircraft to rise as high as possible before opening the throttles of the inner engines. The purpose of this was to cut down the amount of spray from the bow wave that would strike the propellers when the inner engines were opened up. In heavy seas especially, spray would cause 'pitting' of the propeller tips. With the nose at its maximum height, the inner engines were gradually opened up until the props were finally clear of the spray. Full throttle was then given to all four engines. With the aircraft now coming up 'onto the step' (in other words 'planing'), the control column was centralised with the speed reaching about 50 knots. At about 85 to 90 knots the skipper eased back on the stick and the aircraft rose gracefully into the air.

Once airborne, the aircraft was held straight and level until normal climbing speed was reached at 105 knots. Throttle and propeller pitch settings were then reduced in exactly the same manner as in the Hampden. Unfortunately, the engines had the same drawback as those in the Hampden, in that the propellers could not be 'fully feathered' to stop them from 'windmilling' with the throttles closed and the fuel turned off. This was a serious drawback in the event of an engine failure or fire.

As we climbed away from the Sound, Drake's Island passed under the starboard wing and we set course on 080° for Poole.

It was a beautifully steady trip as we flew at 1,000 feet, a popular height with Sunderland skippers. The navigator set up the folding platform directly under the astrodome and motioned me to climb up for a look out. The astrodome was a Perspex 'bubble' which protruded up through the top of the fuselage. Designed for taking 'astro shots' for navigation, it afforded a splendid view through the whole 360° around the aircraft. It made an excellent lookout point and was always manned by one of the crew in an area where enemy aircraft might be encountered. In the event of aerial combat, it was usual for the navigator to man this position as Fire Controller and keep the pilot in touch with all that was happening around the aircraft. Soon Dartmouth was behind us, and we set course for Portland Bill some thirty-five miles away. The weather was cold, crisp, and clear, and I could see the coast of Dorset away on the port side. Looking aft, I watched the rear and mid-upper gun turrets traversing as they kept a sharp lookout for any sneak raiders that occasionally flew in low under our radar cover. Standing in the astrodome I felt master of all I surveyed and suddenly immensely glad that fate had given me the chance to fly in such a splendid aircraft. I wondered how long it would be before I was given a spell at the controls, and how long before I would have the immense pleasure of flying solo in this superb monster. Little could I have guessed how soon this would be.

Portland Bill came into sight and I settled down to study the coast and memorise its outstanding points. For I was to be stationed here, and in bad weather it behove every pilot to know the surrounding countryside like the back of his hand. With Portland Bill now behind us, we made for Durleston Head from where we would fly due north for our final run into Poole. Arriving at Poole we circled the harbour until Control had given us permission to land. Looking down, I was amazed at the shallowness of the water and the comparatively narrow channel in which we had to land. Clearly, our skipper was familiar with the peculiar layout, as we were soon down safely after the smoothest of landings. We had been in the air just an hour and a half, but already I was feeling completely at home in this new aircraft.

Once the mooring-up procedure had been completed, I went ashore with the skipper and other officers. The rest of the crew were to follow after the aircraft had been refuelled and prepared for its next assignment. A dinghy took us direct to the quayside, which was in the middle of Poole itself, and right opposite the sergeants' mess located in a small requisitioned hotel. Thanking Plt Off Stely for the lift, I headed for the mess while he and the other officers waited for transport to take them to the officers' mess. This was in the larger Harbour Heights Hotel, also taken over by the RAF and located out of Poole towards Sandbanks. I was given a room on the first floor overlooking the harbour. It was my best billet so far, the room being large and airy, and I had to share it with only two other aircrew. In the afternoon I went down to Squadron HQ, where I reported to Wg Cdr Lovelock, the CO. He was a pre-war officer who was extremely courteous and friendly towards me. There can be no doubt that from then on, every new contact that I made would be much smoother for me because of the DFM ribbon I was wearing. It automatically gained me respect and attention, for, correctly or incorrectly, it indicated that I was ex-operational, had seen action, and was not just another new boy fresh out of training. So I found myself chatting to my new CO in a manner that I had never previously experienced. At the end of my interview he invited me to fly with him the next day when he would be giving some dual instruction to three other pilots on the squadron. The next day I was up in Sunderland DV968, standing behind the first pilot's seat while the CO gave instruction to the other three pilots. However, we seemed to spend more time on the water than in the air, since the narrow channels in which we had to land made it necessary to do much taxiing downwind before every take-off.

After almost three and a half hours, when the CO had finished with the other pilots, he turned to me and asked if I would like to have a try. I had watched very carefully all that had gone before and had already decided that the aircraft looked just too easy to take off and land. The only difficulty I could see was in handling it on the water. So, like a shot I jumped into the first pilot's seat and prepared to have a go. It was obvious that the main essential during take-off was to keep the wings absolutely level. For, if you were unlucky enough to dip a wing, then the float beneath might easily be ripped off if it hit a wave at speed. Clearly, vigorous use of the controls was required, especially before the aircraft had gained much speed. As I had expected, I had no difficulty at all and soon we were airborne and climbing away happily. I adjusted the controls much as I had done on Hampdens, and noted that when the flaps were brought in, the attitude of the aircraft varied but little, and practically no change was required to the fore and aft trim. At 1,000 feet the CO let me fly it around for a while to get the feel of the controls. The long nose with its gun turret way out ahead made positioning against the horizon very easy. Turns could be made without any fear of losing or gaining height while banked over. I soon felt extremely confident, and when it was apparent that I had got the feel of it, the CO instructed me to go in for a landing.

The procedure was perhaps more simple than in land-planes, as, with an ample water 'runway', there was not the specific requirement to arrive just over the boundary fence as on an airfield. Neither was there an undercarriage to mess around with. Simply run out two-thirds flap and re-trim the elevator controls. Then, on the final approach put the airscrews into fully fine pitch and ease back on the throttles. At 300 feet, bring up the nose and reduce the airspeed to 80 knots, opening up the outer engines to 2,100 revs. Then, using the inner engines, adjust the rate of descent to 200 feet per minute. At night, or when there was a glassy sea, one only had to sit tight and wait for the aircraft to hit the water. In daytime, at the right moment a little holding-off with the control column usually resulted in the smoothest of landings.

Of course it was daytime and a beautiful day at that, nothing like some of the weather conditions under which I would be called upon to land in the coming years. But today, my first ever flying-boat landing was a beauty, and I was particularly pleased with myself for I had not landed an aircraft on my own for over five months. The CO expressed satisfaction with my efforts and told me I could go up again the next day with the Flight Commander for some more dual. My first flight at the controls had lasted just twenty minutes.

The next day I flew again with the same crew and fellow-pilots, but this time our instructor was Sqn Ldr Raban. For an hour and a half, I watched as I had done the previous day while the other fellows had their share of dual. Then Raban motioned me to take over in the first pilot's seat. I don't know what the CO had told him about me or, in fact, if he knew anything about me at all, but he gave me three circuits and landings in fairly quick succession. Then, after the third successful landing he casually said, 'Okay, taxi back to the take-off point and you can have a crack at solo.' I was absolutely astonished, for I had my first sight of a Sunderland just two days previously, and the two sessions of dual I had been given totalled one hour and ten minutes. At least half of that time had been taken up in taxiing around on the water. However, I did not argue, but taxied back to the take-off point and turned into wind.

Raban now left his position in the instructor's (second pilot's) seat, and ushered everybody bar me off the bridge, leaving just the flight engineer, who remained at his panel behind the main spar. I gathered that this was usual when sending a pupil solo, it being too long a procedure to get a dinghy alongside to off-load the instructor. Certainly, the instructor needed to have plenty of confidence in his pupil to risk his own neck every time he sent a new pilot solo.

I began my cockpit drill with extra thoroughness and then, after a look around the sky, opened the throttles. Once up on its step, the aircraft planed along like a high-powered speedboat. With the waves tearing past under the hull the pilot gets a tremendous feeling of elation. Of course, a fully laden aircraft on a rough sea at night is an altogether different kettle of fish. Yet I don't think I ever did a day take-off in a lightly laden aircraft without getting this same wonderful feeling.

I climbed to 1,000 feet, flying round the circuit in complete command and loving every minute of it. Reluctantly, I brought the aircraft round for another quite nice landing. Raban now returned to the bridge, making the customary noises such as 'Good show! Good show!' as was usual on such occasions. I still find it hard to understand how I was ever allowed to go solo after so little time. Perhaps it was the almost magical influence of my 'ribbon' that had given my instructor such confidence in me. It may also have been assumed that I had flown a lot more than was actually the case, for I had not yet handed in my flying log book for certification, which was done at the end of each month.

Having settled into my new squadron, I now looked around for some digs in Poole so as to bring Betty and Jill away from the dangers of air raids in London. I soon found a place just out of Poole on the Bournemouth road and arranged for the two of them to come down during the following week. Before they arrived, I did two operational trips down into the Bay of Biscay on anti-submarine (A/S) patrol, flying as second pilot. As each flight was of twelve hours' duration, I did one hour on watch from the second dickey's seat, then one hour at the flying controls.

The first trip was with a Flt Lt Manger, and the second with a fellow named Dods, both of whom were Australians. At the end of each trip we landed at Plymouth for refuelling, staying overnight and returning to Poole the next morning. I found the trips very interesting, but as we were out of sight of land for more than eleven hours of the flight, it did become very tiring. However, the necessity of keeping a careful lookout, not only for U-boats but also for German JU 88s, who in turn searched for us in flights of six or more aircraft, kept us from the dangers of boredom.

As I referred to earlier, being an NCO meant that I had to do boat-guard duties for twenty-four hours at a time. If this clashed with a couple of operational flights, it was not uncommon to be cooped up in the aircraft for up to fifty or more hours. In winter weather, this could be pretty arduous, for there was no heating in the Sunderland, not even when we were flying. However, there was always plenty of food on board as we drew rations for every flight, and usually had at least one hot meal every day. The meal was usually either steak and potatoes, or bacon and eggs. Also someone on the crew was forever brewing up a cup of tea or coffee. I liked Dods and Manger, as I did all the other Australian pilots that I flew with. But, I did not fly with either of them again, and I am sorry to say that Dods came to an unfortunate end. In the latter part of February 1943, he had to ditch after a disastrous fire in one of his engines. Then on 29 April, he was flying as second pilot to a fellow named Gipps when they sighted and made a successful attack on a U-boat. After flying many hundreds of hours searching in vain, he had to be on a trip when he was not captain but merely acting as a safety pilot (usually known as 'screening pilot') to Gipps, who had only just become a skipper. Then on 28 May he was killed in an abortive attempt to rescue the crew of a Whitley aircraft that had been shot down by enemy fighters.

On 15 October I changed crews again; this time flying with a skipper named Cooke. We flew to Mount Batten to take on a full load of fuel, as our trip the next day was to be down to Gibraltar on an A/S (anti-submarine) patrol and ship recce. This created a devil of a problem for me, as I was expecting Betty and Jill to join me the following day. I dared not ask the CO to move me on to another crew, as we were not allowed to live out while serving on an operational squadron. Having wives around the station was severely frowned upon. Although I felt that I was getting on famously, I had been on the squadron for only two weeks and was not yet in a position to start asking favours not available to other crew members.

The next day we took off on the long trip across the Bay of Biscay and then down the Spanish and Portuguese coasts to Gib. We flew at about 4,000 feet, which was pretty high for a Sunderland on patrol, since we never flew in or above cloud for obvious reasons. However, on this patrol we were relying mainly on radar to pick up any contacts that might be in our search area.

At that time, the aircraft were fitted with the early type of radar without the PPI (Plan Position Indicator) tube with which Sunderlands were equipped later in the war. Forward-searching aerials carried under the outer wing areas could pick up the return from a ship at anything up to twenty miles, depending on the size of the ship and the state of the sea. The aircraft also had to fly at sufficient height to allow for the curvature of the earth, as radar beams, like television, travel only in straight lines. If the sea was rough, a lot of 'mush' appeared on the screen, caused by the radar beam bouncing back off the steep sides of big waves. In these conditions, a weak signal might not show at all. In addition to the forward-looking aerials, others carried on the sides of the fuselage searched on each beam. The radar tube had a centre scale calibrated in miles with three settings looking ten, thirty and ninety miles ahead respectively. Searching for surface targets was normally initiated on the thirty-mile scale, switching to the ten-mile scale when any blip came within that range.

As happened quite regularly, on this particular trip the radar produced only a couple of blips, which both turned out to be Spanish fishing boats. This did not mean that our trip had necessarily been a waste of time; for the U-boats operating in the Atlantic from their French ports had to cross and then re-cross the Bay of Biscay. Our constant patrols caused them to stay below surface throughout daylight hours, and consequently their speed was kept very low. Thus, the longer they took to get through the Bay, the less time they had to operate against our shipping in mid-Atlantic. It should be noted that the U-boats had radar receivers capable of picking up the probing fingers of our radar beams long before our operators were able to identify their tiny blips at long range. So there must have been many occasions when the enemy crash-dived before the searching aircraft was aware of his presence.

After nearly eleven hours of flying, we reached Gibraltar and landed in darkness. This was my first night landing on water, using a technique utterly different from that used on an airfield. There was no glide path indicator to bring us in at the right angle of descent; neither was there a long runway with its double row of lights. The only advantage was the fact that the flare path, as it was known, was laid generally dead into wind. Lights mounted on three eight-foot-long pram dinghies illuminated it. The lights were fixed to the top of six-foot masts, and powered by twelve-volt car batteries. As it was necessary for the lights to be visible from all directions, reflectors could not be used to increase the intensity. They were so dim that they were only just visible from the circuit height of 1,000 feet.

Before an aircraft was due to land, a pinnace would tow the dinghies to the landing area. With the pinnace heading into wind, the Flying Control Officer would anchor one of the dinghies and then steam off into wind. At 800 yards he would anchor the second dinghy, and after a further 800 yards release the third one. The pinnace would then return to the downwind end of the flare path and take up station abeam of the position where it was estimated the aircraft would touch down, usually adjacent to the first light. Here the pinnace would assume its secondary duty as the crash boat. That was the complete set-up. About a year later, the number of dinghies was increased to five, the first and last ones having a red light to mark the extremities of the flare-path, beyond which landing was forbidden.

At Gibraltar, as the depth of water in Algeciras Bay was too great to anchor the dinghies, the procedure was slightly different. Here, they were strung behind the pinnace on a line about a mile long and towed very slowly into wind. Of course, this called for a quick landing on the part of the pilot, before the pinnace ran out of water and had to turn back to the starting point. However, our experienced skipper soon had us on the water and moored to a buoy alongside the runway. Most of the crew slept on board while the skipper and the officers went ashore for debriefing.

For some unknown reason we were kept at Gibraltar for a couple of days. During this time, Betty arrived at Poole and went to the digs I had found for her but did not think much of them. So she started to look around for something better. She was not unduly alarmed when I had not met her at the railway station, as she knew that flying boats were often away from their base for several days.

The next day I had still not returned, and not having any news of me she found herself in a bit of a quandary. So, while she was out with Jill she spotted a young NCO; stopping him, she explained her anxiety. He must have been a decent chap, as he understood that as an unofficially accompanied wife Betty was unable to make an approach to the Squadron HQ. He took her address and told her he would try to find out where I was. Whether he was aircrew or worked in the ops room I did not know, but he managed to find out that I was still in Gibraltar and advised Betty accordingly. The next day she continued her search for better accommodation and was successful in finding a couple of rooms in a huge house much nearer to Poole, and opposite an attractive park.

On 19 October, Betty's birthday, we returned from Gib. We left about three hours before dawn so as to cross our search area in daylight. At that period of the war, Sunderlands had no means of attacking U-boats during darkness, though some Catalinas were being fitted with searchlights, known as Leigh lights after the officer who designed them. The flight home was uneventful, albeit not without risk. JU 88s were on patrol in the Bay most of the time, and had shot down several Sunderlands. Although well armed, the aircraft stood little chance against a 'pack' of aircraft equipped with four cannon apiece.

Back at base, I got away as soon as I could to join Betty. Obviously glad to see me, she was full of the news of the superior digs she had found us. Arriving at what was to be our new home and standing proudly outside it, Betty exclaimed, 'There, that's better, isn't it?' I looked in amazement, covered my eyes in mock horror, and said,

'Oh Gawd! Didn't you see the flag?'

'Flag, what flag?'

I pointed to the big house next door, and there, fluttering proudly atop a tall flagstaff was the RAF ensign. Of all the houses in Poole that Betty could pick, she chose the one next to Station HQ that contained the operations room and was bursting at the seams with Top Brass. Yet she knew that I was not allowed to live out in the way that ground crew were. In the event, I found the location of our new digs to be perfect. If any senior officers did find out that I was sleeping off the station on my free nights, they must have turned a blind eye to it.

I flew with Flt Lt Cooke and his crew for some three weeks, doing fifty-five hours' flying with them. They were a good bunch and I felt really at home with them. By then, I knew every inch of the Sunderland and was able to pull my weight as a crew member. One morning, I was summoned to the CO's office and told by Wg Cdr Lovelock that a new crew was being formed and that he had selected me to be its permanent second pilot. My new captain was, of course, an Australian, by the name of Dudley Marrows. He had not gone through the OTU course, where he would have picked up a crew, but had been given dual instruction while a second pilot on the squadron. His crew was to be picked from a variety of odd bods like me. The CO assured me that Marrows was a good man, and I had been picked to join him as he thought I would be a good stiffener for the crew as a whole. It was not often that one received praise in the RAF, so I left the CO's office feeling very flattered.

Thus started a partnership that lasted some four months and was, I believe, the most carefree time that I spent during the whole five years of my RAF service. For Flt Lt Marrows was a splendid man. Tall, well built and easy-going, I never saw him ruffled or bad-tempered. The way he handled his crew was just about right: friendly, but with no nonsense and with everybody pulling his weight. For flying was but a small part of our job, there being much actual hard work for a Sunderland crew to perform. The 'boat' had to be kept clean, for a start. This was no easy task, as there was always grease and hydraulic oil around on the decks. With a crew of eleven and most of their flying gear and sleeping bags on board, plus at least two members living permanently on board, life was usually a bit hectic. The crew did all their own gun-cleaning and maintenance; all the refuelling and checking of batteries, radio and bilges; and, not least, keeping the windscreens and turrets clean. With all the salt spray flying around on each take-off and landing, the latter alone could be quite a task. It was very much a full-time job.

I got on well with the crew and soon became one of them. I liked and admired Dudley Marrows, and never felt at odds with any of his ideas or with his flying. He shared the flying with me, giving me the occasional daylight take-off to keep my hand in. Yet I never really became pals with him, not because of any incompatibility in our characters, but simply because he was an officer and I an NCO. Also, away from the aircraft we were never together, chiefly because the sergeants' mess was miles away from the officers' mess. Neither was there any social life, such as existed on a permanent RAF station.

However, several of the crew were great pals, in particular a real Aussie character named Sgt Sidney. He would often drop in to see Betty and me in our digs. He usually brought a few odds and ends of food that he had scrounged off the aircraft. This food was especially welcome since, not officially living-out, I was not issued with a ration

Dudley Marrows and his crew. Marrows is second from the end on the left.

card to eke out the meals I had at home. Everything was rationed: meat, bread, butter, margarine, cooking fats, dried fruit, sugar and much else, including milk. Occasionally, we got whale meat off the ration, or even a frozen rabbit. We were never short of food on the aircraft as we drew excellent rations every time we flew a long operational trip. Sergeant Sidney, a gunner, did all the cooking when not in a gun turret, and handled most of the stores.

Before we began operations as a new crew, it was decided to send us on a gunnery course. Not only would this be good for the gunners, but it would also provide a shake-down period for the crew to get used to working as a team. So we flew to Pembroke Dock, where we stayed for six days. We did some fifteen hours' flying, practising low-level bombing at wave-top height, and air-to-air firing at a towed target. We fired off thousands of rounds and dropped dozens of practice bombs. This was all good fun and provided valuable training, especially as Marrows let me have a share of the low-level bombing runs. Perhaps I should explain that the standard bombsight had been removed from Sunderlands early in the war. As the aircraft's primary role was anti-submarine patrol flying, it had been found that 'kills' were much more likely to result from low-level dropping of depth charges than from higher-level attacks with conventional bombs.

This meant that, with the exception of any contribution from the front gunner, the whole operation was strictly a pilot's affair. His job was to pick the course and the moment to begin the attack. Then get the aircraft down to wave-top height and traverse the hull of the submarine slightly ahead of the conning tower, allowing for the boat's forward speed. The bomb release button ('bomb tit' to the pilots) positioned on the pilot's control column had to be pressed well before reaching the target. This was to allow for the forward travel of the depth charges, which had the same forward velocity as the aircraft. In an attack this was usually about 160 mph. Normally, eight depth charges were carried, each containing 250 lb of Amatol high explosive. In an attack, six were released in a stick, set usually with sixty feet spacing. The remaining two would be used if a second attack were required. For practice, a smoke float was used as a target. An 11 lb practice bomb, which released smoke on impact, was loaded on the bomb rack to represent the middle of a stick of six. Thus it was possible to tell if a good straddle of the target had been made.

The weapon release mechanism was operated by an automatic timing switch, known as a 'Mickey Mouse', located on the bridge beside the first pilot's seat. This could be set to vary the time between each weapon release to shorten or lengthen the spacing of the stick.

The aircraft armament at that time consisted of four .303 Browning machine-guns in the rear turret, two more in the mid-upper turret, but only one piddling little .303 Vickers Gas-Operated gun (VGO) in the front turret. Unlike the Browning, each with 500 rounds of ammunition, the VGO was fed by a pan that held only 100 rounds. When the pan had been emptied, the gunner had first to remove and dump the old pan, then turn around in his turret and take a new pan from its stowage. Having fitted the pan, he had to cock his gun twice so as to load the breech, then take hold of the two handles that controlled its operation, re-sight and continue firing. All this meant that, in the case of an attack on a surfaced U-boat, only one gun could be brought to bear on the target, and only one pan of ammo used before the attack was over.

The Germans soon became aware of this weakness and equipped their U-boats with four cannon in quadruple mountings. Their fire-power was therefore so devastating against such a huge target as a Sunderland that it became almost suicidal to attack them if they fought back. For its part, the Sunderland had to make a direct and fairly steady run in to achieve a successful straddle, thus providing a 'no deflection' shot for the U-boat's gunners. We cursed at the stupidity of our one little pipsqueak gun in the nose; while aircraft in Bomber Command carried two Brownings in their front turrets, in spite of the fact that bombers were never attacked head-on at night. In fact, the only crew member of a Bomber Command aircraft who ever actually saw a night-fighter was the rear gunner, and then usually only in the last few seconds of his life. Nevertheless, like everything else in the war we accepted things for what they were, and not what they should have been.

After our stay at Pembroke Dock we returned to Poole and commenced regular patrols in the Bay of Biscay, usually as far south as the coast of Spain. About a month later, we flew our first convoy escort duty, and this I found very satisfying. I remembered very well how I felt when crossing the Atlantic, and the comfort everyone on board ship had felt at the sight of our aircraft patrolling around the convoy. To be aloft now, watching over twenty or thirty ships with hundreds of sailors and tons of precious cargoes, was a great feeling. How different from the emotions one had when going out on a destructive bombing mission. So, I never felt bored or tired while guarding a convoy, and I am sure no one searched the sea and sky more diligently than I did. It is worth noting that I never heard of a convoy being attacked while actually under the protective umbrella of an RAF aircraft. The only snag with both A/S patrols and convoy duty was the need to be there during daylight hours. Being wintertime with only about nine hours of daylight meant that our thirteen-hour flights both started and ended with night flying. Fully laden Sunderlands were never too easy to get airborne, and even more difficult in the darkness. Although night landings with an empty aircraft were quite straight-forward, the identification of the coast, especially in conditions of low cloud, was always tricky at night. I suppose, in those days the old saying, 'Only birds and fools fly, but birds don't fly at night', had not then been overtaken.

The time when we were most needed by a convoy was around dusk. Once a U-boat had located a convoy, it usually followed astern during daylight, keeping the tops of the ships' masts in view, while remaining unseen by the ships' lookouts. Then just before dark, having worked out the average course and speed of the convoy, it would race around ahead on the surface, submerge, and wait for the convoy to come into view through its periscope. So, we stayed with the convoy until this period of danger had passed and were unable to be of any further assistance. Thus, the final leg of our patrol was usually in darkness.

Once back at Poole the night landing was none too easy because of the harbour's narrow channels. Mount Batten was very much worse, as landings were made in the open waters of Plymouth Sound, which, if the wind was from the south, could be distinctly rough. Also, Plymouth was ringed by barrage balloons. A very tight circuit had to be made to avoid flying over the town and getting involved with the balloon cables. Happily, balloons close to the landing area were usually close-hauled during our flying operations, although AA gunners with itchy trigger fingers were known to pose the occasional threat.

The work, though quite different from that in Bomber Command, was very rewarding, and a feeling of camaraderie seemed to prevail in every crew. The ever-present danger of being pounced upon by a pack of JU 88s certainly kept us all on our toes, and grateful to be back on terra firma after each flight. For there were regular interceptions of our aircraft patrolling the Bay, with the Aussie 10 Squadron at Mount Batten seeming to get more than its fair share. Regrettably, many aircraft failed to escape, even after giving a very good account of themselves.

Nevertheless, our crew did not go without the occasional bit of excitement, as the following incident will show. One night, while returning from patrol after a purely routine trip, we ran into a most peculiar cloud formation. Suddenly, the tips of the blades of our propellers became luminous, and the arcs that the props described became huge glowing circles. Gradually, the glow increased until the whole length of each blade seemed to be alight. Then the guns in the turrets began to glow with increasing intensity. Soon the entire nose of the aircraft took on this strange blue-tinged light, as did the leading edges of the wings, the tailplane and the fin. At the first sight of this phenomenon, our wireless operator had wound in the trailing aerial. Now there was nothing we could do but sit and wonder anxiously what would happen next. We did not have long to wait, for suddenly there was a blinding flash and a terrific bang, followed by complete darkness. The effect on everybody was shattering and we all seemed to come up on the intercom at the same moment. The front gunner was sure that his turret had been hit by lightning, similarly the rear and mid-upper gunners. The truth was that we had some-how become charged with a huge amount of static electricity. Then on entering a different cloud, had discharged into it in just the same way as lightning. The phenomenon, known as 'St Elmo's Fire', is not a rare occurrence. It happens occasionally to church steeples in storm con-ditions when there is an abundance of electricity in the clouds. However, the magnitude of the bang that we heard was deafening, and it seemed impossible for us to have escaped damage.

Just after we had recovered from the first shock, the props and guns again began to glow. Again, we sat apprehensively, but we must have flown clear of that particular cloud, as slowly it all died away again. Our experience must have been an extreme example of the phenom-enon, as I never heard of it happening in similar fashion to any other crew. At the end of the trip we landed back at Mount Batten. Returning to Poole the next day, we promptly set off on a fortnight's leave.

It was now all too apparent that I would soon be moving on from 461. An Australian named Wg Cdr Douglas had already replaced the CO, and Sqn Ldr Raban had also gone. Indeed, I was the only RAF pilot left on the squadron and I knew that I was now believed to have sufficient experience to be given my own crew. I had been promoted to flight sergeant, with a pay increase to the fabulous sum of 16/6d (82½p) per day. I had applied for a commission and had been for an interview at Group HQ. The interviewer was a group captain, and a friendly old soul too. He questioned me only on personal matters, and I assumed that my DFM ribbon saw me through the operational aspects.

While I was in a position to help with the move, Betty and I decided to give up our digs in Poole, and we returned to our home in Whetstone. Happily, I was able to spend quite a time with my father, who was still running the firm on his own, and making a good job of it too – quite remarkable for a man in his sixty-ninth year.

At the end of the leave, I returned to Poole and to a room in the sergeants' mess. Marrows and our crew had also been on leave while our aircraft was undergoing a major inspection. Our first job was to air test another Sunderland that had been up on the hard for repairs. It was Sunderland W6050, and the date was 6 February 1943. We did not go very far from base, which was indeed fortunate; for on the return to Poole our port inner engine caught fire. It is difficult to describe fully the terror of having an aircraft on fire in the air, and the feelings of the crew unlucky enough to experience it. For me, it was no new feeling, but one I hope I never have again. However, we landed in double-quick time and were fortunate in getting it quickly under control.

About this time, I had a funny experience that was in no way connected with my duties as a pilot. I should explain first that a ground staff sergeant from Group HQ had been billeted in the same room that I occupied. He stayed with us for a few days, during which I learnt that he was the NCO in charge of pigeons. Before the war, he had been an expert pigeon fancier. In those days we carried pigeons in the aircraft in case we were forced down in the 'drink' without first being able to radio our position to base. The practice was abandoned shortly afterwards, as only true homing pigeons are happy flying over water. There were cases in which ditched crews in dinghies had released birds that had then been reluctant to fly away. Sometimes, after circling the dinghy they returned to squat amongst the crew. The regular joke was that we could always eat them if they refused to fly.

The reason for the sergeant's visit to Poole was that a vigilant coast-guard, who also knew about pigeons, had on several occasions seen a pigeon cross the coast and fly straight out to sea. Before disappearing from sight they were flying strongly and obviously had just been released. It appeared therefore that they were being released from close inland and were on their way to northern France. This could only point to one thing: a spy network operating in the Poole area. Of course, one wondered how the pigeons had come from France in the first place. The pigeon sergeant had been sent down to Poole to make contact with known pigeon fanciers. He was with us for a few days, then one day after I returned from a trip he had gone. I never heard the outcome of the story, but this simple account is only the lead-up to what came next. One Saturday evening, having nothing to do I went with a couple of aircrew friends on a pub-crawl in Bournemouth. We ended up in a pub somewhere between Bournemouth and Poole. By closing time, we were all in a happy mood, my two friends especially.

Although happy, I was by no means 'full', not being a pint drinker, and four or five half pints have always been my limit. We were returning to Poole by way of the white line down the middle of the road. In the blackout, this was the only way to avoid walking into unlit lamp-posts. Also, we were singing, I regret, in a most undignified manner not in keeping with our rank. So, it would have been natural for a bystander, of which there were few around, to assume we were just three young soldiers much the worse for wear. However, as we were going through Parkstone, a man joined us from out of the shadows and asked if we would like to have a few beers with him. Immediately, I was a bit suspicious, thinking that we might be lured into some sort of shady place and divested of our money.

My two companions were all for it, with expressions like 'Lead on Macduff!' Soon we had turned around and were following our new 'friend' a little way back up the street. Entering a small shopping centre, we arrived at a large brick building, which was of course in total darkness. Our friend then produced a key, and opening a door led us into the building. He did not turn on the lights but, with the aid of a torch, led us to a room at the rear. Much to my surprise, I realised that we were in a bank; we soon found ourselves in a small room that was obviously the manager's office. It seemed totally impossible, but there was no disguising the row of cashiers' desks behind the brass grilles in the room we had just passed through. Our friend then closed the door between the office and the main bank area and turned on the light. Pulling up some chairs, he bade us sit down while he got some bottles of beer and glasses from a cupboard by his desk.

When the light first went on he took good stock of us and appeared a little surprised to find that we were all senior NCOs, not just ordinary soldiers or airmen. After we sat down, his first remark was, 'Oh, you're the British Air Force.' This had me completely puzzled, as it would have been normal for him to say, 'Oh you're in the RAF', or 'Air Force'. The term 'British Air Force' I had never heard before, or since. I looked at my two companions, but the detail seemed to have escaped them. We started on the beers he set before us, and I went along with this apparent charade, pretending I was as merry as my two companions were. From the way our friend sat comfortably behind the desk, there was no doubt that he was the manager of the bank. But whatever was a bank manager doing inviting three unknown drunks into his bank after 11 o'clock on a Saturday night, in wartime in an important town like Poole? Perhaps he had a son in the Forces and would soon turn the conversation on to him and bring out some photographs. This often happened to servicemen who were offered a

155

drink in a pub by some well-wishing civilian. Yet nothing like this happened during the couple of hours we sat in his office being plied with beers. Neither did he tell us anything about himself or his family. He certainly tried to keep the talk on Service matters, and although we did not discuss any secret matter, I felt that on many things my companions had been highly indiscreet. I wondered what the devil was going on, and finally made up my mind that our friend was one of two things: either a German spy out to pick up what information he could, or a British Intelligence agent out to catch indiscreet servicemen.

Soon we got quite a shock that made me certain that our friend was indeed a spy. For, at about 1 o'clock in the morning, the bell on the front door of the bank rang loudly. Our host then turned off the lights in the office, leaving us in complete darkness. He made his way to the front door and opened it, letting someone in without a word being spoken. Then he returned with another man and switched on the lights again.

Much to our amazement, the other man was an Army despatch-rider clad in uniform. That he was actually on duty was apparent from his remark to the bank manager that he had left his motor-cycle in an alley at the rear of the bank. Clearly, he had been at the bank many times at night before from the casual way he came in without any explanation of his clandestine visit at dead of night. He sat down and was soon drinking beer, but had little to say and appeared somewhat ill at ease to find us there. We now sensed that the bank manager wished to get rid of us as soon as possible. Consequently, after a little more conversation we found ourselves out in the street again. The mode of our exit was the same as that of our entry, for we were let out in complete darkness with just a curt 'Goodnight', and no mention of anything such as a return visit.

I was now certain that we had unwittingly stumbled into something sinister, and I was ninety-nine per cent certain that our manager was some sort of enemy agent. The episode of the pigeons was still fresh in my mind, also what I had seen going on in Belgium and France when I was there only months before. I still had the niggling thought that our man might be working for Counter-Intelligence. If this was so, we must report what had occurred that night immediately, and not wait until the morning. My two colleagues were not so sure, only wishing to get their heads down on a friendly pillow, but I prevailed on them to go along to HQ with me.

At Station HQ we told the sentry to call out the Duty Intelligence Officer. As there were no operational flights that night, the officer had gone to bed and the sentry was loath to disturb him. However, as we insisted, a bedraggled fellow in pyjamas under his raincoat appeared. To say he was annoyed was the understatement of the year, but we told him our story from start to finish. Not knowing what to make of it, he called out the Senior Intelligence Officer and we repeated the story. At the conclusion, we were told to return the next morning and make a full statement. Looking back, I am sure we did the right thing in reporting everything that night, as it gave my companions time to sober up and so remember all that had occurred when we reported it again the next morning.

At HQ the following day, the whole episode was discussed in detail. Our Intelligence Officers were now of the same mind as I was, and a report was made out for transmission to Group HQ. Before this happened, it was necessary to identify the bank we had been in. So, I was detailed to return and establish its location. I set off wearing my greatcoat well buttoned-up to hide my 'wings' and medal ribbon. These would have been a dead give-away for our bank manager to recognise me if he lived over or near the bank.

It was a pleasant Sunday morning, but there were not many people about and I did not want to look as if I was snooping around. Spotting a young WAAF walking some way ahead, I caught up with her and asked if she minded if I walked with her. She must have thought it was just an ordinary pick-up and readily agreed. I realised that I would have to tell her something, for once I had identified the bank in question, I would have to drop her just as quickly as I had picked her up. So, in my best cloak-and-dagger manner, I told her I needed her as a cover while I had a look round the Parkstone area on behalf of our Intelligence Section. She fell in with the request and we walked on together chatting amiably.

I had no trouble in finding the bank, as the night before on the way back to Poole I had memorised where we had been. When we were well clear of the place and I was sure I had not been seen by my friend of the night before, I told the WAAF that I had found what I was looking for. Instructing her not to talk to anyone about our meeting and what had transpired, I thanked her for her help and returned to HQ with the information required. I heard nothing more for a couple of days until I was again summoned to HQ and interviewed by two senior NCOs from Group who had been sent down to investigate the incident. They had already made some enquiries and had ascertained that the only person who possessed the keys to the bank was the manager. It appeared that he did not live on the premises, nor was he permitted to be there late at night after working hours. He certainly did not belong to any Counter-Intelligence organisation in the area.

Before going any further, they required me to make a positive identification of the man himself. Accordingly, an interview was arranged with the manager on some quite legitimate banking transaction. I was not told what this was, but the investigators wanted me to follow them to the bank and enter it shortly after they did. I was to go to the cashier and change a note, and while there have a quick look at the manager in his office. He could be seen clearly through the glass partition that separated his office from the main part of the bank. To make myself less recognisable, I was given an airman's greatcoat to wear without any NCO stripes.

The two NCOs set off for the bank with me following at a discreet distance. I entered the bank, got my change, and had a good look at the manager, who was now talking to my RAF colleagues. I was able to identify him without any doubt whatsoever. I was sure I had not been seen or recognised, and left the bank to return to HQ, to be joined later by the two NCOs. Having now established the identity of our 'man', the NCO investigators told me to keep right out of it, as they would hand the whole matter over to the Police and MI5. That was the end of it for me, but I would love to have known the outcome of this most unusual occurrence.

On 16 February our aircraft's inspection had been completed and we took it for a test flight. Two days later we were sent to have a look at two northern bases in case we might one day be diverted to them. We flew first to Stranraer and then to Oban, where we stayed the night. It was an attractive place, but in winter terribly remote, and I would not like to have been stationed there.

Returning to Poole on the 19th, I found that not only had my commission come through, but that I had received a summons to Buckingham Palace to receive my DFM from the King. I was given another short period of leave and jubilantly set off again for London. I went to the Palace on 23 February with Betty, my parents, and Betty's parents, but only two people were allowed to accompany each recipient at the investiture. So the honour went to Betty and my mother, while the others waited outside the Palace. Over three hundred people were to be decorated, an awfully tiring job for the King, especially as he had to say a few words to each recipient. In view of his well-known stammer, it must also have been terribly nerve-racking, something I could sympathise with only too well. My impression at the time was that he looked somewhat unreal, with the made-up look of an actor.

The ceremony for each individual was very brief. We took our turn in a long line, and as our names were called, we took a few paces forward until we were directly in front of the King. Then we did a smart left turn, bowed and then took another step forward. By this time, the King's aide had passed him the medal, which he attached to a small hook that had earlier been fixed to the left side of our tunics. Then he murmured a few words and shook hands. We bowed again, took a pace to the rear, turned, and moved off. We now crossed to another room where the medal was taken from us and placed in a small box, while the hook was removed from our tunics. The medal box was a poor thing indeed: just simply made of white cardboard, having one's name in ink in copperplate writing; a very poor companion to the DFC given to officers, in its beautiful leather-bound case with the letters DFC embossed in gold. But no matter, the DFM is generally looked upon as being harder to win than its counterpart. A rather strange thing about the DFM was that it had the holder's name engraved round the rim, while the DFC had only the year it was awarded on the reverse.

The ceremony over, we waited outside the Palace until our relatives joined us. They were required to remain until the entire investiture was completed, with the King leaving first. Chatting with other recipients, it became apparent that the King used but a few different phrases for each of us, quite understandable in the circumstances. It reminded me of the silly joke concerning investitures that went around during the war. The King was decorating an airman and asked him how he won his medal. 'Well, Sir,' said the airman, 'a couple of months ago I shot down two Fokkers. Then a week later I shot down another Fokker, and the very next week I got two more Fokkers.' The King, now very brassed-off, replied, 'I don't care h-how many F-Fokkers you shot down, you're only g-getting one F-Fokking medal.'

However, the investiture was very impressive in spite of the large number of people being decorated. I felt very proud of the fact that I had shaken hands with the King and received my 'gong' from him. Afterwards we all went to the Trocadero for a slap-up lunch. I can well remember my father walking along the street ahead of us, swinging his umbrella around jauntily, rather like Charlie Chaplin in the old silent films. For such was his evident joy at my award of the DFM. Next, we went to a military tailor, where I was measured for my officer's uniform.

It was a happy leave indeed, following which I returned to Poole and moved into the officers' mess. I might mention that when a serviceman is commissioned from the ranks, he is first discharged from the Service. He receives a new identity, including a new Service number. Although I did not know it at the time, the award of the DFM also carried with it a cash award of £20. This is given to an airman at the end of his service career, or to his next-of-kin if he is killed.

However, having been discharged from the service as an airman, the twenty quid was paid to me immediately. It came in very handy, as my initial clothing allowance barely covered the cost of my new uniform.

Back at Poole, I started on what I can only describe as a totally different life style. At first I felt very ill at ease in my new surroundings in the officers' mess, as I had not been used to rubbing shoulders with everyone from the CO downwards. However, the Aussies were a decent bunch, and Marrows did his best to make me feel at ease. A brand-new pilot officer in the mess is very small fry indeed compared with a flight sergeant in the sergeants' mess, and quite a period of time is required to make the adjustment from one to the other. I can well understand why an officer newly commissioned from the ranks is posted away to a new unit, especially in the Army and Navy.

Hardly a week had passed before a posting came through for me to join No. 4 (Coastal) Operational Training Unit, where I was to undergo a Captains' course. I did only four more trips with Marrows, none of them operational, before leaving 461 Squadron. I had learned a tremendous amount since joining the Squadron, and I really missed Marrows and his crew, all of whom I liked and whose company I enjoyed. I had now amassed over two hundred additional flying hours, and was a far more proficient pilot than I was on the day I joined the OTU at Cottesmore. Although flying held no fears for me, I hated all the moving from base to base, and did not relish the idea of going, yet again, to a new station where I would not know a soul. The day of parting finally came and I found myself on the way to London and then to the North. One of the advantages of being commissioned was being able to travel first-class, and this certainly made the journey tolerable.

On 10 March 1943, I arrived at Alness on the Cromarty Firth, just west of Invergordon, which was the home of No. 4 (C) OTU, Coastal Command's main flying-boat training unit. About forty-five aircraft were based there, roughly half Sunderlands and half Catalinas. Our billets were in Nissen huts, with about twenty of us in a hut. We were made up into crews; mine consisted of five officers and only four NCOs, which was really rather top-heavy for a flying-boat crew. It meant that the officers would have to do at least their fair share of work when we had our own aircraft to look after. All the crew were new boys except one gunner and me.

The gunner really was a most unusual character, and I guess a book could have been written about him. He was forty-seven years old, of solid build and elderly ways; he had been a designer and inventor in Civvy Street, and I gathered he had forty-seven patents to his credit.

He was a flight lieutenant and therefore the most senior-ranking member of the crew. His name was Thimblethorpe, but at school he had been nicknamed Tinkerbell, which had now been shortened to Tinkle. In spite of his age and quite unusual nature, he turned out to be a hard-working and utterly reliable member of our crew, and he gave me undivided loyalty. He always called me 'Bav', except when with the other crew members, when it was just the usual title of Skipper. In some ways, he really was the epitome of a crackpot inventor. He always kept his watch seven and a half minutes fast, so as never to be late. 'Surely,' I once asked him, 'don't you rely on your watch being fast and so lose the advantage of it?' 'No,' he replied, 'I think of it being only five minutes fast and that way I always arrive two and a half minutes early.' He carried baggage with him that far exceeded that of two other crew members. It included a portable typewriter, camera, civilian clothing, and even a personal revolver. He had been a gunnery instructor on Wellingtons, and in spite of his age, had requested a posting to an operational squadron.

The second pilot was a young flying officer named Harry Holt. He was single, being hardly out of college, and very inexperienced in every way. He was an amusing chap who loved a silly story, but always made a complete hash of re-telling it later. However, he was a good sort and I grew to like him very much. My navigator was another flying officer named Eric Harrison. He turned out to be good at his job, though a bit sharp on the tongue, and always referred to pilots as 'airframe drivers'. It was a good job he was not in the RAF thirty years later, when navigators rose to be Commanding Officers, as I am sure he would have been intolerable. The other two officers were Plt Off Boorman, a WOp/AG, and Plt Off Hards. Don Boorman had been a policeman in peacetime and was a true cockney. He got his commission because of his prowess at sport, and had done quite a bit of boxing. He was married and had a small son whom he always referred to as 'my little bloke'. His wife Joyce was a kind and sincere girl whom Betty and I met several times, and again after the war.

The two other WOp/AGs were Sgts Perry and Elliot. Elliot was also our WOM (Wireless Operator Mechanic) and was the best of the three when it came to actual wireless work. The last, but by no means least, members of our crew were Sgts Wright and Curwen. The latter was a decent fellow but not really the aircrew type at all. He lasted with us until we joined a squadron, but, unfortunately, hardly ever flew with us without being airsick. I tried hard to cure him of this, even allowing him to have spells at flying the aircraft, but finally had to give up and get him taken off flying.

Jock Wright was a character much in the same vein as Tinkle, and came from Glasgow. He was about my own age and also married. He was short and stocky, and one only had to look at his battledress to know that he was a flight engineer: the spots of grease that adorned his uniform were a dead give-away. Yet, a bond of friendship grew up between us that exceeded that of any other, even including Tinkle.

The OTU course was designed on much the same lines as that at Cottesmore; except that we had proper dual instruction from experienced pilots, all of whom had done an Instructors' Course. This resulted in thorough flying training, and I realised how inadequate I had been when I left my first OTU.

We did not fly with our own crews at first, but with staff crews who were 'on rest' from operational flying. While we pilots were doing the 'circuits and bumps' part of our training, our crews were getting ground instruction. I flew with another pupil named Hazeldine; our instructor for day flying was Flt Lt Logsdail. For night flying we had Sqn Ldr Bennett. I stood and watched while Hazeldine was given four and a half hours dual before going solo. Owing to my previous Sunderland experience, I had only a couple of check circuits before going off on my own. At the end of five weeks, when we had also both flown solo at night, we joined up with our allotted crews and started on long oversea flights. The longest of these, on 7 May, lasted nine hours.

Group HQ then laid on an operational A/S patrol, for which our aircraft was fully armed with guns and depth charges. At the end of this operation we were diverted to Sullom Voe in the Shetlands where we stayed overnight and returned the following day. I had never been as far north as 60° and was fascinated by the fact that it was never really dark at night. At one o'clock in the morning there was enough light to read the large print of a newspaper. I would have hated to be there in winter, for even on good days the sun made only a brief appearance. Our landing at a different base seemed to set the seal on the completion of our training, and we felt full of confidence from then on. I was immensely pleased at the way we had all settled in and were working together as a team. I knew that I had been lucky to get a good crew, and in my heart I felt that they were also happy with me. It was a great feeling for me, and I now believed that I really belonged in the RAF more than at any time previously.

After nearly three months of intensive training, our course ended. We were given a fortnight's leave, and as I travelled south to London, I wondered which squadron we would be posted to on our return. Not that I was really too bothered, as I was particularly pleased that again I had received an assessment of 'Above average' at the end of the course. Nevertheless, I had missed Betty and Jill terribly, though her letters, which arrived almost daily, were a great comfort. With five married men on our crew, we dreaded being posted to some out-landish place such as Bathurst in West Africa, or worse still, the Seychelles in the Indian Ocean. We need not have worried, for during our leave we received notice of our posting to 201 Squadron, based at Castle Archdale on Lough Erne in Northern Ireland. We all had a great leave, for it was midsummer, and although the end of the war still looked many years away, the dark days of 1940 and 1941 were now far behind us.

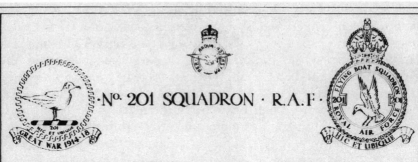

·No· 201 SQUADRON · R.A.F·

FORMED AT GOSPORT 15ᵗʰ OCTOBER 1914 AS Nº1 SQUADRON R.N.A.S ·· PROCEEDED OVERSEAS ON
26ᵗʰ FEBRUARY 1915 ·· BECAME Nº1 WING R.N.A.S JUNE 1915 ·· "A" SQUADRON Nº1 WING R.N.A.S,
FORMED AT Sᵗ POL, DUNKIRK 1ˢᵗ MARCH 1916 ·· DESIGNATED "DETACHED" SQUADRON 3ʳᵈ JULY 1916
BECAME Nº1 SQUADRON R.N.A.S. 6ᵗʰ DECEMBER 1916 ·· RENUMBERED Nº 201 SQUADRON R.A.F
1ˢᵗ APRIL 1918 ·· RETURNED TO ENGLAND 15ᵗʰ FEBRUARY 1919 ·· DISBANDED AT LAKEDOWN
31ˢᵗ DECEMBER 1919 · · Nº 480 (COASTAL RECONNAISSANCE) FLIGHT AT CALSHOT.
REDESIGNATED Nº 201 (FLYING BOAT) SQUADRON JANUARY 1929

COMMANDING OFFICERS		LOCATIONS			EQUIPMENT	
SQUADRON COMMANDER A.M. LONGMORE	15·10·14	GOSPORT	ENGLAND	15·10·14	AVRO. BRISTOL SCOUT	
		NEWCASTLE	"	23·11·14	CURTISS, HENRI FARMAN	FEBRUARY 1915
SQUADRON COMMANDER F. K. HASKINS	1·3·16	DETACHMENT	TO	2·2·15	MAURICE FARMAN	TO JUNE 1915
		DOVER	"	JAN. 15	MORANE PARASOL	
SQUADRON COMMANDER R.S. DALLAS	14·6·17	Sᵗ POL (DUNKIRK)	FRANCE	26·2·15	VICKERS FIGHTER	
		FURNES	BELGIUM	10·6·16	NIEUPORT SCOUT	
MAJOR C.D. BOOKER	18·3·18	CHIPILLY	FRANCE	15·2·17	NIEUPORT TWOSEATER	MARCH 1916
MAJOR C.M. LEMAN	18·8·18	LA BELLEVUE	"	11·4·17	SOPWITH TRIPLANE	TO JANUARY 1917
	1015·2·19	BAILLEUL	"	1·6·17		
W/C D.G.MACDONALD D.F.C, A.F.C	·1·29	MIDDLE AERODROME (Nᵗ BRAY DUNES)	"	2·11·17	SOPWITH CAMEL	NOVEMBER 1917 NOVEMBER 1918
S/L E.F. TURNER , A.F.C	·30		"			
S/L C.G WIGGLESWORTH A.F.C	·33	DOVER	ENGLAND	10·12·17		
S/L J.D BREAKEY D.F.C	·35	TETEGHEM	FRANCE	16·2·18		
W/C C.H.CAHILL D.F.C, A.F.C		Sᵗ MARIE·CAPPEL	"	27·3·18		
W/C C.S.RICCARD	14·8·40	FIENVILLERS	"	28·3·18		
W/C W.G ABRAMS	9·4·41	NOEUX	"	12·4·18		
W/C J. L CROSBIE	23·12·41	Sᵗ MARIE·CAPPEL	"	20·7·18		
W/C J.B BURNETT	19·8·42	POULAINVILLE	"	6·8·18		
W/C R.E.G. VAN DER KISTE D.S.O.	4·5·43	NOEUX	"	14·8·18		
		BAIZIEUX	"	19·9·18		
		BEUGNATRE	"	14·10·18		
		LA TARGETTE	"	27·10·18		
		BÉTHENCOURT	"	22·12·18		
		LAKEDOWN	ENGLAND	15·2·19 TO 31·12·19		
		CALSHOT	"	JAN·29	SOUTHAMPTON	JANUARY 1929
		LONG HOPE	ORKNEYS	22·5·39	LONDON	TO MARCH 1940
		SULLOM VOE	SHETLANDS	7·8·39	SUNDERLAND	MARCH 1940
		CASTLE ARCHDALE	N.IRELAND	1·10·41		

No. 201 Squadron history at the time when the author joined.

Chapter 12

I JOIN 201 SQUADRON

At the end of the leave, Betty came to King's Cross station to see me off on the night train to Stranraer, together with members of the crew who lived in London. It was a long tiring journey there, with a ferry to catch to take us over to Larne, then a train to Belfast, followed by several hours' wait until we caught the slow train to Enniskillen. Finally, RAF transport took us to Castle Archdale after a journey of almost twenty-four hours.

On arrival, we found our new home was composed entirely of Nissen huts, apart from the ops room which was located in the old castle. The huts where we slept were partitioned off into small rooms, each to take two officers. Tinkle was my room-mate, and once I got used to his idiosyncrasies, of which there were many, I found him an agreeable companion, tolerant of my shortcomings and appreciative of my virtues. This was fortunate, for we shared our tiny room for nearly ten months.

Having got ourselves dug in, I reported to the Adjutant, who arranged for me to present my crew to our new CO. He was Wg Cdr Van der Kiste, and like many senior officers in Coastal Command was a pre-war officer. He was no 'desk wallah', as the DSO ribbon under his wings indicated. I soon found that I liked him immensely, for in some ways he reminded me of my father. 'Van', or the Flying Dutchman as he was often called, was from the mould of pre-war types who in most ways were unlike our group of 'hostilities only' officers. Each morning at 9 o'clock there would be a conference attended by all skippers who were not actually flying. He would ask us what our crew programme was for the day. Maybe one crew was due for a fighter affiliation exercise, or perhaps a test flight. Whatever it was, once he had cleared it, he left it entirely to the individual skipper to carry out. He trusted each skipper to look after his own aircraft like the captain of a ship. This included the welfare and discipline of his crew. After two years of being an NCO and a second pilot, I liked my new authority and was inspired to carry out my duties in the best way I could. My main thought, however, was to get my crew through our tour of Ops all in one piece and, in so doing, keep my own neck tightly screwed on as well.

Our first flight with 201 Squadron was a local trip, and a senior pilot named Flt Lt Sanderson came with us to point out the salient features of the countryside. An important one of these was the narrow 'air corridor' over Ballyshannon, where we were allowed to cross neutral Eire between Lough Erne and Donegal Bay. We completed our flight by carrying out some low-level bombing and gunnery on a flame float that we dropped in Donegal Bay. The next day we got the job of testing another aircraft following an engine change, and enjoyed being entirely on our own.

Then followed two more local trips, the last of which was to practise QGH procedure. This was the only means then available by which we could be guided down to a landing in bad weather, caused by either low cloud or poor visibility. The procedure consisted of our sending out signals on W/T (Morse code) that were picked up by a D/F (direction-finding) operator at the base. He would then rotate his D/F loop aerial and get a compass bearing on us while our WOp held down the key of his transmitter so as to send one long un-interrupted signal. Having got our bearing, the ground operator would relay it to the ops room. Another operator would then call the aircraft on R/T (short-range voice communication) and give the pilot a

Short Sunderland NS-Z of No. 201 Sqn builds up speed on take-off.

magnetic course to fly. At this stage, the aircraft would normally be approaching base at a safe enough height to clear all high ground. When directly over the D/F station, the pilot would be given fresh courses to fly to take him out from the station and then bring him back overhead again. He would now be sent out on a predetermined course, during which he would be directed down to a lower height. After flying out about ten miles, he would be brought back to the landing area again, at the same time being given instructions to reduce height at a rate of so many feet per minute.

This may all sound straightforward, but it is very difficult for a pilot to carry out to perfection. Of course, the pilot would be flying blind in cloud in conditions that might be tossing the aircraft about all over the place. Also, a strong wind could be pushing it continually off course. Additionally, the pilot was required to maintain a steady airspeed, which, in bumpy conditions, was quite difficult, while at the same time losing height at a constant rate. Ever present in the pilot's mind was the fact that alongside our landing area was a hill some 1,200 feet high. So, one can well imagine our thoughts when, as was often the case, we did not break cloud until we were below 500 feet. Even when below cloud, it was sometimes necessary to do a circuit before landing. Doing split-arse turns at about 400 feet, with this bloody great hill alongside, was never my favourite recipe for reaching old age, especially at night.

Our first operational flight came on 19 June, when we did an A/S sweep down to Gibraltar. Again, Sanderson came with us as the 'screening' pilot to provide a safety check. I really felt this to be quite unnecessary, as I was familiar with Bay patrols and had already been to Gib. The trip was uneventful, apart from the fact that the oil temperature on our port inner engine started to soar before the end of the flight. Much to my dismay, Sanderson merely reduced the revs on the engine to offset this trouble, without reducing the boost. I suggested to him that the boost should also be reduced to allow the engine to run lightly. But he disagreed with me, and used his position as a senior pilot (in both rank and experience) to overrule me. As this procedure was akin to trying to make a car go uphill in top gear with the throttle fully open, I was much annoyed, and perhaps a little alarmed as well. However, this was the last time that any decision I made in the air was overruled.

On arrival at Gibraltar, we moored up alongside the airstrip where we had been on my previous visit. Going ashore, and with our de-briefing over, I decided to try to find Mr Darling. After a few enquiries, I located him and he was most pleased to see me. He told me I was the only airman who had come through the Escape Line that he had ever met again. The first enquiry I put to him was, of course, of Dédée de Jongh and the rest of the Escape Line team. He shook his head sadly. 'I am afraid I have only bad news for you', he said. 'Dédée has been arrested, as have most of the people who helped you last year. They are either in prison or have been shot.' He went on to tell me that they had tried everything possible to get Dédée de Jongh released. They had even approached the King of Italy to obtain her release by offering to exchange her with any political prisoner that we held in custody, but all to no avail. I learned too that little Dédée Dumont and her father had also been arrested. The Steenbecks had also been arrested, the father having been shot. At the time, he had been trying to warn the Evrards of the raid by the Gestapo; it had happened in the underground basement through which Bob and I used to pass every evening. His sacrifice had been in vain, for the Evrard family had all been arrested; the last Darling had heard about them was that they were imprisoned in Essen. He had no idea whether they were still alive.

Deeply shocked and saddened by the news, I felt guilty that I was alive and free; the very thought of it filled me with despair. If I could have put the clock back, I would willingly have gone to a POW camp if, by doing so, their capture could have been avoided. I could not forget the wistful eyes of little Dédée Dumont, or the young beauty of Gisèle, nor the courage and determination of Dédée de Jongh.

After a couple of drinks with Darling, I rejoined the crew. Although I am very talkative by nature, I was unable to speak about my news to any of the crew, since they were not allowed to know anything about it, except the bare bones of my escape after the raid on Cologne. It was a long time before I was able to get those wonderful people from my mind, although I was then unaware of the horrors that they were going through in the concentration camps. Many years later, I was to find out at first hand.

The next day we were sent down to Port Lyautey on the west coast of Africa, where we landed on the river, but the purpose of the flight was not made known to us. We were only there a couple of hours and then returned to Gibraltar. However, we did know that Churchill was at a conference in Algiers and would obviously be travelling back to the UK via Gib. For a while, we thought we might have been tasked with bringing him back, but this did not happen. Looking back on the incident, I think it was possible that we could have been sent there as a decoy. Since Sunderlands were not based at Gib, German agents in La Linea would have noticed our arrival there. We stayed at Gibraltar until 23 June, by which time Churchill was safely home. We learned later that he had left at night, flying back in a Liberator. On our long trip back across the Bay of Biscay we fully expected to be intercepted by JU 88s. We knew that they would be out in force in an attempt to shoot down the aircraft that Churchill might be on. Luckily for us, we got home in one piece, only to hear on the news that an unarmed civilian aircraft flying northwards across the Bay from Lisbon to Britain had been attacked and shot down by JU 88s. There can be no doubt that the Germans had hoped that Churchill was on board. Of course, the passengers and crew perished, one of the passengers being the film star Leslie Howard. Our trip home was blessed with a following wind and took only twelve hours; the flight out had taken sixteen.

Our next three trips were all training exercises, practising low-level runs and gunnery over a smoke float used to simulate a U-boat. It now appeared that all German submarines were staying on the surface and fighting back when attacked by aircraft. This made life particularly difficult for Sunderlands and Catalinas, which both had only one forward-firing gun, and only .303 calibre at that. So, in order to get in over a target with the minimum chance of being hit, I developed a strategy that I would adopt when and if the opportunity ever came. This way the crew would know just what to expect, and would not be put off balance by my approach. The technique was to approach the target at an oblique angle so as not to provide enemy gunners with a straight no-deflection shot at us. Then I would dive steeply to wave-top level to a point some way to the side of them. This would mean giving them a double-deflection shot at us. This would be followed by a quick turn on to target for the run-in, during which I would fly an undulating path whilst maintaining my correct approach. The problem for the front gunner was to assess the correct moment to open fire. If he fired too soon, he would run out of ammunition at the point when we were in the most vulnerable position. If he fired too late, then he would not use all the ammo, reducing his chances of knocking out the enemy gun crew before they hit us.

My only problem was that Tinkle was determined that in an attack, he would be the one to man the front gun, and he absolutely hogged the use of it. When on A/S patrols, being the senior gunner he arranged the roster for the gunners, and always took the front turret when we were in the patrol area. I had the greatest difficulty getting him out of the turret, even for meals. However, he was very good at his job and the rest of the crew seemed quite willing to fall in with his wishes. It certainly gave more practice for the other gunners in the rear turret. They had to be ready for the quick pull-up of the aircraft after an attack and have their guns at just the right angle to open fire imme-diately. So this was the way we usually practised, using up untold amounts of ammunition in the process.

Our final acceptance as a fully trained crew came after three and a half hours of night flying with Sqn Ldr Flint as our watchdog, while we practised circuits and bumps. From then on we were on our own, and, I might say, were a very highly trained crew indeed. On 28 June, we flew our first operational patrol. It was a convoy escort task that lasted over sixteen and a half hours, all very worthwhile. We stayed with the convoy until darkness had fallen and their risk of U-boat attack had decreased. Then followed a five-and-a-half-hour night flight home. After debriefing and a hot meal, we tumbled into bed well satisfied with ourselves.

We now thought that our training programme was finished for good, but how wrong we were, for we spent another whole week doing fighter affiliation, air firing, QGH practice and actual submarine attacks carried out on a 'tame' submarine of the Royal Navy. The time spent on the latter was especially valuable, as the 'victim' always took evasive action in an attempt to keep us from running directly over him, showing us his limitations.

As well as the small practice bombs that we aimed at the sub., we carried a rear-facing camera that operated as soon as a bomb was released. This allowed our efforts to be analysed back at base. I got quite good at it, and was sure I would not have any difficulty in getting a straddle across a U-boat, provided, of course, that we did not get clobbered on our way in. I enjoyed the work with a submarine, but I must confess that I hated fighter affiliation. The fighters scared the living daylights out of all of us. We used to meet up with three Beaufighters from a local fighter squadron. Being similar in perfor-mance to JU 88s, they would carry out dummy attacks on us in formation. Of course, no fire was exchanged, but there times when we felt like giving them a warning burst in an attempt to keep them off. In fact, their attacks were not at all like the real thing. Armed with cannon, the JU 88s could open fire from a much greater range than the Sunderland with its .303 guns. They seldom came in close enough to expose their soft underbelly to our four tail guns as they broke off the attack. Whereas the Beaufighters, having no such fears, came right in to point-blank range, breaking off their attacks only feet above our fin and rudder. When attacking simultaneously from all sides, the danger of a mid-air collision from these young fanatics was terrific.

It was always with a sigh of relief that we finished these frightening antics. Of course, we threw our Sunderland all over the sky to avoid an attack, as we would have done in real combat. Thus, the danger of collision was magnified many times. Without parachutes, a collision would have been catastrophic for the whole of our crew, but I do not think the Beaufighter pilots appreciated this. By the middle of July, our intensive training course ended, and we returned to the main task.

A few weeks earlier, I received a pleasant surprise when I walked into the mess and saw my old friend Brazenor standing at the bar. At Castle Archdale, in addition to 201 Squadron there were two Canadian squadrons, Nos 422 and 423. Brazenor was a member of 422 Squadron. He had been on leave for part of the short time that I had been with 201, and when he returned our paths had never met. It was the same within 201, where sometimes I would go weeks on end without seeing particular colleagues. This was quite unlike Bomber Command squadrons, where usually the entire aircrew complement was briefed and flew off on the same mission. A few days later, who should turn up in the mess but Alexander, another old friend whom I had last met when he was a PT instructor at Babbacombe. He was now a flying officer, and had come to us as a second pilot in the same manner I had first been sent to 461 Squadron. It was great to see him, and later he flew with me as my second pilot on one occasion. His story ended sadly: for later in the year he was with some other second pilots getting night flying instruction, and they crashed while doing circuits and landings. It seemed the Sunderland touched the water in a slightly nose-down attitude, dug in its nose, cartwheeled over, smashing itself to pieces, and sank. Several of the crew, including Alexander, came to the surface, as we always wore Mae Wests (life-jackets) when flying. But he was badly injured, and later found to have broken his back, with the result that he was permanently paralysed from the waist down. I often wondered what became of him, for I felt more sorry for him than for the crew members who were killed. Surely, theirs was the lesser fate.

It may sound heartless, but we never really had time to grieve over a comrade who had been lost or killed, for generally we were kept far too busy. As an example, during the last ten days in July we did five operational trips with a total of over seventy-seven hours' actual flying time. The average airborne time was fifteen and a quarter hours. Added to which would usually be at least two hours of briefing and preparation before flight, and sometimes three hours after a flight between landing and finally getting to bed. This timespan would be considerably expanded if several Sunderlands from the three squadrons had landed at around the same time. There could be a long wait for a refueller before we could leave the aircraft, and then ages waiting for a dinghy. Sometimes we would even have to wait to be debriefed if several crews were ahead of us. We had two mottoes that covered this eventuality: 'They also serve who only stand and wait', and, 'Never in the field of human conflict have so many been buggered about by so few'.

I have already described the various procedures we had to go through to get a Sunderland airborne. Once in the air and at our cruising height, things quietened down somewhat, except for the navigator, who worked continuously throughout the entire trip. His only breaks were for quick mugs of tea and a snatched meal in the galley. We navigated by DR (Dead Reckoning), using aids such as radar, loop bearings and the occasional star shot with a sextant as a check on our DR plot. To fly by DR, we had to find the exact wind speed and direction every fifteen minutes if our 'air position' was to be correctly transposed to our 'ground position'. Of course, we did not have the modern electronic wizardry that is available today. To find the wind speed and direction, the aircraft had to be flown on three courses at sixty-degree angles to each other. The 'drift' of the aircraft on each course was measured and entered on a small hand-operated Wind Speed and Direction calculator to work out the wind information. In daylight, the navigator himself could measure the drift, by peering through a drift recorder that protruded from the side of the aircraft. At night, we dropped a flame float into the sea on which the rear gunner took a series of bearings on each heading. When our position had been determined, it was passed to the wireless operator. Thus, in any sort of emergency, or when we obtained a U-boat sighting or radar contact at night, the WOp could flash a position signal to base.

The next most arduous job on board was that of rear gunner. He sat in a terribly cramped space, rotating his turret from side to side while the tail of the aircraft gyrated in a slow circular motion. In Sunderlands, although the turrets were not heated, the job was not so bad as it was in bomber aircraft, since our rear gunners were relieved every hour. In a Lancaster, for example, the rear gunner would normally remain there for anything up to eight hours. He would certainly never leave his turret while over enemy territory.

As the skipper, I always did each fully laden operational take-off and flew the aircraft for the first hour until everything had settled down. Then I would change seats with the second pilot and keep an eye on things while he did the actual flying. For me, the most worrying event was a night take-off with a fully laden aircraft, especially at Castle Archdale, as Lough Erne was fresh water and therefore not so buoyant as the sea. This meant that the hull of the aircraft sat deeper in the water, and it took greater speed to get the aircraft up onto the step and planing. Sometimes the take-off run took as long as two minutes, and all the time the throttles were wide open and the engines on maximum power. At night, the exhaust rings round the engines glowed almost white hot, not a very pleasant sight for someone with a vivid imagination. I rarely left the bridge, particularly when flying at night, and usually just to dash below to snatch a quick meal. I always got a spare member of the crew to take my place in the second pilot's seat to assist in keeping watch and to double-check that the second pilot didn't suddenly doze off. There were always plenty of volunteers when I needed someone for this job. Long before we reached the coast I would be back on watch and would not leave the bridge again until we had landed.

Most of the skippers of other Sunderlands flew the aircraft themselves during the hazardous time of locating and crossing the coastline. Unlike the east coast of England, where the complete absence of mountains and the profusion of aerodrome beacons made identification of one's position easy, the west coast of Ireland had no such aerodrome lights, very few lighthouses, but plenty of jagged cliffs and mountains along most of its length. Also, the weather was much more likely to be bad, with a cloud base often down to mere hundreds of feet. Although our navigation was pretty good, it should be remembered that we were often out of sight of land and without any positive fix of our position for perhaps fourteen or fifteen hours. So, when still many miles out from the coast, I would get the second pilot to take over the demanding job of instrument flying. I would then sit in the second pilot's seat and devote the whole of my attention to establishing just where we were. Sadly, so many of our Sunderlands crashed into hills or mountains that my main worry, especially when in cloud, was to make sure that our cloud was not hiding anything solid. I used every aid available to us to achieve this.

The navigator would continue with his job, while I would search out all the information I could get for him to plot on his chart to help him to verify the position he had worked out for us. If we were returning from a patrol well out in the Atlantic, I would first get the wireless operator to tune in to the radio station which sent out a radio beam, known as Lorenz, along which we could fly. If we were to either the north or the south of the beam we would hear either a Morse signal letter 'A' – Dot Dash – or a letter 'N' – Dash Dot – in our headphones. This was followed every minute by an identification signal. When we were aligned with the beam the two signals would merge to form a continuous signal, which we would hold to reach our base.

This system was called Radio Range, and transmitted in a westerly direction from Castle Archdale through Donegal Bay and out over the Atlantic. It sounded fine, but in practice was not always satisfactory owing to atmospheric interference. Once we were on the beam, the navigator would lay off the reciprocal line from our base so that he could check it against his DR plot on his chart. At a point 100 miles from base the radar operator would turn on his forward-searching aerials and switch to 'long range'. If we were high enough, which was not always possible if the cloud base was low, our radar could often pick up the base responder beacon at over ninety miles. The navigator could now calculate our ETA (estimated time of arrival), which would be radioed to base.

Once we were over Donegal Bay, radar returns on the land on each side of us would be relayed to the navigator. If the visibility was good, we might be able to pick up the beam of a lighthouse in neutral Eire and identify its signal. A bearing on the lighthouse using a hand-held compass would be passed to the navigator. He would plot a reciprocal of the bearing, and obtain a good right-angle fix (estimated position) using a bearing from the base radar beacon. Where there was the slightest doubt, I would instruct the WOp to call base and request a bearing on which we should fly to reach them. If I still did not feel entirely happy, or if the cloud base around the coast was too low for safe flying beneath it, I would abandon that particular approach, slam on power and climb to at least 4,000 feet. I would then call base and ask for a QGH (controlled descent through cloud).

One of our trips at the end of July required us to provide cover for the *Aquitania* on her way in from America. Our duty was to patrol ahead and ensure that no U-boat lay in wait for her. Her speed was such that no submarine could follow her, much less catch up with her. On this trip, I took with me a new member of the squadron, who came to us straight from Bomber Command, having completed two operational tours and twice been awarded the DFC. He was Flt Lt Ruth, known of course as 'Babe' Ruth. This was not after his namesake in America, but rather because of his round baby face. Very soon he was promoted to squadron leader and became our Flight Commander. Having completed two operational tours, he could have become more or less 'chair-borne' for life, had he wanted to; but he was not that type at all, in spite of his nickname. He quickly began learning all about 'boats', and flew with different crews to obtain a variety of experience.

With our new Flight Commander on board, we took off several hours before dawn, and once things had settled down, I handed him the controls. To say that he was an expert at night flying was certainly an understatement, for he never bothered to use 'George', our automatic pilot, but flew manually all the time, entirely on instruments. He never seemed to wander off course, by even a degree or two. I felt humbled by his skill, learned not only in Bomber Command, but also during his time in the pre-war Air Force. He became very popular with everyone in the mess, and would probably have become our next CO, but for the fact that he was killed before a year had passed. His name is engraved on the RAF Memorial at Runnymede, along with the names of over twenty thousand airmen from the European Theatre of World War II who died with no known graves. (I will refer to this again later, as I was deeply involved in the affair.)

At the beginning of August, I was detailed to go on an Engine Course for pilots at the Bristol Aeroplane Company. I spent a whole week at the Filton Works with about a dozen other fellows, attending lectures given by a civilian instructor. Being always very interested in engines, I quite enjoyed the course and at the end of the week there was little that I did not know about the workings of radial engines.

Returning to the squadron, I found that our Sunderland was in the workshops for a five-hundred-hour inspection. To my surprise, Tinkle was busy ripping out all the fittings and hydraulics from the front turret. Like the rest of us, he had always chaffed at the stupidity of the single gun in this turret and believed that something had to be done about it. He had the full support of our CO, who was just as concerned as his crews about U-boats that fought back on the surface. There were plenty of VGO guns in the station armoury, and Tinkle had drawn up plans whereby he intended to fit three such guns in the turret instead of just one. The only snag about the idea was the lack of space for the hydraulic mechanism as well as the extra guns. However, Tinkle felt sure that it would be possible to swing the turret bodily from side to side, and to alter the elevation of the guns by means of a system he had thought out. While he was doing this I joined him in the workshops and made up an extra escape hatch to go in the top of the aircraft hull. I should have mentioned earlier that the mid-upper gun turrets of the aircraft at Castle Archdale had been removed to reduce the load. Also, we now carried only six depth charges instead of the usual eight. Several unnecessary stowages and various items not generally required, such as high-level flares, were also removed. In this way, the aircraft were able to carry more fuel, allowing us to stay longer on convoy patrol, or fly further out into the Atlantic where the U-boats were more likely to be lurking. The extra escape hatch I made up I fitted into the space vacated by the mid-upper turret. When these tasks were completed we were given some leave, but not before I had sharpened and reset the 24" blade of the workshop saw, much to the surprise of the workshop staff, I might add. My leave was marred only by the fact that my father looked far from well. He had suffered from acidity of the stomach for many years (his love of tasty food, perhaps?), and we thought it was but a recurrence of this old complaint. Everything at the factory was going well and he looked upon his work as his 'war effort'. Yet, I felt unhappy about him, for, in spite of his sixty-eight years he had to do duties as a firewatcher at night.

I returned to Castle Archdale eager to find out how our three-gun turret would work in the air. I was much amused to find that while Tinkle had been on leave he had drawn up some proper blueprints of his design and had gone to the Patent Office to taken out a Provisional Patent. He showed me the finished drawings and I hooted with laughter when I saw that he had patented it as 'The Thimblethorpe Quick-fit Turret'. Unfortunately for Tinkle, the CO took a dim view of his patent, as he wanted the turret, if it worked, to be regarded as a squadron effort.

Nevertheless, on 17 August we flew our aircraft to let Tinkle try out his new baby. Unbeknown to us, he had instructed the armourer to load all the pans of ammunition entirely with tracer bullets. His argument was that a tracer bullet would kill a U-boat gunner just as well as any other bullet, and three streams of tracer fire would look deadly to whoever was at the receiving end of it. Usually, our pans of ammo were loaded in the standard pattern of two ball cartridges, one armour-piercing, one incendiary and one tracer. So, by using only tracer bullets in our three guns, there would be fifteen times the number of bullets visible when the guns were fired. Certainly, this would be an enormous deterrent.

Out over Donegal Bay, we dropped a flame float into the sea and came round for one of our normal attacks. Tinkle held his fire until I had completed our final turn-in; then he started firing. Most of the crew had gathered on the bridge behind the pilots' seats. Everyone gasped at the fantastic firework display provided by the three continuous streams of tracer that Tinkle let loose. What's more, he was able to swing the turret and almost obliterate the flame float target with his accurate fire. We made several more such attacks and I was exhilarated to see that in spite of my jinking the aircraft up and down during a dummy attack, Tinkle never failed to plaster the target through sheer bodily effort. At the end of two and a half hours we returned to base feeling confident that from then on we would be able to give an excellent account of ourselves if we were ever required to attack a U-boat.

Thus, the Thimblethorpe Quick-fit Turret was born and more of our

Sunderlands were fitted with it. The squadrons operating in the Bay of Biscay, however, were not at all keen to have our turret, for they were being attacked almost daily by packs of JU 88s and were suffering many losses. They were more interested in how the turret could be used in an aerial fight rather than a U-boat attack. They did not believe that anybody would be able to work the turret manually while the aircraft was being thrown about the sky during a dogfight. So some bright fellow at Group HQ decided to send us down into the Bay to join the other squadrons operating there and see how we got on if we were attacked. Here I must confess that I would be a liar if I pretended that I was at all thrilled with the idea. For one thing, we did not have our mid-upper gun turret, without which we would be a sitting duck during a beam or quarter attack; while our front guns would be of little advantage to us, since it was not normal for JU 88s to attack Sunderlands head on.

Nevertheless, on 24 August we flew down to Pembroke Dock ('PD', as it was better known). We took up a couple of fellows from the other squadrons there, but they did not seem to be much impressed. A spell of bad weather did not allow us to fly again until 31 August, when, during a fourteen-hour flight, we saw not a thing. I reckon we spent more hours scanning the sky than the sea. On our return, bad weather prevented us from landing at either PD or Mount Batten and we were diverted to Poole, where I was glad of my earlier time there and my knowledge of the channels. The next day our aircraft was checked over and we flew back to PD on 2 September.

The following day, our CO arrived. We took him up and gave him a demonstration of our new turret. He then arranged for Wg Cdr Hartnell, CO of one of the PD squadrons, to fly with us, and let him see how Tinkle could operate the turret successfully. We dropped a flame float well out in the Irish Sea and I handed the controls over to the Wg Cdr. He really threw the aircraft around the sky during his run-in to the target. Each time, by a supreme effort Tinkle kept control of his turret and was able to obliterate the flame float with concentrated fire. Even then the issue was not decided.

The next day saw us on patrol down in the Bay again. When nearly halfway to our most southerly point, Harry Holt suddenly spotted some aircraft on our port bow about three or four miles away. I grabbed hold of the field glasses and had a look at them. My heart sank as they broke cloud cover and I could count eight JU 88s. They saw us at about the same time and turned towards us. Fortunately, there was a long bank of cloud away to port, and instinctively we turned towards it. I was in a precarious position to say the least of it; for we

---

had been sent down there to see how we could manage to use our front turret during an actual attack. How could we find out if I ran for cover? I knew very well that we could never hope to survive a fight with eight enemy fighters equipped with longer-range firepower in the shape of thirty-two 20 mm cannon between them. However lucky we might be, we could not possibly hope to shoot down or drive off all eight of them, especially as we didn't even carry enough rounds of ammunition for such a task. So to engage could only mean one thing – the loss of our aircraft and the crew. So I did the only thing possible and ran for cover. On arriving at the cloudbank I did not enter at once but watched as they got into formation for an attack. I did this more to annoy them than anything else. Then, when I judged the right moment had come, we ducked into cloud. Had there been no cloud, we would have turned due west to lead the fighters away from their bases in France, and dropped down low near the sea so as to prevent any fighters from getting beneath us. We would also, of course, have immediately jettisoned our depth charges.

Once in the safety of the clouds we all breathed a little easier. We altered course every minute or two in case the JU 88s were fitted with radar like some German night-fighters. Fortunately, they appeared unable to follow us, and when we flew out of cloud cover a few minutes later, they were nowhere to be seen. When we had first sighted them our WOp had sent out an OA signal and our position; this told base that we were with enemy aircraft. Our main reason for sending the signal was to warn any other Coastal Command aircraft that might be in our vicinity. I suppose that after we got safely away we should have cancelled it, but in the excitement, both the WOp and I forgot about it. The outcome was that when we arrived back at PD we collected one hell of a raspberry, for it was assumed we had been shot down. I truly think our colleagues there were almost sorry to see us back, as our demise would have settled the affair of the Thimblethorpe turret once and for all. After this inconclusive débâcle we were sent back to Castle Archdale. It left a bit of a sour taste in our mouths, but my crew knew that I had done only the most sensible thing in refusing such an unequal combat. However, I did have a niggling conscience for some time, for it did not match up with my medal ribbon.

It was good to be back at CA, which had become our home. Not that there was much to do in our spare time but stand around the bar and drink awful beer brewed in the Irish Republic and known to us as 'Liffey water'. Straight out of the River Liffey I reckon it came, too. We had now been together as a crew for some while, and I was happy to find that we had developed a marvellous team spirit, with little or no

178

bleating about the multitude of jobs that befell a flying-boat crew. We all got on famously with each other, and rank made not one jot of difference between us. When we did have any spare time, we usually spent it on our aircraft, for it became a sort of home from home. Our Sunderlands were moored in a sheltered spot among the islands to a line of buoys that were known as 'trots'. We spent many a time out there brewing up cups of tea and Camp coffee and making a few slices of toast, safe from outside interference.

On one particular occasion when our CO was away, we had a visit from an air vice-marshal from Group HQ who was in charge of training. For days the station had been getting ready for his visit. On the day in question we all got up late, the crew having been flying the night before until the early hours. So after lunch when the crew reported to me, I thought it was a good idea to lie low and get out to our Sunderland for an afternoon cuppa and a quiet 'skive'. When we arrived on the aircraft it was in a filthy state, as was quite often the case. Before we had our tea, everyone, including the officers, took off their tunics and laid into the job of giving the boat a good clean-up.

I can well remember the occasion, for I was in the galley in my shirt-sleeves attempting to remove the thick layer of grease that covered the cooking stove. The gunners were cleaning out the turrets and the guns, Harry Holt was up on the fuselage polishing the Perspex windows, and everyone was gainfully employed. Suddenly, one of the engineers burst into the galley saying, 'You had better get your tunic on, Skipper. The Station Commander has just come on board with an officer with a double row of 'scrambled eggs' on his hat, and he wants to see you.'

Anxiously I looked around for my tunic, but before I found it, the AVM strode into the galley. I stood to attention and hastily apologised for my appearance, but he quickly put me at ease and asked what we were doing. I told him that we were preparing the aircraft for our next trip and answered several pertinent questions that he asked. Then I took him round the aircraft and introduced him to all the crew. He stayed on board for some time and seemed very interested in every-thing that he saw. He even shook my greasy hand before departing. Together with the rest of the crew, I thanked goodness that we had not reached the tea-drinking stage when he came aboard. Going ashore about an hour later, I returned to the mess to find that our bigwig had left the station. I breathed a sigh of relief and forgot all about it.

A few days later, on the return of our CO, I was summoned to his office. He appeared to be as happy as a sand boy, shook my hand, and said, 'Good Show, Bav, Good Show.' I was at a loss to know what it was all about until he explained. It seemed that before the AVM left the base after his visit, he complimented the Station Commander on what he had seen, making much of what he thought of the morale on the base. He made a direct reference to the wonderful way in which he had found our crew working in their spare time and put in a report to Group HQ commending everyone. Of course the group captain had been much pleased, and had told our CO all about it. So, instead of getting a blasting for what we had intended to be a quiet skive, we became the blue-eyed boys of the squadron. There must have been a moral in this somewhere, though I failed to recognise it. Anyway, it did serve to blot out our ignominious return from PD and our débâcle in the Bay.

After this amusing incident we settled into a routine way of life, which usually meant doing an operational trip every three or four days. As winter approached, life on the station became a little more tedious, and the trips became more hazardous because of bad weather. North-west Ireland is notorious for rain, even in summer. Regrettably, there was the occasional loss because of the weather. One of our aircraft, flown by Flt Lt Crossey, in conditions of low cloud and poor visibility crashed into the mountain on Brandon Head in South-west Eire. There were only three survivors, including the flight engineer, whose position with his back up against the main spar was the safest in the aircraft; also the rear gunner, whose turret broke free from the aircraft and rolled down into the valley. Thanks to sympathetic locals, all three avoided internment and were able to return to the squadron. Another Sunderland returning from convoy escort in bad weather flew into a mountain to the north of Lough Erne, with no survivors. In another tragic accident, an aircraft from one of our Canadian squadrons was on a transit flight to the RAF engineering base at Wig Bay, near Stranraer. With a reduced crew of eight, they also carried eight passengers. The aircraft struck a hill in North-east Ireland, and all eight passengers, who were on the lower deck, were killed, while the entire crew survived. One of the passengers was an AC 2 (Aircraftman second class). He was going on leave originally by way of the long train and ferry journey. Anxious to obtain another day with his wife, he thumbed a lift on the ill-fated aircraft. It is difficult to imagine how his wife must have felt when, knowing he had a safe ground-staff job in about the safest part of the UK, she learnt that he had been killed on his way home. This was a situation far worse than that for an aircrew wife who lived daily expecting such news.

Of all the crashes we had on the squadron, the one that sickened and saddened me the most was the one that involved my old friend Brazenor who had trained with me in Canada. He was skipper of an aircraft that took off in daylight in terrible weather to find and give protection to an Atlantic convoy. Shortly after take-off, while still out over Donegal Bay, they sent out a signal saying that they had engine trouble and were returning to base. A few minutes later they sent out a hurried SOS followed by silence, indicating that they must have crashed into the sea. There could have been only one explanation for the suddenness of the disaster. A faulty engine must have seized up, and the reduction gear, with the propeller attached, would have sheared off. Instead of falling clear of the aircraft, it would have either struck the propeller of the adjacent engine, causing disastrous damage, or sliced into the pilots' cockpit, killing the pilots or severing the control rods located under the flooring. The signal had been picked up by three D/F stations, which obtained a good position fix on the aircraft. Search aircraft found no trace of the aircraft or crew in the heavy sea. Like most other aircrew, I had become impervious to losses among crews, but the loss of a close friend is hard to recover from.

On 11 November I had the most worrying QGH that I have ever

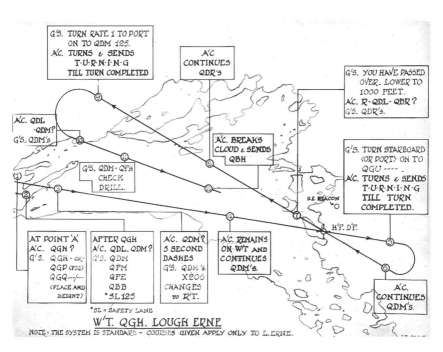

The QGH approach and descent system used in poor visibility to fly over Lough Erne for a landing at Castle Archdale.

had. We were returning from a patrol at night when our WOp picked up messages between base and two other aircraft that were returning ahead of us. Apparently, in bad weather and a very low cloud-base, they had been instructed to gain height and adopt QGH procedure for a controlled descent through the cloud. Knowing that I would have to do the same when my turn came, I climbed up through the cloud-layer into clear conditions with a full moon shining. We flew along just skimming the tops of the clouds almost as easily as in daylight. As we approached base, we picked up the radar beacon. Knowing just where we were, we enjoyed the sheer beauty of the moonlight on the cloud tops.

Before we arrived over base, the first aircraft had landed, and on our arrival, the second aircraft was under QGH control. As soon as an aircraft breaks cloud, the skipper tells the Ground Controller, and then, flying visually, completes a circuit and lands. As soon as one

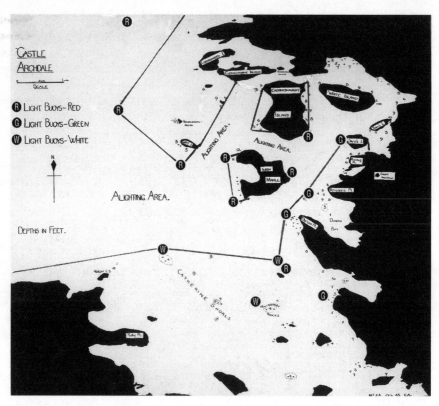

The light buoys and landing areas surrounding Castle Archdale.

I JOIN 201 SQUADRON

aircraft goes 'visual', the Controller calls the next aircraft in the queue to start its controlled let-down in the same way. Starting the procedure, we flew off on our first leg, having first descended to a safe height, but still in cloud and flying blind. We then did our second leg, and were on the final worrying run-in, coming down to about five hundred feet but still without breaking through the cloud-layer. As usual, Harry was calling out the airspeed to me every few seconds, leaving me one fewer instrument to watch. Suddenly, the Ground Controller, who up to now had been giving us continuous courses to fly, came on the R/T and, in an agitated voice, directed us to abort the QGH and climb quickly to a safe height.

By now, we were well down among the hills, and fearful that the Controller had suddenly found that we were heading straight into the 1,100-foot hill that bordered the Lough. With a sick feeling in my stomach and sensing that our end was near, I opened the throttles wide as Harry adjusted the airscrews into fully fine pitch to give us maximum power. I pulled the nose upwards and climbed as quickly as we could. Slowly the altimeter needle rose while the whole crew, who of course were listening in on the intercom, bit their fingernails down to the elbows. At last, we reached fifteen hundred feet, safe from oblivion.

I continued to climb until we were in the moonlight and above the cloud-layer again. As we flew around in a gentle circle, we could hear all sorts of reports coming in on the R/T that gave us the reason for aborting our landing. The previous Sunderland had broken cloud successfully and had made a normal circuit and approach, but the skipper had misjudged his touchdown. The aircraft flipped over on to its back, broke up and sank. Fortunately, most of the crew, who were in their 'ditching' positions, as is normal on night landings, came to the surface, supported by their Mae Wests. Tenders and motor launches were everywhere, scouring the water for survivors. On a pitch-black night when the moon was obscured, this was an extremely difficult task, and not without considerable risk to aircrew in the water. Later it appeared that searching boats speeding to the rescue ran down two of the crew, who had been alive in the water. Their bodies were picked up later.

Clearly, our appearance on the scene would only have added to the confusion. While we circled, I got Eric Harrison to work out a course to our nearest diversion base. This was PD, and we soon received instructions to go there. It took us another two hours of flying before we landed in the night-flying area in Angle Bay. This meant a wait for a refueller to come out to us. Then, after refuelling and making everything secure, we had to wait for a dinghy to collect us and take us to the night-flying pinnace. Here we waited for another pinnace to transfer us to PD, some three miles to the east. We walked to the ops room for debriefing, then to the aircrew mess for a meal before we could find a bed for the remainder of the night. Thus, another day of twenty-five hours' work lay behind us.

Next day we had to return to Angle Bay to bring our aircraft back to PD for its usual pre-flight check before flying it again. We taxied 'on the step' at about 75 knots all the way back to the moorings. This was quite exhilarating, especially for the two mooring crew who, with the front gun turret wound back, stood in the bow enjoying the thrill of planing along at high speed.

It was four days before we flew back to Castle Archdale, as a defect was found in our port outer engine. We next flew on 17 November, for the purpose of a compass swing, a check that had to be carried out at periodic intervals. On a land-plane, the swing was carried out on the ground at a point well away from magnetic interference. With flying-boats, this was not possible as wheels had to be attached to the hull to bring the aircraft up onto dry land, and the steel in the wheel assemblies would have interfered with the compass. So, compasses had to be checked in the air by comparing their reading with the angle of the sun, which was done using an astro-compass. The check had to be carried out on each of the eight points of the compass, which meant flying for several minutes at a time on each particular heading, with the sun bearing directly on to the astro-compass. This was nearly impossible in the winter when a cloudless day was a rare thing, unless we tried to climb above the cloud. On this occasion, I took our Sunderland up to over 14,000 feet, where it wallowed and gasped for breath. Strangely enough, for an airman who spent five years in the RAF, this was the highest altitude that I ever flew at, the highest previously being 12,000 feet in a Manchester.

On 20 November we did another convoy escort well to the south off the African coast. As we were too far away to return to Castle Archdale, we were ordered to stay with the convoy as long as our fuel allowed, and then divert to Gibraltar. Convoys that had been attacked were not always in their expected positions, but we found this one without much trouble. We stayed around them for almost five hours until it was dark and the danger from U-boat attack had subsided. It is worth mentioning that convoy patrol was quite hard work for the pilot, as the aircraft had to be flown manually when manoeuvring in the convoy's vicinity. Apart from searching for U-boats, a lookout was also kept for long-range enemy aircraft, usually Focke-Wulf Condors, shadowing a convoy and reporting its position to the U-boats. For the navigator, time spent with the convoy was comparatively restful, since there was no requirement to maintain the normal DR plot, with the business of finding three-course wind speed and direction every fifteen minutes. He had merely to plot the speed and course of the convoy and apply it to the first position in which the convoy was met. As convoys did not move faster than the slowest ship, they did not travel very far, even in five hours.

With our convoy now behind us, we set course for Gibraltar. Picking up what we thought was the coast of Spain, we went in as close as we dared in the darkness, positioning ourselves on our radar. However, we were unable to see any identifying lighthouses or landmarks, and were uncertain of our correct position. So, Eric suggested that we should climb up above the clouds and take a sextant shot on our old friend the Pole Star. This would immediately give us our latitude and let us know if we were off the coast of Spain or North Africa. It was a

The author, standing on the right, and his crew, after the convoy escort duty flight of 14hrs 50min, landed at Gibraltar on 21 November 1943.

very cold day, and as we climbed higher and higher, the cold in our unheated aircraft became intense. The normal temperature drop at altitude is three degrees for every thousand feet of height. When we finally reached 10,000 feet the cold was intense, reading fifteen degrees below freezing point. My hands got so cold and painful that I had to hand over to Harry, leave my seat and bang my arms together in order to get the circulation going again. Eric's hands suffered similarly, and he was quite unable to take a reading on his sextant. So we abandoned the effort and descended to warmer air.

I then instructed the WOp to call Gib and ask for a QDM bearing. At first we got no reply, so I told him to preface the signal with an O priority, which was the last step before an SOS. Their reply was prompt, giving us a bearing, which showed we were well south of our estimated position, and the land to our east was indeed Africa. Gratefully, we acknowledged their signal. As we were not sure of the height of the land in North Africa, I flew above cloud which now was not so high as previously. I knew we could establish our position once we were in range of Gib's radar responder; and could then let down over the Mediterranean. Before reaching that point, we sent them an ETA.

Still with some way to go, we spotted a patch of light on the clouds ahead. We thanked goodness, for evidently an astute Controller was on duty in Gib; knowing that we were an aircraft from another base, he had ordered some of the searchlights on the Rock to be shone on to the clouds. This was the patch of light appearing through the clouds that we had seen. We stayed at Gib for a week, doing another A/S patrol from which we were recalled because of bad weather. We finally left to patrol another convoy coming up from the South Atlantic. A short time after leaving this convoy, and while heading north across the Bay, we ran into engine trouble. Without warning, the constant speed mechanism on the port inner airscrew went U/S (unserviceable), and automatically the blades went into fully fine pitch. The revs on the engine immediately rocketed off the clock, and we had to close the throttle rapidly before the engine blew itself to pieces.

As I explained earlier, when a Pegasus XVIII engine failed, it was impossible to stop the motor completely as the propeller blades could not be 'feathered', that is turned so that the blades were edge-on to the airflow. Consequently, the propeller continued to rotate at about 1,200 rpm, even with the blades in the fully fine position. With the constant speed unit unserviceable, we were unable to alter the pitch of the propeller. This caused considerable drag, and to offset it, our three good engines had to be run at higher power. So I left the power on our bad engine and opened the throttle just enough to bring the revs up to match those of the serviceable engines.

Mindful of the fate of my friend Brazenor, I could not ignore the possibility of the engine reduction gear breaking off during our flight home. Accordingly, I instructed the WOp to send a WJR signal to base reporting our problem. Group HQ picked up the signal and ordered us to divert to Mount Batten. This I was more than happy to do. We altered course, though we now realised that we would be crossing the Bay of Biscay much closer to the French coast, and would therefore have to keep a good lookout for enemy fighters.

About one hour later, Group sent us a signal instructing us to report our position. This threw me into a real quandary, and I cursed the well-meaning but stupid Duty Controller. For we knew very well that the enemy listening posts would have picked up our first signal and taken a bearing on us. However, they would not have known how far along the bearing we were, or whether we were heading north or south. If we now sent a second signal, even in code, they would get a second bearing on us and then be able to fix our position. If we ignored Group's signal, this would imply we were down in the sea, and that would have initiated all sorts of action. The outcome would have been my collecting one hell of a raspberry when we arrived safely home. So I did the only thing possible and acceded to their request. I now knew in my own heart that it was almost certain that we would be intercepted, long before we had completed our crossing of the Bay.

I handed over the controls to Harry Holt and went back to have a look at Eric's navigation plot. We drew a line due west of the German airfields which we knew lay around Brest, and then worked out the time we would intersect it on our present course and speed. I passed this information to the crew to make them extra vigilant in searching the sky. We had been flying just under cloud at about 1,500 feet, to allow some spare altitude should our prop have given further trouble. When we were about fifty miles short of our estimated interception point, we descended to wavetop height, where our camouflage would make us difficult to spot. Now all eyes were directed above us, for the crew undoubtedly felt as apprehensive as I did. When we were only five minutes from the interception point, our WOp picked up a signal prefaced with the ominous OA priority, and it was from a Sunderland of my old squadron, No. 461. They followed their OA with the message that they were being attacked by eight JU 88s and were fighting back. They gave their position in uncoded latitude and longitude. When Eric transferred the position to our own chart, they were only ten miles from us. There was no way in which we could possibly help them, for they would be heading rapidly west to draw the enemy away from their base. With only three serviceable engines, we had insufficient speed to participate. Yet we guessed that they had strayed into the pack of fighters that lay in wait for us. The skipper of the Sunderland was a fellow named Howe, and instead of the usual ten or eleven crew, there were thirteen men on board. All of them perished in the unequal combat when their aircraft was shot down. Their deaths resulted in our being unmolested, and we arrived safely at Plymouth and landed on the Sound.

We taxied up the Cattewater and moored to a buoy close to the slipway, as our aircraft would have to be brought ashore in order to change the airscrew. Later, however, we found that a complete engine change was necessary. As 10 Squadron were very busy with the maintenance of their own aircraft, it would be some time before we were in the air again. So, I obtained permission from my CO for the crew to go on leave while the work was being done. As always, it was great to be home again. The bombing of London appeared to have ended, and life at Raleigh Drive was almost normal, except of course for the severe rationing and the lack of personal transport. Although it was winter, the blackout made it practically impossible to go far from home. So, I spent some time with my mother and father, and accompanied my father to the business where he still worked every day. He appeared far from well, though still in good spirits.

On return to Mount Batten, we found that our aircraft was not yet ready, and had little to occupy our minds. While we were there, we met a very pretty Canadian Section Officer named Margaret Cookson. She had been at Mount Batten for some time, but had now been posted to Castle Archdale. Rather than take the long journey by train, ferry and then another train across Northern Ireland, she asked if she could fly back with us. I told her that I would be delighted if she could get the necessary permission from the Station Commander. This she did, and from then on until we left, she spent most of her time with us.

Eventually, the aircraft was ready, but as it had had an engine change, it required an air test. On the afternoon of 19 December I took off with a scratch crew, including our new friend 'Cookie'. The wind was very strong and coming in from the south, which made sea conditions on the Sound quite rough. We got off easily enough as the aircraft was lightly laden. After flying around for about half an hour we came in to land, finding that the wind had got up and the sea was quite rough. I made a normal touchdown but hit quite a big chop and bounced back into the air. I eased open the throttles a little to ease the aircraft down but bounced again. We finally settled on the water after two or three of the wildest bumps that I made in the whole of my RAF career. I apologised to Cookie, but she was quite unperturbed, saying, 'Oh, I thought you always landed like that', a sure sign she had never been up in a Sunderland before. In fact, I doubt if she had ever been up before in anything.

We finally left Mount Batten the next day, having been away from the squadron for over three weeks. The weather was fine, and we were able to have a good look at the coastline of Eire. As Eire was neutral, we were not allowed to overfly the country direct to Lough Erne. Our route took us round the south-west corner of the country and up the west coast until we reached Erris Head and Benwee Head. We then crossed Donegal Bay to our air corridor over Ballyshannon and back to base. The crew enjoyed having a pretty girl on board, and I can well remember Jock Wright bringing her a meal to eat on her lap while she sat in the second pilot's seat enjoying the flight. From somewhere or other Jock managed to find a nice clean tea cloth that he used to cover the battered tin tray on which he served her meal. Cookie had been rather miserable when we first met her. She had become extremely popular with the Aussies at Mount Batten, and having made many friends, bitterly regretted having to leave. Going to Northern Ireland, so far from London and the major war effort, did not appeal to her, but having got to know our crew, she felt that she was not going off entirely into the unknown. Our flight home lasted just over five hours and was enjoyed by us all. For much as we had all welcomed our un-expected spot of home leave, the idle days afterwards at Mount Batten had left us more than ready for active life on the squadron again.

After mooring up, we sent Cookie ashore in the first dinghy, while we refuelled and secured the aircraft. Once ashore we cleaned up and changed into our 'best blue', as was required by mess rules for officers not due off on flying duties. As usual, Tinkle and I joined up with Harry Holt, Don Boorman and Eric Harrison at the mess, and made our way in for a quick drink where there was a group of chaps around the bar. In the midst of them was our CO with Cookie, who already had a crowd of eager beavers around her.

Seeing us, the Wg Cdr called us over to join them, and jovially waved to Cookie for us to be introduced. He said to Cookie, 'Meet one of my crews just back from Mount Batten. This is Baveystock, their Skipper.' With a big grin, Cookie held out her hand. 'There's really no need to introduce us,' she replied, 'you see, I am one of Baveystock's crew. I flew up with them today.' The CO said nothing, and somehow I felt embarrassed at having stolen his thunder. It passed off with banter and good humour, and after a few drinks we all went in for our evening meal. The next morning after our usual skippers' conference in the CO's office, my feeling of the evening was confirmed, for after the meeting was over,the CO called me to one side. 'Oh, Baveystock,' he said, 'I have no objection to you bringing up Section Officer Cookson on your aircraft, but I do think that you could have done me the courtesy of ringing through first and asking my permission.' Immediately, I realised that he was right and that I should have indeed done so. For a second or two I fumbled for a reply. I genuinely liked Van, and certainly did not wish to offend him, or to put up a black so early in my tour on the squadron. So I apologised and admitted that I had thought about it, but had been in a bit of a predicament. Since Cookie had obtained permission to fly with us from the Station Commander at Mount Batten, a group captain, I did not think I could very well go over his head and request further permission from my own squadron. The CO thought for a moment, and then replied, 'Oh yes, I understand', and that, fortunately, was the end of it. I must admit that I was immensely relieved to have wriggled out of an awkward situation. When I look back after all these years, I am even more pleased than I was then; for Guy Van der Kiste was certainly the best Commanding Officer that I ever served under.

Chapter 13

BLOCKADE-RUNNER
ALSTERUFER

We flew again on 21 and 22 December, and on Christmas Eve (1943). On coming ashore, we were all somewhat dismayed to find that we were detailed to carry out an anti-shipping reconnaissance on Christmas Day itself. It was to be a night take-off, getting us to the patrol area by dawn. We would fly though the day and return that night. Meanwhile, the station would indulge itself in Christmas festivities, which, though by no means up to pre-war standards, would be a great shame to miss. With a 2 a.m. call, we would need to go to bed soon after our evening meal if we were to get any sleep at all.

As usual, once I had turned in, sleep just would not come, and I lay awake pondering the task ahead. For it appeared to be something quite different from the routine A/S or convoy patrol. Also, our aircraft was but one of six Sunderlands all going off from our base at the same time, which was highly unusual. I envied Tinkle, who slept soundly in our tiny room. Obviously, he had more confidence in me than I had myself.

At 2 a.m. the Duty Orderly called us. Having checked that Eric, Harry and Don were about, we had breakfast, and then hurried over to the ops room. The place was buzzing with conversation and crews were surveying the huge map of the Atlantic and Western Approaches almost covering one entire wall. Marked out was a large area of the Bay of Biscay divided into six smaller areas lying to the west of Brest. It was apparent that each of the six crews would be covering one such expanse of the Bay, but just what we would be looking for, we all wondered.

We did not have long to wait before the briefing commenced, and we found out what the score was. Our quarry was a fast blockade-runner named *Alsterufer*, which was carrying supplies to Germany of immense value to their war effort. She had left Japan several weeks earlier, and in spite of searching by the Navy, had not yet been found.

191

A Short Sunderland of No. 201 Squadron, having just taken off, with a Catalina flying above and to the right.

However, she was confidently expected in the Bay during the next few days, and it was believed that she would make a run direct to Brest. It was our job to make sure that she never got there. The area that our aircraft had been given to search was the corner in the south-east and the nearest to Brest itself. This meant that we would have to keep a sharp lookout for enemy fighters, which no doubt would be watching for *Alsterufer* as well. As usual, at the end of the briefing questions were invited. I asked if we had been armed with bombs instead of our usual six depth-charges. This would permit us to attack our quarry if we found her. The answer was no, and we were told our job would be to home in other attacking aircraft using our radio. To me at least, this was rather disappointing. However, briefing was soon over and we made our way down to the jetty and out to the aircraft.

Once airborne we climbed to fifteen hundred feet, just under the cloud base. About two hours later, after we had been flying entirely on instruments, the dawn broke, but the weather was foul with poor visibility that continued throughout the long day. We searched almost entirely relying on our radar. Still lacking the Mark 3 radar with its PPI (Plan Position Indicator) tube, operation of the radar was completely manual. Switching first on to the forward-looking position, and then after a few minutes going on to the beam aerials and searching each side of the aircraft, we found nothing. As no signals were heard from our other five aircraft, they too presumably had seen nothing.

Completing our search, we set course for home. It was some hours after dark before we arrived back at base after a flight of fourteen and a half hours. By the time we had got ashore, been debriefed and fed, the Christmas Day festivities were over. Not that it mattered, for we were all so dog-tired that we just piled into bed and slept almost until next midday. Arriving in the mess for lunch, I looked at the notice-board, more out of curiosity than anything else. To my amazement (and horror) I found that we were scheduled for another trip that same night. Usually when we were due for a 2 a.m. call we went to bed in the late afternoon. But this was ridiculous for we had only got out of bed a few hours earlier. After hanging around the mess for a while after lunch, I went back to the billet and wrote a few letters home.

Tinkle and I turned in at about 10 p.m., and as usual Tinkle was soon away in the land of Nod. On this occasion, I too was soon fast asleep. The next thing I knew was a gentle tug on my shoulder from our Mess Orderly. Back in the ops room again, our briefing was the same as for the previous trip, except for the bit given by the Armament Officer. Apparently, he had taken up my query of the previous trip and now told us that four of our depth-charges had been off-loaded; in their place we now had two 500 lb bombs. Then he proudly told us we could have a crack at our quarry if lucky enough to locate her. When I asked what delay had been put on the tail pistols in the bombs, the Armament Officer hesitantly informed us that both nose and tail fuses were instantaneous.

Bloody hell! He had forgotten that we did not carry bombsights for high-altitude bombing as our depth-charge attacks were all made at wavetop height. HE (high-explosive) bombs with no time delay could not be dropped from zero feet without blowing up the aircraft as well as the target. So I asked one more question: could he tell us what was the minimum height at which we could release the bombs without damaging our aircraft?

'Well, the absolute minimum would be 500 feet.' I sat down in disgust, not so much that we would not be able to use our bombs, but

A No. 201 Squadron Short Sunderland on her way out for a convoy protection mission.

because it would mean we had to drag another 1,000 lb dead weight around the sky for the whole trip. The chances of hitting a ship from over 500 feet without a bombsight seemed pretty slim indeed.

One other important thing we were told was that there were two Irish ships in the vicinity that were not to be confused with the blockade-runner. However, as they were of only some 1,000 tons displacement, it seemed unlikely that they would create any confusion. (Little did I know!) The weather, although reasonable at the beginning of our patrol, was expected to worsen with heavy rain squalls and low cloud. In other words, just a typical winter's day in the North Atlantic.

The open area of Lough Erne was east–west, as was the prevailing wind. This meant that we had a long stretch of water ahead of us once we were committed to our take-off run. This was most helpful when one remembers that flying-boats sit lower in fresh water than they do in seawater. Thus, they require more time to reach the planing attitude before actual lift-off. Arriving in the take-off area we were soon roaring down the flare-path (what a misnomer for flying-boat pilots that is!) and about to lift off the water. The first few minutes once you have become unstuck are the hairiest part of a flight, when one's life literally hangs on the reliability of four man-made monsters belching flames from their exhausts. Having climbed a couple of hundred feet and throttled back the engines a great sense of relief was felt, not only by the pilots but also by the whole crew.

After a long straight run down to our patrol area, during which the regular course changes for our navigator to check wind speed and direction were the only diversions during a boring few hours, we finally arrived at the patrol starting position and began to sweep northwards. Not that any of us expected to find our quarry, bearing in mind that, as previously, we were on the inside of the whole patrol area that had now been covered by searching aircraft for the previous two days. It seemed highly unlikely that any ship could have slipped so far through our screen of searching aircraft. But the unexpected happened, for after some thirty minutes on patrol the radar operator reported a firm contact seventeen miles away. He believed that it might be a ship of reasonable size. So, full of excitement, we homed onto it. To increase our speed I put the aircraft into a slight dive, levelling out at 1,000 feet, and at a range of six miles we spotted the ship.

The first thing that we noticed was that it was heading due north and not sailing towards France as had been expected. For a good look at it through the binoculars, we closed in to about a mile range. It was a typical cargo ship of some five or six thousand tons, and was heading straight towards Ireland at about seven or eight knots. Somehow it just didn't look right, and was obviously much larger than the Irish ships we had been told to expect. So, I decided that we would need to go in for a close inspection. We knew of course that if it were the German blockade-runner she would be well armed; though there was no sign of guns from our present range.

I warned the crew that I would carry out the manoeuvre we had practised for an attack on a U-boat. Positioning the aircraft about one mile on the ship's starboard beam, I eased back the throttles and aimed the aircraft at a point about six hundred yards away from her, so as to give her gunners a double deflection shot if they fired at us. I levelled-off at wavetop height and then turned hard to port to fly directly across the ship's bows. As we dived, the ship made no response; but as soon as we turned in towards her they obviously thought we were going to attack. Immediately they opened fire on us with several guns we had not seen from far away. They appeared to be 20 mm cannon shells that now streamed towards us, with green and red tracer trails flying around us.

I jinked the aircraft up and down, and keeping as close to the sea as possible, we shot across the ship's bows below her mast height. In fact, our low altitude curtailed the firing during the critical moments we were dead ahead of her within almost point-blank range. Strangely enough, I felt absolutely no fear during this brief encounter, for I was much too busy flying the aircraft. Anyway, the strategy paid off, for much to our amazement, not a single shell hit us, and we had proved beyond all doubt that we had indeed found our quarry.

The ship now turned towards France and increased her speed to about fourteen knots. We circled and sent off a message to base giving the ship's new course and speed, reporting that it was the blockade-runner and that we had been shot at. Of course, the crew were all very excited, not only because our search had yielded results but also because we had been fired at. For the entire crew, apart from me, this was a new and unexpected experience. I now flew well astern of the ship, taking a compass bearing that I passed to Eric. He plotted it from our position and it led, of course, direct to Brest.

By now Group HQ had received our message and soon made their response. To say it dumbfounded us was an understatement, for it tersely said: 'Ignore contact, resume patrol.' As our WOp read it out to me over the intercom a babble of voices from the crew followed, the gist of which was, 'What the bloody hell are they thinking of? They must all be nuts!' So again we repeated our message in more detail, repeating our position and the course and speed of the ship, and confirming that it was definitely our quarry. In due course back came the reply, exactly as before. I discussed it with the rest of the crew, and the opinion of everyone was unanimous, 'Not bloody likely!' So, we continued to shadow the ship in spite of Group's instructions.

We were now circling the vessel at a distance of about three-quarters of a mile. We rapidly increased this when the rear gunner reported a big puff of black smoke some way behind his turret. We concluded that this was our friend having a pot shot at us with a larger deck gun. That the shell had exploded well behind us was not surprising; for the Sunderland is such a big aircraft that it must have appeared to the ship's gunner to be much nearer and flying slower than it actually was. To hit our aircraft flying at right angles to them at long range would require the gun to be aimed at a point well ahead of us. This they had not managed to do. Thus, we continued our waiting game, certain that Group had somehow made a big mistake. Maybe they had the same idea that I had had earlier, that no ship could have penetrated as far as our position.

After about an hour, someone at Group must have woken up, or perhaps there was a change of Duty Officer. For suddenly our WOp was again scribbling away on his pad as another message came through. It carried a high priority and said: 'Regain contact and commence Homing Procedure'. To which we replied: 'Am in contact, will commence Homing Procedure.' Our only problem now was the weather; for rain squalls were coming in from the west. Were it not for our radar, which was working well (a rarity in those days), we would have had quite a job keeping in contact whilst staying out of range of the ship's guns. Within a short time, two of the other Sunderlands that had been patrolling farther to the west of us joined in the circuit. Now our quarry must have realised that their chances of reaching Brest were very slim indeed. We had first picked her up at about 10.00 hours, and we continued our endless shadowing while transmitting our signals on W/T to enable attacking aircraft to find us. For it was obvious that if there were no surface vessels near enough to intercept her, then Group would certainly send long-range bomber aircraft. We worked out our PLE (prudent limit of endurance) as about 15.00 hours. If no bombing aircraft had arrived by that time, I was determined to have a crack at her myself. Despite the fact we could not bomb at a height of less than 500 feet, I felt we had a good chance of hitting her. However, bearing in mind our earlier instructions to ignore the ship, and as our huge size and slow speed would make us an easy target at a height of 500 feet, I believed I should get clearance from Group before risking the aircraft and crew.

Well before we were due to head for home, I had sent a signal to Group requesting the necessary permission. There was no reply, so we repeated the request, and still there was no answer. By this time I was getting somewhat annoyed, so I instructed the WOp to send a signal in plain language (uncoded) asking simply: 'May I bomb? Answer Yes or No.' A bit high-handed perhaps for a lowly flying officer to send to his superiors, but it worked. About two minutes later, back came the reply, 'Yes'.

By now, the weather had deteriorated considerably and the ship was disappearing in rain squalls that covered the whole area. Only our radar kept us constantly in touch with her. Accordingly, I decided to attack from the south, making my approach in cloud and using the radar for guidance. I called one of the other Sunderlands, told him of our intention and asked him to fly round to the north, as close to the ship as he was able, to draw their attention away from my approach. Having got an affirmative, we flew off to the south. We ran out our bombs, fused them and then made an approach at just under 1,000 feet. We were in cloud, flying on instruments, while the radar operator directed us towards the target.

An air of excitement now gripped the entire crew, as this was the first such experience for all of us, and I guess we were all a bit apprehensive, half expecting a hit from the ship's gunners. Trusty old Tinkle was manning the front turret, and I doubt if we could have prised him out with a crowbar. I ordered him to open fire as soon as we broke cloud. The rear gunner sat with his guns fully depressed, ready to open fire as soon as we passed over our quarry. Then, when the range on the radar closed to one mile, I put the aircraft into a dive down through the cloud. I expected to fly out at six or seven hundred feet, with the ship just nicely ahead. However, it was not to be, for she had entered another heavy rain squall, and by the time we saw her we were down to 500 feet, with the ship almost directly below us. Had I released our bombs they would have overshot the target. So I regained the protective cloud cover. Our rear gunner got in a long burst of fire from his four Brownings and swept the decks from end to end. Fortunately for us, they were taken completely by surprise and not a single shot was fired at us. We were all a bit disappointed with the outcome, so I reckoned we would have another try.

My chief concern now was our fuel state, for with all the drag caused by bombs and depth charges extended on their carriers under our wings, instead of being tucked away in the bomb bay, we needed more power on the engines, and that meant more fuel being consumed. Again I flew to the south and, when far enough away for a good run-in, I turned and approached our enemy in cloud, as previously. This time, determined not to overshoot again, I put the nose down at a distance of some two miles from the ship.

Luck still evaded us, for we found ourselves in the middle of a particularly heavy rain squall. By the time we had spotted the ship we were down to 200 feet with our quarry dead ahead in what should have been an ideal position. If I released our bombs we just couldn't miss, but their forward speed, being the same as that of the aircraft, would have resulted in explosions almost directly under us, with consequent dire damage to ourselves. This I could not risk. Not that I had much time to make up my mind, for this time the ship's gunners were expecting us and tracer shells were soon flying around us. Tinkle had a field day with his beloved three-gun turret, and the continuous stream of tracer bullets must have been nerve shattering for the ship's gunners as he sprayed the decks from end to end. We flew over the ship at about 200 feet, and as I climbed to regain cloud cover, our rear gunner got in another long burst of fire. I knew that I just couldn't keep the procedure up much longer and I cursed the stupid Armaments Officer for not giving us delay fuses on our bombs, as he should have done. We climbed up to 1,000 feet again and decided to drop our bombs and depth-charges using radar alone as a means of aiming. This we did on a sort of guesswork pattern, releasing the bombs a quarter of a mile before actually passing over the target, and hoping that the forward speed would carry them to the right place. Then we turned and headed for home.

Once on our course I ordered a good look around the aircraft to see if we had been hit by enemy flak. I also instructed the WOp to send a message to Group telling them that we had broken off the engagement and were returning to base. However, a circuit appeared to have failed on his transmitter and he was unable to send out any messages. We were still able to receive signals on both the WOp's receiver and the receiver used by the navigator for Loop bearings, but this would be all.

Meanwhile, crew members who were looking for possible damage to the aircraft reported that only one small hole was apparent in the bottom of the hull, and this was soon dealt with using a wooden plug from the repair kit. Later, Don Boorman came up on the bridge proudly displaying a 20 mm shell he had found in the bilges. Fortunately for us, it was one of the armour-piercing type that had not exploded, making only a small hole in the aircraft skin. It had cut through a few stringers under the floor, causing insignificant damage. I told Don he could keep the shell as a souvenir, and sometime later, he confessed it had been the means of acquiring numerous free beers.

We now settled into the long journey back to Castle Archdale, Eric working out an ETA of 19.00 hours. Being in the middle of winter, it would be dark by about 17.00 hours, which meant we would be making a landfall in the dark with a night landing ahead of us. This was of no concern to me, though I hoped that the weather would be okay at base. Without our radio transmitter working, it would be impossible for us to do a ground-controlled letdown if we had to approach above cloud. The weather was steadily deteriorating, with almost steady rain and low cloud. I must admit, on our way home I fretted quite a bit about the options open to us. The fuel that we had left would only just get us back to base, with insufficient to go to a diversionary base if so ordered. In Coastal Command we did not carry parachutes and could not bale out if events came to the worst. We could therefore be facing a forced landing. With this in mind, Jock Wright, our flight engineer, and Eric Harrison, our navigator, began to work out just how long our fuel would keep us in the air. Their calculations showed that we might just about regain base, but with little over by way of a safety margin. On the other hand the aircraft was by now very light, for not only had we burnt off nearly all our fuel but we had also got rid of the weight of our bombs and depth-charges and much of our ammunition.

On this trip, it had been obvious to all of us that we would need

199

every drop of fuel we had. So I had instructed Jock to sit with his hand ready on the changeover lever, and wait until the engines started to cough before moving to the fresh tank. In this manner, we had first emptied our four trailing edge tanks, then the front outers, until at last were finally running on our two main tanks.

Just in case we had to come down in the sea somewhere, I descended to sea level whilst there was still light in order to reset the altimeters. This done, I climbed back to 1,000 feet and continued our journey. The crew were in fine fettle and eager to get home and tell our story. The off-duty crewmen got busy on the cooker and soon we were enjoying a good meal. I handed the controls over to Harry Holt and went down to the wardroom when my turn came to eat. It was good to stretch my legs after the many hours I had sat in the skipper's seat during our engagement with the ship.

Some two hours before we expected to reach base we received a signal. While we were on patrol we had been under the direct control of HQ 19 Group at Plymouth, but this latest signal was from our own base at Castle Archdale. It asked for our ETA and our fuel state. Of course, we were unable to reply owing to the failure of our transmitter. This absence of a reply caused the ops room staff some concern for our safety, as they had not heard from us since our acknowledgement of the signal giving us permission to attack.

They were also concerned about our fuel state, and like ourselves had worked out our endurance as ending somewhere around 19.00 hours. So, with the best of intentions they sent us a signal instructing us to divert to the Scilly Islands if unable to reach base by 18.00 hours. The major snag was that they were unable to ascertain just what the weather was like over the Scillies. Hastily, Eric and I consulted our chart only to find that we were just about equidistant from base and the Scillies, and this threw me into a bit of a quandary. I had guessed that their concern was for our fuel state. On the other hand, they could have been concerned about our radio silence. The radio would be essential should we find ourselves having to descend through cloud in poor weather back at base. Thus, I had no option but to obey their signal and divert to the Scilly Islands.

I didn't wait for Eric to work out a new course but turned on to a heading that I knew would be approximately correct, for our fuel supply was now our major concern. Within minutes Eric had worked out our new course, and we settled down to what looked like a dicey future for us all. I had seen the Scillies from the air many times before, and had always been struck by the numerous outcrops of rock that abounded round the main group of islands. It looked as though God had found himself with a bit of extra soil when he had finished creating England down at the Land's End area of our fair country. Not knowing just what to do with this last handful He had loosely cast it out into the Atlantic. I was quite sure that there were no facilities for flying-boats to land there, especially after darkness had fallen, but I kept such thoughts entirely to myself.

At about quarter past six, in what was now almost total darkness, on our forward-searching aerials at a range of seventy miles, we picked up the radar beacon on the main island of St Mary's. This was perfect, and we homed directly on to it, allowing only an offset against the wind. We were now running on the last of the fuel in our main tanks, and it looked as if we would have just sufficient to make it. The aircraft was now so light that the throttles were only half open, and the engines were running at 1,700 rpm. These were the lowest settings I had ever known in a Sunderland.

In case we had to ditch, we got our inflatable dinghies ready under the astro-hatch. I told the crew to have a good drink of water and pocket any spare food. Then, after having a look at the chart and finding that the highest part of the island was some 250 feet, I commenced a gentle letdown as we made our final approach. We crossed the radar beacon at 300 feet, but were still in cloud with not even a glimpse of the land beneath us. I knew that a normal landing on a flare-path was not feasible. So my only course was to try and get the aircraft down on the sea somewhere to the east of the island where there appeared to be fewer rocks to destroy us. I briefed the crew of my intention, and apologised for having got them into our predicament. I told them that we would fly about ten miles east where there was plenty of open water. We would turn around and then endeavour to set the aircraft down on the water when we were about two or three miles from the island. When we turned, the crew, apart from the radar operator, would take up ditching stations. I finished by wishing everyone good luck, and told them to keep their fingers crossed. There were the usual acknowledgements and, happily, no adverse comments whatsoever. Far from feeling scared at our predicament, I felt strongly elated by this unexpected challenge to my flying skill.

At ten miles, we turned around and using our radar we headed back to St Mary's. Gently I reduced height to 300 feet and flew west. I tried our landing light, but it was quite useless as we were still in low cloud. At about five miles Harry Holt ran out the flaps, and set the engine revs as for a normal night landing (2,100 rpm on the outer engines and fully fine pitch on the inners. At about two miles I raised the nose, reducing speed to 80 knots, and adjusted the inner engines to provide the normal 200 feet per minute rate of descent. At about 250 feet we broke through cloud, and again I tried the landing light; but the sea was inky black, and devoid of any white-caps that might well have reflected our light and provided some indication of height. Switching the light off, I concentrated on our flying instruments. Getting the nose a little higher than normal, with a speed of only 75 knots the aircraft sounded unnaturally quiet, and I felt strangely calm. Then there was a sudden 'whoosh' when we were only about a mile from the island. We were down!

Not caring whether we bounced or not, I closed the throttles, for I knew we could not go round again. Jock Wright, whose ditching position was in front of his instrument panel, had already warned me that our fuel tanks were now registering zero. Thank heavens we did not bounce and the landing was as good as any I had ever done. As the noise of our engines died away, a sudden silence descended on us, broken within seconds by a spontaneous cheer from the whole crew. It was a wonderful moment that will never fade from my memory; but I guess the cheer was not so much due to my effort in the landing, but more an expression of relief on the part of the crew. For our flight, which had lasted a total of seventeen hours and twenty-five minutes, had been a trying and nerve-racking one for us all. However, it was not yet time to relax, for there was still the very real danger that we might run onto rocks and still lose the aircraft.

Without any command on my part the crew swung into action continuing our usual drill for ditching which we had practised so many times in the past. By the time that Harry and I had run in the flaps and shut down the engines, the crew had already removed the astro-hatch, and had manhandled the two life-rafts to a position on the wing. They had also checked over the aircraft and made sure that everything was shipshape.

I climbed up through the hatch and joined some of the crew already there. Looking towards the west, we could dimly make out the low profile of the island about a mile away. Our concern now was to prevent the aircraft from being swept ashore. Although the Sunderland was normally equipped with a quite formidable anchor, these had long been removed and replaced by valuable fuel. As a makeshift replacement, two of the crew had attached our No. 5 machine gun to the anchor chain with the idea of tossing it over should we be swept too close to the shore.

We also wondered if the radar operator on the Scillies had seen our blip on his radar screen. Had he noticed that, instead of us showing the normal 'friendly aircraft' return, we were now showing the 'distress signal' that we had switched on when we first approached the island? Just in case he had not done so, we fired off a couple of red distress flares. However, we had no cause for worry. The radar operator, who was accustomed to seeing friendly aircraft homing on to the radar beacon on their way to bases in England, had not bothered to check his interrogator (which would have shown our distress signal). He nevertheless noted that after first crossing the island we had returned, gone out to the west and then turned back again. He had watched our blip on his screen until it disappeared as we touched down on the sea. Of course, he was not aware that we were in a flying-boat, and had assumed that we had crashed into the sea. He had immediately alerted the Navy, as had a coastguard who, luckily, had seen our distress flares.

Of course, we were not aware of this; so we settled down to keeping watch and waiting for our eventual rescue which none of us doubted would soon arrive. About a couple of hours later while I was up on the wing, we saw a thin pencil of light sweeping across the water some few miles to the north. As our expected rescuers drew closer, I fired a double white illuminating flare directly above us. This hung in the air sufficiently long for the searchers to identify us as a Sunderland flying-boat. A naval Fairmile launch was soon with us and threw us a line attached to a strong hawser that we passed over our bollard. Immediately, we were on our way up round the north of the island, arriving in the tiny harbour at St Mary's some two hours later. Quickly, they had us alongside a marine buoy, and within minutes we were securely moored up.

I could now sit back and relax for a few minutes, while the crew attended to the assortment of jobs that always had to be done before the aircraft could be left. Then the Navy sent over a small powerboat to take us ashore, apart from two members who remained as boatguards. I sent Harry and Eric up to the Radar Post, where they were able to send off a signal to base reporting that all was well. By this time, over twenty-three hours had elapsed since we left Castle Archdale, and a very worried ops room staff had all but given up hope of our ever returning.

We were accommodated for the night in a tiny house with a kind landlady whose name I have long since forgotten. The next day we set about getting our aircraft ready for our return to base. Of course, our main problem was how to get sufficient fuel on board for the flight. There was no refuelling tanker available, and no way in which we could tie up to a jetty in the manner of a launch. We overcame the problem eventually, but it proved to be a long and laborious job that took nearly all day. We borrowed a rowing boat some fifteen feet in length, and brought out the fuel in forty-four-gallon drums, one at a time. Then with a two-man hand-pump the fuel was transferred to the aircraft. We took on some 1,200 gallons in this tedious manner (approximately twenty-five trips back and forth between the aircraft and the quayside). That evening we all went down to the village pub and made quite a night of it.

The next day was 29 December. After a fine breakfast of bacon and eggs, we said goodbye to our worthy landlady. Down at the foreshore we found that the local inhabitants had given our crew boxes of fresh daffodils. They were grown on the island literally by the million for the London market. Because of the war and the shortage of shipping between the island and the mainland, the trade had all but ceased. We returned to the aircraft, taking with us the good wishes of the islanders.

The two boat-guards had already prepared the aircraft for take-off and we were soon on our way out into deep water. It was a beautiful day as I opened the throttles, in spite of it being mid-winter. I flew back over the island and dipped low in salute. Then, waggling the wings in a final farewell, we climbed away on our homeward journey. Somehow I felt that one day I must return to St Mary's, for we had found shelter in her waters and the friendship of her people.

There was much time for thought on the flight back, and we all had the feeling that we were returning from an unplanned holiday. After three and a quarter hours we were back on our mooring on Lough Erne, and went ashore to what appeared to be a rather different world. At the ops room, we found quite a big crowd waiting to hear our story. The Intelligence Officer had much to ask us, all of which was recorded for later analysis at Group HQ. Of course our CO was there, as also was a very happy young WAAF, our Cookie. Van was most impressed by our night landing on the open sea, from which we had sustained no damage. It was obvious that he was as pleased as Punch that we were one of his crews.

While we were still in the ops room, a call came through on the 'Scrambler' (secret) telephone from Group. It was Air Vice-Marshal Baker, AOC 19 Group, under whose command we had been operating. When he had finished speaking to the Duty Controller, he asked to talk to me. I took the phone rather apprehensively, but all was well. However, I did get a bit of a reprimand for the message in which I had demanded 'Answer Yes or No' to my request to bomb, although this was mainly on account of cluttering up the radio frequency on which we were working. For the main part, he congratulated me on a job well done. The Admiralty had been very pleased with the original sighting of *Alsterufer* by the RAF, and well they might have been. For when I heard the whole story, I found out just how important it had been. It appeared that when we sent our first sighting report on the blockade-runner, the message was picked up by the radio operators in two cruisers, HMS *Glasgow* and *Enterprise*, that were covering the south-western approaches to France. On receipt of our message they had set course at maximum speed to intercept *Alsterufer* before she could reach Brest. Meanwhile, the ship, aware that their enemy now knew its identity and position, had broken radio silence and requested support from their Navy and Air Force. The German Navy promptly acted on this, and a squadron of destroyers, mainly of the Narvik Class, was sent to escort *Alsterufer* home. However, the Germans were unaware that the British cruisers were on a collision course with them. By the time that the two forces met, *Alsterufer* had been attacked by a Liberator of Coastal Command, set on fire and later sunk.

A running battle ensued between the two forces, which resulted in some casualties aboard the cruisers, and the destruction of three of the German escorts. Aircraft on both sides had joined in, with action between Beaufighters and JU 88s. Two of our Beaufighters had been shot down, together with several JU 88s, so the outcome of the operation was being hailed as an outstanding victory for our forces. It had all resulted from our original sighting and the facts that we had not been fooled by our quarry steering towards Ireland, and our refusal to obey the first order from Group to ignore our contact and continue with our patrol.

Years later, I was to learn that Captain Piatek, flying a Liberator of 311 (Czech) Squadron, had attacked *Alsterufer*. Five rockets had been fired and hits had been achieved with one 250 lb and one 500 lb bomb. The ship was set on fire and abandoned. It was finally despatched four hours later by two Liberators of 86 Squadron. Two ratings had been killed in the attack and the Royal Navy had picked up some seventy survivors from the ship.

It was with some jubilation that we finished our debriefing and returned to our billets. That evening, the station put on a dance for all the aircraft crews who had spent the entire Christmas either on patrol or in bed. I must confess that we were the centre of attraction, and it gave a tremendous boost to my ego. I knew that even if I never found a U-boat during my tour on the squadron, my time would not have been thought wasted.

The next day we brought our Sunderland ashore to have the shell hole repaired. I also handed in my log book for my first six-monthly

Flying Assessment to be recorded. When the book was returned, I was delighted to see that as a captain/pilot I had been assessed as 'Exceptional'. At the bottom of the Assessment Form, in the space headed 'Any points in flying or airmanship which should be watched', the CO had inserted: 'Very experienced in bad weather flying'. Although such a remark might well be a source of pride to its recipient, I nevertheless viewed it with apprehension. I knew only too well that pilots with such an assessment usually got the flights that might be hazardous owing to adverse weather conditions. No matter, I had now completed over one thousand hours of flying, and the butterflies that had roamed in my stomach in the early days had all but completely vanished. On 1 January 1944, while our aircraft was receiving one of its normal inspections, we were given another Sunderland and sent to the RAF station at Aldergrove. There we were to carry out a week's bombing and gunnery practice. Our landing area was on the eastern side of Lough Neagh, which from the flying point of view was an excellent location. The course that was arranged for us was almost identical to the one I had done with Dudley Marrows and, of course, was intended more for the crew than for me. They enjoyed the air-firing part of it that consisted mainly of my diving the aircraft in alongside a towed drogue, and the gunners having a shot at it whenever they were within range. Despite the fun, we looked forward to getting back to our own billets, for we lived in temporary accommodation and had no laundry facilities; neither did we know anyone on the station.

On 8 January we returned to Castle Archdale and our many friends. A Coastal Command station was nothing like one in Bomber Command. With bombers, it was the usual practice for operational trips to involve the whole squadron. The operations room before a trip would be full of the aircrew involved. Therefore one quickly got to know the other skippers and to be at least on nodding terms with most of the other aircrew. In Coastal, it was quite different, since most trips involved convoy duty or escort work, for which only one aircraft at a time was required. A briefing in the ops room would therefore involve but one crew. Of course, I knew all the other skippers, most of whom were officers, but there were many members of other crews whose names I did not know. Even on the rare occasions when more than one crew was being briefed, not all members of the crews would be present. The flight engineers and the gunners went ahead to get the aircraft prepared for its flight.

Naturally, we didn't have the thrill of being in a whole bomber squadron lined up on the approaches to the runway, and then taking off in quick succession. Neither did we have the excitement of landing back on the airfield, perhaps within half an hour of each other, and then congregating in the ops room and messes. For those crews lucky enough to have returned, the relief at being safely back would manifest itself in laughter and line shooting. Grief and sorrow would be expressed for those comrades whose faces were no longer to be seen, and we could only hope that they had landed at some other base, or parachuted to safety. It all made for a special kind of bond between all crew members, similar perhaps to that on a fighter squadron. In Coastal, our ties and friendships were confined almost to one's crew; even then, the crew were split down the middle by the segregation of commissioned and non-commissioned ranks. This to me was very irksome, for I had served as a Senior NCO for a year and a half and was keenly aware of the difference that rank made, especially to a pilot. A couple of days after returning from Aldergrove I received a message to report to the CO's office. I knocked and as I entered the CO rose from his chair beaming from ear to ear. 'Congratulations!' he exclaimed. 'Here, read this.' He passed me a slip of paper that had just arrived from Group: in a daze, I read that I had been awarded the Distinguished Flying Cross. Attached to the paper was the citation that read:

'This officer was the pilot and Captain of an aircraft, which sighted an enemy blockade-runner on 27 December 1943. After signalling his position, Flying Officer Baveystock resolved to attack the vessel. In the face of considerable anti-aircraft fire he raked the ship with machine-gun bullets, and then attacked with bombs that he released on his third run over the target. His aircraft had been hit, but he flew safely back to base. [Not so!] Visibility was extremely poor and no flare-path was to be seen. Nevertheless, in absolute darkness, he brought his aircraft down on the water close to the shore with masterly skill; no further damage was sustained. This officer displayed outstanding keenness, efficiency and determination.'

I could only stand and fumble for words as Van continued to congratulate me. 'Good show, damn good show Bav! What is more, Group has informed me that you are to receive a Green Endorsement in your flying log book.' I had heard of Red Endorsements for bad airmanship, but never before had I known of 'Green' entries.

A few days later, the entry was duly made and signed by Air Vice-Marshal Slatter, AOC No. 15 Group. Under the heading, 'Instances of

YEAR 1943.		AIRCRAFT		PILOT, OR	2ND PILOT, PUPIL	DUTY
MONTH	DATE	Type	No.	1ST PILOT	OR PASSENGER	(INCLUDING RESULTS AND REM
—	—	—	—	—	—	—— TOTALS BROUGHT FOR
DEC.	19.	SUNDERLAND	DP.185	SELF.	F/O HOLT + CREW	AIR TEST.
"	20	"	"	"	" " " "	TRANSIT M.B. – BASE
"	21	"	EJ.137	"	" " " "	AIR TEST.
"	22	"	EJ.137	"	" " " "	COMPASS SWING + AIR FIRI
"	23	"	EJ.137	"	" " " "	ANTI- SHIPPING RECCE.
"	24	" 'T'	EJ.137	"	" " " "	BOMBING + CIRCUITS
"	27.	"	EJ.137.	"	" " " "	ANTI- SHIPPING RECCE. F
						BLOCKADE RUNNER-ALST
						ATTACKED WITH MACHINE GU
						2 × 500 GP. BOMBS. SUNK LAT
						LIBERATOR. LANDED IN SE
						OFF SCILLY ISLES.
	29	"	EJ.137.	"	" " " "	SCILLY ISLES TO BASE.
			SUMMARY FOR DEC 1943		AIRCRAFT	SUNDERLAND
			UNIT 201 SQD			
			DATE 31.12.43			
			SIGN. [signature] S/L			

FLIGHT COMMANDER, 201 SQUADRON.

GRAND TOTAL [Cols (1) to (10)]
1050 Hrs 15 Mins.

TOTALS CARRIED FO

The author's log, covering the period of the discovery of and attack on the *Alsterufer*.

PERIOD IN.201 SQDN.

(*11212) Wt. 40572—2665 20,000 1/43 T.S. 700
(*12278—11212) Wt. 15036—517 50M 6/43 T.S. 700

FORM 414 (A)

SUMMARY of FLYING and ASSESSMENTS FOR YEAR COMMENCING 1st...10·6·43...*19......

[* For Officer, insert " JUNE " ; For Airman Pilot, insert " AUGUST."] TO 31·12·43

	S.E. AIRCRAFT		M.E. AIRCRAFT		TOTAL for year PERIOD	GRAND TOTAL All Service Flying
	Day	Night	Day	Night		
DUAL	✓	✓	✓	✓	✓	77·30
PILOT CAPTAIN.			310·10	70·10	380·20	2ND PILOT 166·05 / 1ST PILOT 787·10
PASSENGER	—	—	GRAND	TOTAL		1050·15

ASSESSMENT of ABILITY

(To be assessed as :—Exceptional, Above the Average, Average)

(i) AS A CAPTAIN† PILOT (F.B).......... Exceptional

(ii) AS PILOT-NAVIGATOR/NAVIGATOR...........

(iii) IN BOMBING...........

(iv) IN AIR GUNNERY...........

(v) IN S.B.A...........

† Insert :—" F.", " L.B.", " G.R.", " F.B.", " Instructor ", etc.

ANY POINTS IN FLYING OR AIRMANSHIP WHICH SHOULD BE WATCHED

VERY EXPERIENCED IN BAD WEATHER FLYING

Date...1 / 1 / 44

Signature...R.E.? *ander*...

Officer Commanding...20? Squadron. R.? F.

	30·30		15·00						

34·50	26·35			64·20	64·50	43·10	13·10	111·45	122·55	26·45	
(1)	(2)	(3)	(4)	(5)	(6)	(7)	(8)	(9)	(10)	(11)	(12) (13)

avoidance by exceptional flying skill and judgement of loss or damage to aircraft or personnel', was written:

> 'On arrival at a diversion base the weather was bad and no flare-path was visible. Flight Lieutenant Baveystock, by use of his 'SE' positioned himself five miles from land, and using his landing light made an entirely successful night ditching in the open sea from which his aircraft sustained no damage whatsoever.'

Of course, the five miles and the use of the landing light were not correct, nor unfortunately was my rank, but these did not detract from the entry. 'SE' stood for Special Equipment, i.e. our radar.

As soon as the interview with the CO was over, I hurried away to tell the members of my crew. They were all delighted, as a 'gong' for a skipper is really one shared by the whole crew, and I told them that was how I felt about it. Of course, it is only the skipper who receives the award, as indeed it is the skipper who collects the raspberry when things go wrong. To celebrate the occasion, I decided that I would put on a party for the whole crew. It would have to be off the station, as we were a mixed crew of officers and NCOs. So we decided to have a night out over in Eire. We chose the little village of Pettigo, where there was a woman with a small cottage who could put on a meal for us. The crew elected to invite Section Officer Cookson, whom they had adopted as their mascot.

A few days later, clad in civilian clothes, we crossed the Border and arrived in Pettigo. It was the tiniest of villages, but typical of the hundreds scattered over the West of Ireland. We had a few drinks in the village pub and bought a bottle or two of wine to have with our meal. I saw a large doll in a local shop, which would have been un-obtainable in England, and this I bought to send back to Jill. Then we invaded the small cottage where we had arranged to spend the evening. The good lady had arranged tables down the centre of the room and we sat down with Cookie at the head. As we were unable to have our wives or girlfriends with us, Cookie was the token substitute for all of them, and we loved having her with us. No doubt she enjoyed being the only girl invited to this otherwise all-male gathering. We had an excellent meal, and it was great to have home-cooked food for a change. Needless to say, it was a splendid laughter-filled evening. Having thanked our kind Irish lady we returned across the Border to that small part of Northern Ireland we called 'home'.

We did little or no flying at all during the rest of January, except for some dual instruction that I gave to two of our second pilots. One was a Swiss fellow named Regensburger, the other a Northern Irishman, Flg Off McCready. It was thirty years later that I next heard from 'Red'. He had stayed in the RAF and had risen to the rank of wing commander. He had also been CO of 201 Squadron (a good effort indeed).

At the end of January, the crew had a spell of leave and we went off together as several of us lived in London. It was marvellous to be home again, as we had felt cut off in Northern Ireland. Everyone made quite a fuss of me, since in addition to my new medal I had been given the acting rank of flight lieutenant. It was quite a leg up; I had been commissioned for less than twelve months, and promotion to the substantive rank of flight lieutenant normally took two years. It also meant that my pay had risen to £1 2s 6d (£1.12) a day. Consequently, I was now able to cope quite easily with my mess bills and to enjoy a reasonably good standard of living.

At home, I found that my father was far from well, yet he was still working the normal week. So I spent several days with him at the business. I didn't think that I was able to help very much, but he enjoyed having either Sidney or me with him. All too soon the leave came to an end, and with members of my crew I travelled back to Castle Archdale.

Our flying programme resumed with a couple of local trips, one of which was my old worry of a Fighter Affiliation exercise. Again, the dreaded Beaufighters scared the living daylights out of us by their 'near misses' on our Sunderland. Sometimes I felt that the practice attacks were more frightening than the real thing might have been. Fortunately, fate continued to smile on me and I never had to put the theory to the test. Nevertheless, we did have one bit of bad luck during those dismal winter days.

We had been briefed for a Convoy Escort patrol that originally was scheduled for a night take-off, but the weather was atrocious and a gale warning was in force. The wind was from the west and had whipped up the ten-mile Lough into a wild sea. So, we were held over until dawn with instructions to go out to our aircraft and assess the conditions ourselves. The final decision was to be mine, but the Operations Officer stressed the importance of providing the convoy with an escort if possible.

We slipped our moorings soon after dawn, and taxiing out into open water, we met the full force of the gale that was blowing at about fifty knots. I knew at once that it would be impossible to get airborne without risking damage to the inner airscrews, and even perhaps to the hull, the waves being about five feet in height and with a very short chop. However, the importance of the convoy made a decision to abort the sortie a difficult one to accept. I then decided to see whether it would be possible to take off in the smoother water in the shelter of the islands.

Normally, this would be quite out of question with a fully loaded aircraft, but the strong wind would mean our getting airborne in a much shorter run than usual. At the starting point of our intended run lay an area of water into which we did not normally go. The chart of the Lough indicated that there was adequate depth of water in the area provided we kept to the middle. I taxied into quite a large bay, and when I judged that we had a long enough run for take-off, I turned the aircraft into wind. As I did so, a shudder ran through the hull of the Sunderland and we ground to a stop. It was the most sickening sensation that I had ever had, and I could have cried at my bad luck. Had I turned around only a few seconds earlier, all would have been okay.

We shut off the engines and called for assistance over the R/T. Then I went to have a look at the damage. Lifting the floorboards we were surprised to see that the damaged area was quite small, some rocks having penetrated the hull about twenty feet back from the bow, with a hole no more than a foot square. In an attempt to get the hull to float clear, we decided to lighten the aircraft by jettisoning all thousand gallons of fuel in our main tanks. Calling on the R/T again, we warned all powerboats to stay clear to avoid any risk of fire until the fuel had been jettisoned. The strong wind soon dispersed the huge slick of fuel that trailed out behind us. When the danger appeared to have passed I gave clearance for a boat to come alongside. The Marine officer-in-charge came aboard and I proposed that a cable be attached to the towing eye at the rear of the aircraft's hull. We could then be pulled off from astern, the way we had gone in. This was not accepted, and instead it was decided that the depth charges would have to be taken off first. The Marine officer had the odd idea that if we were to sink, the DCs might explode. He then called for a bomb scow to come alongside to remove them. To me, this decision was bloody stupid. If an armourer were sent out to remove the detonating pistols, the DCs would have been as safe as houses.

The bomb scow arrived and tied up under our starboard wing. A bomb scow is a huge steel barge some forty feet in length and weighing several tons. So one can imagine the drag it created alongside us in the strong wind that was still blowing. To make matters worse, it was decided to bring out a refueller and pump out the fuel in the other tanks that could not be jettisoned. The refueller, also of enormous size and weight, tied up on the port side of the aircraft. Both vessels dragged their anchors, and by the time the Sunderland was pulled clear of the rocks the hole in the hull had grown to about ten feet in length. However, the hull did not flood completely, thanks to the watertight compartments. Finally, it was towed back to the slipway, where it was brought ashore.

I returned to the ops room sick at heart, but our CO was just fine about the episode and supported me throughout. I learned later that Group was pretty mad about it and demanded my scalp; but the CO would have none of it. He told me that he refused to let one of his crews 'carry the can' for trying to accomplish an almost impossible task. I heard no more about it, though it might well have incurred a Red Endorsement in my log book, which would have looked very odd alongside my Green one.

This particular episode had not yet ended, for the aircraft was given a temporary repair and then flown back to Short and Harland for repair. It arrived at Belfast and touched down on a calm sea, only to bury its nose, cartwheeling over and smashing itself to pieces. Whether the pilot misjudged his height over the calm water, or whether the temporary plate ripped off the hull, we never discovered. However, as so often happened, one by one the entire crew bobbed up to the surface where the aircraft had gone down; fortunately, without serious injuries. Of course, all aircrew wear life-jackets, even in the gun turrets where space is very restricted; they were never discarded.

Chapter 14

INVASION LOOMS

The loss of our aircraft curtailed our flying for a while. During this period I was sent on an engine course at the Bristol Aircraft works at Filton. It lasted a week, and by the time it was over my knowledge of aero engines had grown considerably. Back on the squadron, where the first two weeks in March were busy ones, we were given a new aircraft. In addition to local flying, which included yet more Fighter Affiliation, we did five operational flights. The weather was awful most of the time, and at the end of the last two flights we had to make an approach in cloud at night, then do a QGH.

After one of our morning sessions in the CO's office, I was told that Harry Holt was to be made a skipper. He had completed an OTU course as a second pilot with me, and it seemed unnecessary to put him through it all again. The CO asked if I would mind handing over my crew to him, as it would obviously be easier for him to start on his own with a familiar crew. Much as I regretted losing my team, I could see the good sense in doing so, and I readily agreed. Meanwhile, it had been decided that I would be sent on an Advanced Officers' course at the RAF College at Cranwell.

Halfway through March I presented myself to the College Adjutant. The course was for three weeks and included instruction on Boards of Inquiry, Courts Martial and other related matters that senior officers were required to know. Our instructors were either wing commanders or group captains, and the Chief Instructor was an air commodore. We were very well looked after, the food and service in the mess being just as I imagined they would have been in peacetime. It seemed strange to think that only three and a half years previously I had been an 'erk', and not at all used to such treatment; but I enjoyed it immensely.

By the time the course had ended, much had happened. With the date of the invasion of Europe drawing ever closer, the squadron had received orders to move to Pembroke Dock to join 461 and 228 Squadrons who were already operating there. The intention was of course to give maximum cover to the invasion forces from the attention of the U-boats based in the west-coast ports of France, which were expected to attack in force. Accordingly, I received orders to report direct to Pembroke Dock.

A few days earlier I had had a letter from my mother telling me that my father was now very ill, and could I possibly get to see him. So I rang my CO and asked for a 48-hour pass that would allow me time to drop in as I passed through London. This was readily approved, and I was soon at my parents' home in Finchley. I was terribly shocked to see how thin my father had become, and that he was now confined to his bed. A few days earlier his doctor, Florence Bibby, had sent him to a specialist for an opinion; but it was obvious that the kindly doctor had not told my mother the complete story. So I made an appointment and went to see her that evening.

I liked her very much and respected her knowledge – she had saved Jill's life only a year or so earlier. This time she could do nothing, for my father suffered from an advanced state of cancer in both his lungs, and had only a few weeks of life ahead of him. The pain in his chest that he had earlier complained about would become so acute that he would need to go into hospital, where he could be given pain-killing injections. She suggested the Finchley Memorial Hospital, when the time came. Meanwhile, we should tell him that he had a slight infection on his lungs that might require hospital treatment. This would spare him the knowledge of his impending death. I felt utterly shattered at the prospect of losing him. After all he had done to keep the business going, he would never have the joy of seeing us back there again when the war was over. To my astonishment, my mother took the news with complete calm. Although she had not been told, she nevertheless had a shrewd idea of what was wrong. I told her what Dr Bibby had suggested, and in due course, my father readily accepted the necessity of going into hospital.

The next day, I went up to our factory in London to arrange for work to continue, as I knew that Dad would never return there. Fortunately, we had two faithful employees who had been with my father for over twenty years. One was a spinster in charge of the office and ran it single-handed. Her name was Winifred France, an extremely efficient person some twenty-five years younger than my father. Of course, the news distressed her badly, but she assured me that she would do her best to keep the business running until Sydney and I would return at the end of the war. We also had a good man in the business who did all the packing and saw to the dispatch side of the work; his name was Charlie Davis. I knew that the two of them would keep the business ticking over. Later, Sidney managed to get leave one day a month from the Admiralty to visit the factory to sign cheques and attend to the necessary paperwork.

Having made my farewells with my parents, I took the train to Pembroke Dock to rejoin the squadron. I arrived late at night and reported to the CO the next morning, eager to get on with the job. The CO was aware that my father was very ill, and as he rose from his chair to welcome me back, he asked how he was. Unfortunately, this was too much for me. I had managed to get through the last two or three days without too much display of emotion. Yet Van's genuine concern, and perhaps the empathy that existed between us, triggered something inside me, and I sat down in the chair in front of his desk and just about burst into tears. For a few moments, I buried my face in my hands, utterly overcome and terribly embarrassed by my inability to control my feelings. In a flash, the CO bounded from behind his desk, crossed to the door and hung up the 'Do not disturb' notice that he used during our morning conferences. A short while later, I had regained my composure and was able to tell him the sad news the doctor had given me. He was very kind about it and I must say handled the situation extremely well, so much so that when I took my leave, I was able to do so without any embarrassment.

I did little flying during the rest of April, only some twenty hours in which two flights were with my old crew, with Harry still as my second pilot. On one of these flights we had to return early with two engines in trouble. Happily, our old Thimblethorpe three-gun front turret was now no longer with us. Our new Sunderlands had turrets equipped with twin Brownings, each carrying 500 rounds of ammunition. Better still, they had also been equipped with a long-range 0.5 inch American machine-gun that was operated by a crew member from a position between the front gunner's legs. However, this gun was difficult to aim and would have been useless at night. Best of all, the new aircraft were now equipped with four additional Browning guns, fixed two on each side of the bow. They were sighted and fired by the pilot, and aimed by pointing the aircraft, as in a fighter aircraft. To complete our armament, two more Vickers guns had been fitted in the galley and were fired from the galley hatches. Now at last I believed we had a good chance of successfully attacking a U-boat, even if it stayed on the surface and used its multiple cannon to repel us.

I did one trip as a screening pilot with a new skipper, an American who, however, will be nameless. Our flight was a five-hour one to familiarise the pilot with the south coast, and let him have a look at Mount Batten and Poole. Unfortunately, his conduct as a skipper left much to be desired, and I gave him a bad report when I returned to base. There were still sneak raids being made along the coast during daylight by enemy fighter-bombers. In spite of this danger, he did not make his crew keep proper lookouts, or keep the turrets constantly manned and on the alert. For most of the flight he sat back in his seat enjoying a cigar, while the automatic pilot flew the aircraft. The laxity of a skipper soon spreads through the entire crew. Perhaps I was the jittery type of skipper, never without some pangs of fear, and perhaps never completely at home in the unnatural element of flying under wartime conditions. I believed that one needed an element of fear in order never to miss the important details that needed constantly checking and rechecking.

At last I was given another crew, and our first flight together was on 17 May. This was an A/S patrol down in the Bay that lasted just over thirteen hours. We were now carrying eight depth-charges instead of the six we carried while at Castle Archdale. Also, we were doing only thirteen-hour patrols because of having the mid-upper turrets refitted, together with the extra guns and ammunition. My new crew were experienced and had previously flown with Flt Lt Longland. He had been unlucky enough to break a leg, and was now hobbling around the station with his leg in plaster.

They were quite different from my old crew, and, for want of a better word, I could only describe them as 'gentle'. A crew seemed to identify itself with the character of its skipper, and Longland was a quiet un-ruffled fellow, easy-going but efficient. He was certainly not a bit strung up like I was. There had been many occasions, generally at night, when I had let fly on the intercom at one of my crew who had not responded to an order quickly enough.

To return to my new crew, my co-pilot, Colin Griffith, was younger than me, and very friendly and co-operative. I liked him at once, and we got on like a house on fire. My navigator was Peter Hunt who had shared our billet at Alness at the beginning of 1943. He was a good navigator and very conscientious. Happily, he lacked Eric Harrison's caustic tongue. Both were officers, and we had two more flying officers, Philip and Anderson. The other crew members were Flt Sgts Hobson, Currie, Humphrey, Sharland, Watson, Foster and South. They were a well-knit team and all expressed pleasure in having me as their replace-ment captain. Naturally, they would have preferred their previous skipper, but they knew that I was now one of the most experienced pilots on the squadron. Of course, the main thing that every crew member worried about was not the colour of the skipper's eyes, but whether he would always get them home again in one piece.

Our aircraft was one of the new ones, with all the additional guns already mentioned. It also had the new ASV Mk 3 Radar, similar to that carried in Bomber Command Pathfinder aircraft and known there as 'H2S.' It consisted of two rotating scanners, one under each wing, outboard of the engines. They were synchronised to sweep 360° around the aircraft. The radar beams transmitted by the scanners that struck an object like a ship or a surfaced U-boat bounced back and showed up on the PPI tube in the aircraft. It was also able to show the coastline around us – an altogether revolutionary piece of equipment. At night, or pre-dawn, we could not only find a convoy, but could even count the number of ships, provided the surface of the sea was not too rough. Of course, the main drawback in attacking U-boats picked up by the radar at night was that we could not see them. Numerous Catalinas and Liberators had been fitted with powerful searchlights known as Leigh lights, but for a variety of reasons the Sunderland was not so equipped.

However, some ingenious Boffin hit upon the idea of Sunderlands using fighter flares. I believe that these 1.7 inch flares were originally developed for use by bombers under attack by enemy night-fighters in order temporarily to blind them. They were dropped manually through a flare chute in the rear of the aircraft, and were fired by electrical contacts at the base of the chute. Igniting immediately on leaving the aircraft, they burst into three sections burning together for three seconds and giving out three million candlepower. A good operator could drop one in little over a second, so it was possible to get anything up to nine million candlepower alight at one time. The light was so bright that when we first dropped some for practice over an unoccupied island, we could see hundreds of rabbits running for cover from a height of fifty-five feet. The only snag, which was serious, was that they lit up the white undersides of the Sunderland's wings, making it a first-class target for a surfaced U-boat.

The general effects of the flares were uncanny. Using them on a clear night with even a little haze, it was like flying in a huge white bowl, because of reflection from the haze. During practice attacks on a British submarine, when illuminated at a range of half a mile it did not appear to be on the surface of the sea at all. Diving the aircraft at the sub., the pilot had the impression that the target was up in front of him, and that he could in fact fly under it. Such was the peculiar illusion caused by the brightness of the flares. We soon became familiar with this strange phenomenon, and with practice found we were able to make very accurate runs over our 'tame' sub., once we had it clearly on our radar screen. Of course, the sub. took evasive action as soon as it was illuminated, and we had to respond quickly to avoid missing it. Flying at between fifty and a hundred feet over the sea on a dark night was all rather dicey.

Before D-Day burst upon us, I did manage to get a few days in London to see my father. He was in a private room in the Finchley Memorial Hospital. He was heavily sedated and would drop off to sleep from time to time. He was delighted to see me, saying how much better he felt and how kind everyone was to him. He thought he was regaining weight, but this was not so. His arms and legs were indeed getting puffy, but, alas, it was the approaching breakdown of his system that was causing it. He told me that as soon as the war was over he would retire and buy a little place out at Potters Bar. I stayed with him for about an hour, and when I kissed him goodbye and left his room I knew very well that I would never see him again. Before returning to Pembroke Dock, I spent a little time with my mother, who was strangely calm and unruffled throughout the whole time of my father's illness. I was reminded how unconcerned she had appeared to be when I first returned after being missing. Then I remembered that she had seen five of her brothers die while she was still young, and had nursed her mother until she too had died. Later her father and my Dad's father had died during her lifetime; so perhaps she had become inured to death, which was no stranger to her.

On 17 May 1944 I did my first ops flight with Longland's crew in Sunderland 'S', ML 760. It was a standard A/S patrol, well down in the Bay of Biscay. We were airborne for over thirteen hours, flying the last three hours and making the final landfall in darkness. I found the crew to be quietly efficient, and I hit it off fine with all of them. Rather like 'Tinkle' in my first crew, I had one elderly crew member, elderly by wartime flying standards, that is. He was Flt Sgt Hobson who was 48 years of age. He had served as a pilot in the RAF in World War I, and when he first joined the squadron he wore his pilot's wings. However, he wanted it known that he was an operational crew member. So he removed his pilot's brevet and wore that of a flight engineer, which was his position in the crew. Back at base, I was sure that I had been given an excellent team, and together we could tackle anything.

By the end of the month, we had made several more flights, including another night exercise with our tame submarine. We would have made at least a dozen radar homing runs and simulated attacks during that exercise, and we all believed that we had the whole procedure well buttoned up. All that remained was to find that real live U-boat.

At the beginning of June, it was obvious that D-Day was drawing close. All leave was cancelled for aircrew and groundcrew alike.

Indeed the groundcrew had not had leave for some weeks, owing to the necessity of keeping every aircraft fully serviceable. In many ways, it reminded me of the big flap before the Thousand-Bomber Raid.

On 1 June, we did another night exercise, this time using a specially constructed radar buoy that was anchored in the sea north of Milford Haven, instead of the submarine. As usual for night landings, we had to anchor in Angle Bay and go down by pinnace the next morning to bring the aircraft back to PD. On 3 June we did a further night exercise on the radar buoy lasting six and three-quarter hours, when we dropped literally dozens of flares. During this exercise, I flew the aircraft manually at anything between fifty and a thousand feet, which, to say the least of it, was very nerve-racking and extremely tiring.

The most amazing flight was on the afternoon of 5 June. Our Sunderland needed to have several engine cylinders replaced, owing to the usual trouble of excessive wear in the exhaust valve guides. This work required a test flight. We took off to the west and climbed clear of the coast, where we saw an amazing spectacle. A few miles out from the coast was an armada of naval ships of every type and size. They stretched as far as the eye could see from north to south, and there must have been a hundred or more. There were destroyers by the dozen escorting a variety of 'battle-wagons' and cruisers. This could mean only one thing: the Invasion fleet was under way, and D-Day for the landings would be 6 June.

The fleet that we could see stretched out in front of us was on its way to begin the softening-up process of enemy coastal positions, and their big guns would be belching death and destruction within twelve hours. We returned to base full of exhilaration at the prospect of the great news that would burst upon the world the following morning. Burst it certainly did, for the news of the Invasion was on everyone's lips by the time I reached the mess for breakfast. There was terrific excitement knowing that, at last, the most critical stage of the war had arrived.

Chapter 15

THE SINKING OF U-955

On the morning of 6 June, I went along to look at the operations board for the day's flights to see if I would be flying on this most memorable of days. There was my name, well down the list, showing we were due for an all-night special A/S patrol, with take-off at 19.30 hours. Colin was with me and we speculated about what it might be. However, our speculations were cut short by a message that I was wanted on the public phone in the mess. When I heard Betty's voice I knew at once what to expect. The news that I had dreaded had come at last: my father had died the previous night.

The funeral had been arranged for three days ahead, and Betty asked if I could possibly attend. As the Invasion was only just beginning, I told her that I very much doubted if I could be released. Later that morning after the usual CO's conference, I told the CO my bad news. He asked me if I would go ahead with that night's flight as the job called for an experienced pilot who was fully trained in low-level flare attacks. Then perhaps he could allow me time off for the funeral.

Picking up the crew, we spent the rest of the morning preparing our aircraft for the coming night trip. I had arranged to take a passenger with us, though this was not my custom at all. For I made a fetish of keeping the aircraft as light as possible and never allowed the crew to keep unnecessary personal gear on board. Every 100 lb of weight counted on a fully loaded night take-off, and its absence added to our ultimate flight endurance. On this occasion, our passenger was our Squadron Intelligence Officer, Flg Off Malcolm Anderson.

Some days earlier he had told me that he would like to do an ops trip, if possible on D-Day, so that in the years ahead he could tell his grandchildren about it. I had agreed that if the CO approved he could join us. When the day came, I was pleased that, although we would be flying throughout the night, we would take off in daylight. Although we now carried 100 gallons less fuel than we did from Castle Archdale, we would still have a heavier load. With twelve men on board, together with fifteen guns and their ammunition, a mid-upper turret, two extra depth charges and scores of flares and flame floats, we were very

221

heavily laden. Frequently a long take-off run was necessary to unstick the aircraft, particularly in calm conditions with little or no wind.

That afternoon we did little but listen to the BBC News, whenever it came on. It was useless to try and get any sleep, as there was far too much noise in the mess. Our bedroom being on the ground floor, one could always hear the fellows in the room above as they walked around on the uncarpeted floors. At 17.00 hours we all met in the aircrew mess, which was open 24 hours a day where the entire crew could eat together before flights. Regardless of the time of day, we always got an egg and bacon 'breakfast'. After the flight, we had a meal (usually steak) in this mess. We were also given rations for the flight itself. This may have seemed generous under wartime rationing; but it should be remembered that by the time we had eaten our so-called breakfast, been briefed, taken to the aircraft, made ready for the flight, slipped moorings, flown for perhaps thirteen and a half hours, followed by mooring-up, refuelling, cleaning and stowing guns, then returning to

No. 201 Squadron staff at Pembroke dock in 1944.
Standing, left to right: Johnny Wheeler (Navigation Leader), Malcolm Anderson (Intelligence Officer), Ivor Wiles (RAAF), 'Doc' Lineham (Medical Officer), Waterland (Engineering Officer), Johnny Mallet (Signals Leader), Ernie Norris (Adjutant), Harry Marten (Gunnery Leader) and Bob Rainbeck (Radar Leader).
Seated: Wally Walters, Babe Ruth, Guy Van der Kiste, Lionel Powell and Bav Baveystock.

222

the ops room for debriefing, the total time between 'breakfast' and 'dinner' could be anything up to twenty hours. So, a meal in the air was in no way a luxury if we were to remain alert throughout the whole period. Returning to the briefing for this particular flight, as we entered the ops room everyone's eyes were on the end wall. Covering most of it was a huge chart showing the approaches to the Eastern Atlantic seaboard. On it were plotted all the aircraft in the area, with their patrol areas clearly defined. All shipping and the positions of U-boats, known or believed to be in the area, were also shown.

Our aircraft was detailed to carry out a Creeping Line Ahead search along the expected track of a known U-boat. Its estimated position had been established after it had stopped a Portuguese liner, *Serpa Pinto*, on 26 May. In mid-ocean, the passengers and crew had been ordered into the lifeboats, where they had been held for several hours. Three passengers, including a young baby, lost their lives during transfer to the boats, and two American passengers were taken aboard the U-boat, which had been attacked (by Johnny Posnett) on the morning of 5 June. Thereafter, other aircraft had kept it continuously submerged for most of the time. So, there was a fair chance that it would have to surface to charge its batteries during the period of our patrol. One other aircraft was to patrol with us. This was N/461, which was due to take off sometime ahead of us and would be farther along the estimated track of the U-boat by the time we arrived.

At the end of the briefing we were all full of excitement, albeit perhaps a little apprehensive. For we were going after a known target, and not on just another patrol where there might be no target at all. I felt quite elated at having been selected for this opportunity. We slipped moorings and got airborne at 19.42 hours. The run down to the patrol area, some fifty miles north of Gijon on the Spanish coast, was uneventful. I gave Andy, our passenger, the job of lookout in the astro-dome, as I guessed that he would be more apprehensive than any crew member. He would therefore keep an extra-sharp lookout for enemy fighters as we crossed the Bay before darkness fell. By 22.00 hours, it was completely dark and we would be free of enemy fighters, at least until dawn.

A voice on the intercom informed us that a hot meal was ready. I always allowed the crew to sort out their shifts in the gun turrets, only fixing the times when my co-pilot and I would have a break in the wardroom. This time I elected to go first so that I would be back on the bridge well before we reached the patrol area. I was soon tucking into an excellent steak. With only a double-burner Primus stove in the galley, it was amazing what some members of the crew could turn out after only a few months aboard a Sunderland. I enjoyed the meals in the air as much as anybody; as well as bucking us up, the food helped to offset tiredness. At about half an hour before midnight, we reached our patrol area. We now adopted a new course pattern, creeping back and forth across, and progressively along, the estimated course of the U-boat. Each leg was of about fifteen miles, first to the north and then to the south, with the legs about ten miles apart. In this way, our radar coverage would normally have ensured that if the U-boat was on the surface we would pick it up on our PPI screen; and pick it up we did, just before midnight. Dennis South was on the set and suddenly reported a firm contact on our port beam at a range of about nine miles. Excitedly, I asked him,

'What does it look like?'

'It looks good, Skipper. Just about the same size as our tame sub-marine did at the same range.'

'Okay, let's go down and have a look at him', I shouted.

Without waiting for any further instructions, the whole crew went into action, with Colin sounding a series of three short blasts on our Klaxon horns to warn any of the crew who might not be plugged into the intercom. First, the WOp would send out an immediate 'First sighting report', giving our callsign, followed by Code Number 465 (suspected U-boat contact), our last DR position (supplied by the navi-gator every fifteen minutes) and, of course, the time. The flare chute would be manned, and the operator would report that he was in position. Meanwhile, I ran out the eight depth-charges, of which the first six would be dropped, spaced at sixty-foot intervals. At the same time, the co-pilot would be increasing engine power and airscrew revs. This was partly to overcome the extra drag of the DCs, and to provide greater manoeuvrability during the attack at low level.

I had now turned the aircraft towards our contact and reduced height to 300 feet. This was not quite as fraught as it may sound, for we had a low-level radio altimeter that worked like radar. Trans-missions sent down to the sea from an altitude below 350 feet were reflected back and converted into precise heights. (This was another new gadget that I could have done with when we landed in the sea off the Scillies.) As well as being extremely accurate, it could be set to operate warning lights on the instrument panel at a pre-selected height. When flying at the pre-set height a green light would show. Above the height, an amber light would show, and at a lower height, a red light would appear. As one can imagine, if a steeply banked turn was made at under three hundred feet it would not have taken more than a few seconds to hit the sea.

Flight Sergeant South was now giving me bearings every few seconds as we rapidly closed in on our contact. One of the things that we had to do during this critical run-in was to try and assess the amount of drift that a crosswind approach would have on the track of the aircraft. If we found the bearings given by the radar operator needed constant adjustment, we would offset the course that we were flying by a few degrees. It did not matter if our target lay a few degrees to one side of our heading, as long as the bearing remained constant. A similar situation applies when a land-plane is making an approach on a runway in a crosswind. On this particular run-in, our bearing with the contact remained very steady. So, perhaps the direction of our target was cancelling out the drift effect of the wind.

Flying entirely on instruments, and guided by Dennis South, we closed on our contact. There was an electric air of expectancy among us all, though, apart from the radar operator, the intercom was completely silent. Would it be our U-boat, or just another harmless Spanish or Portuguese fishing-boat, many of which sailed without navigation lights? Gently I caressed the button that fired the four Browning guns that pointed out from the Sunderland's bows. Then, at half a mile range I shouted: 'Flares!' Colin, with his hand already over the flare switch, quickly made the flare chute 'live', lighting a red warning light on the top of the chute to start the operator dropping the flares. As the warning light came on and he heard my call on the intercom, Flt Sgt Sharland began dropping the flares as fast as he could, not stopping until the light on the chute was extinguished.

Igniting immediately, the first flare burst into its three million candlepower. As it did so, I put the aircraft into a shallow dive, transferring my eyes from the blind-flying panel to the sea ahead. The result was an anticlimax, for the sea ahead was devoid of our target. Suddenly, Colin let out a shout and pointed to a white swirl ahead and a little to the right of us. A couple of seconds or so later we tracked just about over it. By craning his neck out of the side window, he was clearly able to see bubbles coming up through the swirl where the U-boat had crash-dived. By this time, of course, it was too late to attack, as our depth charges would have overshot the target by a considerable distance. 'Hell!' someone exclaimed over the intercom, 'the bastard has crash-dived.'

Reluctantly we climbed away but we knew that we had missed him through no fault of our own. U-boats had a radar receiver tuned to pick up the pulses from our searching radar beams. The U-boat commander must have decided to crash-dive when attack appeared certain. Full of disappointment, we switched off the flare chute, climbed to 450 feet and brought in the depth-charges. We then radioed base, stating that the U-boat had dived and that we had tracked over the swirl. We ended the transmission with the cryptic message, 'Am baiting'. Group would know that we would stay in the area until either the U-boat re-surfaced, or we ran short of fuel.

I turned the aircraft around and saw the light from the flame-float that one of the crew had dropped from the galley as we tracked over the target. Then we headed back west again in the direction the U-boat was believed to be travelling. Suddenly, all hell broke loose as the whole area lit up. Coming straight towards us at a closing speed of about 300 knots was another Sunderland. In the excitement of the moment, we had forgotten all about N/461. They had picked up our original signal to base, and turned towards us to join in the fun. Instinctively, I hauled back on the stick, and thank God the other skipper did not do likewise. He passed harmlessly but uncomfortably close below us.

His radar had picked us up as originally we flew below him, and he had mistaken us for the U-boat. Since our radar aerials were housed under the wings and swept forwards and downwards, we were unable to see him on our screen. He should really have been alerted by the speed at which the two aircraft were closing. However, there was so much to think about in such a situation that failure to do so was more than understandable. We heard later that they were as shaken as we were, for the nearness of a head-on collision was apparent to us all. It took us a little while to settle down after that episode, and from then on we kept a lookout for them.

We now began the lengthy process of baiting our enemy, starting from the brightly burning flame-float that marked the position where he had dived. For one hour we flew north, south, east and west, going out only four miles on each leg before returning to our marker. As each flame-float showed signs of burning out, we dropped another beside it to maintain the position. At the end of one hour, the procedure required us to increase the sides of the square to eight miles, and after two hours to twelve miles, and so on.

During the early part of the first hour, I had a discussion on the intercom with Anderson and with Colin and Peter Hunt. We firmly believed that the U-boat had only just surfaced when we picked him up on radar, for, if he had surfaced earlier, N/461 would surely have found him. We also knew that the U-boat had been kept under water for the previous thirty-six hours by other searching aircraft. So, he must surface for at least two hours to charge his batteries. With dawn breaking at about 06.00 hours, he should therefore surface again at about 03.00 hours. We also guessed that the U-boat commander would not anticipate our being in the area, as we were so far from England, our nearest base. Of course, he would not have known that we had only just arrived on patrol when we first detected him. Neither would he have known that we had worked out our fuel consumption and found that if we landed at the Scillies instead of going back to PD, we could in fact stay until just after dawn. We could then hand over to other aircraft if we had been unsuccessful. However, in the event, this proved unnecessary.

During this long vigil, I dared not leave my position in the first pilot's seat in case our enemy surfaced earlier than we expected. I found flying low on instruments over a dark sea, with constant changes of course, to be most tiring. Time passed terribly slowly, broken only when we were rewarded by one of the crew with a cup of hot sweet tea and a slice of NAAFI cake. The relentless flying north and south, and then east and west, went on until we were into the third hour. At 02.30 hours Flt Sgt Currie relieved Dennis South on the radar and settled himself into watching the ever-rotating luminous line on the PPI tube.

Suddenly, at 02.44 hours, when we had just turned at the end of one of our twelve-mile legs, Currie broke the silence of the intercom to report a contact at eleven miles. We knew that it must be our U-boat, as N/461 had left the area at 02.20 hours, and Group had sent us a signal that another Sunderland would relieve us at 04.15 hours. So there were no other aircraft in the area. Once again we carried out the pre-attack drill, exactly as before, and started our run-in. Every one of the crew (especially me) was keyed up as never before; since we all felt certain that the U-boat commander would elect to stay on the surface and fight back; he must now charge his batteries or perish.

From the bearings that Currie gave me, I found that the aircraft was drifting slightly to starboard. So I offset our course a few degrees to port to compensate. About three degrees port was sufficient to keep the target on a constant bearing, and this was exactly what was required. Another signal had already been sent to base, and the flare chute was manned and ready. With Colin in the second pilot's seat, Andy under the astro-dome and two gunners in their turrets, four pairs of eyes searched the darkness ahead. My own never left the blind-flying panel, watching airspeed, course and the altimeter, while listening to Currie's constant repetition of the bearing of the enemy ahead.

Then suddenly, without warning when we were about three-quarters of a mile away, gunfire opened up ahead and below us. Two long streams of coloured tracer bullets that at first seemed to be travelling quite slowly, swung towards us and accelerated rapidly past us.

Although we were flying only 300 feet above the surface of the sea, I instinctively dived below them and turned slightly to starboard. At the same time Anderson shouted 'There's the U-boat', and Colin switched on the flare chute. At once, Sharland began dropping the flares. Immediately, the whole area lit up like day, and there was our U-boat, fully surfaced about half a mile away and a little to our left.

The U-boat commander was no fool, for on the first occasion he steered straight towards us and presented the smallest area for our radar to detect. With the wind now drifting us to the north, he turned sharply south, compounding our difficulty in getting him lined up. It was essential for us to pass over him forward of his conning tower if our DCs were not to explode astern of him. As he turned broadside on to us, his quadruple-mounted cannon opened fire, surrounding us with streams of tracer shells. The intensive training of the last few weeks now came to my aid. I banked the aircraft around and aimed the nose amidships at the U-boat. Our front gunner had already opened fire, and, lining up the target, I fired the four fixed Brownings. Our mid-upper gunner also opened fire; although he could not depress his guns low enough with the astro-dome in front of him. Andy must have had quite a shock as the streams of tracer flew low over him.

A maze of criss-crossing tracer filled the air with literally hundreds of bullets hitting the U-boat and surrounding sea, many of them ricocheting high into the night sky. I held my gun button down for six or seven seconds, then had to stop firing in order to bank slightly to port for my final run. Fortunately, our combined fire-power had been enough to knock out his gun crews, and our final few seconds of attack were unopposed. At just the right moment, I pressed the 'bomb tit' and our stick of six depth-charges fell clean across his hull, just forward of the conning tower. Immediately, I pulled hard back on the control column to avoid diving into the sea. As the aircraft's nose started to lift, a tremendous shock wave hit the underside of the hull. Usually, the aircraft does not feel exploding DCs as their concave noses are designed to make them go twenty-five feet below the surface with thirty-six feet of forward travel. Thus the explosion was underwater and the column of water that rose from the sea was well behind our tailplane by that time. My first thought was that a lucky shot from the U-boat's deck gun might have hit us. With deep relief, I found that the aircraft was still responding normally to the controls.

As we climbed away, Currie reported that the blip on his screen, which he had held quite firmly for the previous eleven miles, had vanished. As there was no sign of the U-boat attempting to crash dive only seconds earlier, we felt certain that it had been well and truly sunk.

Anderson in the astro-dome and our rear gunner had both seen plumes of water rising high into the air around the U-boat.

However, there was more excitement to come. On the intercom, Sharland suddenly reported that we were on fire. For a couple of moments I felt utter panic and called for a further report. Happily, the panic did not last long, as Sharland announced that he had been mistaken. Our front guns alone had fired well over 1,000 rounds, filling the whole of the forward compartment and wardroom with dense smoke and fumes. An open galley door had allowed the smoke to pour through into the rear of the fuselage. This was pierced by the glow from the dim red lights in the wardroom (used to protect the night vision of off-duty crew). What with the smoke, the red glare and the shock of the explosion that he had felt in the rear of the aircraft, Sharland had jumped to the conclusion that we were on fire.

A unique photographic record of anti-U-boat warfare in World War II. It shows the 1.7 inch flares illuminating the delivery of the Sunderland's No. 4 depth-charge that sank U-955 on the night of 7 June 1944.

YEAR 1944		AIRCRAFT		PILOT, OR	2ND PILOT, PUPIL	DUTY
MONTH	DATE	Type.	No.	1ST PILOT	OR PASSENGER	(INCLUDING RESULTS AND REMA
–	–	—	–	—	—	—— TOTALS BROUGHT FORW
JUNE	1.	SUNDERLAND	ML760	SELF.	F/O GRIFFITH & CREW	RADAR BUOY & PINNACE
"	2.	"	ML760	"	" " " "	RETURN FROM ANGLE AND TE
"	3.	"	ML760	"	" " " "	RADAR BUOY & PINNACE
"	5.	"	ML760	"	" " " "	TEST FLIGHT.
"	6.	"	ML760	"	F/Os GRIFFITH, HUNT,	SPECIAL ANTI-SUB. PATRO
					PHILP, ANDERSON,	SIGHTED SWIRL AFTER S.E CO
		U/BOAT WAS U/955.			F/SGTS HOBSON, CURRIE	BAITED FOR THREE HOURS.
		KILL CONFIRMED BY			HUMPHREY, SHARLAND	HOMED ON CONTACT FROM 11 MIL
		AIR HISTORICAL BRANCH			WATSON, FOSTER	ILLUMINATED U/BOAT & ATTAC
					& SOUTH.	PHOTOGRAPHS CONFIRMED STRA
						6 × 250 lb. TORPEX & 1200 round
"	16	"	ML768	F/O MOLD	SELF & CREW.	TRANSIT TO WIG BAY
"	16	"	ML772	SELF	SKELETON CREW	TRANSIT TO BASE.
"	24	"	EJ150	SELF.	SKELETON CREW.	TEST FLIGHT.
"	25	"	EJ150	SELF	F/O LANDERS & CREW	A/S PATROL
"	29	"	EJ150	SELF	" " " "	A/S PATROL
				SUMMARY FOR JUNE 1944		AIRCRAFT 1. SUNDERLAND.
				UNIT 201. SQD.		
				DATE JUNE 30th 44		
				SIGN. ~~Powel~~ S/Ldr.		
				FLIGHT COMMANDER, 201 SQUADRON.		
NOTE		ML760		SHOT DOWN ON THE NIGHT OF 12-6-44 IN POSITION		
		48° 15' N	09° 45 W BY U/BOAT. ALL CREW PERISHED.			
			THE TEMPORY CAPTAIN OF A/C WAS SQD/LDR RUTH – DF			

GRAND TOTAL [Cols. (1) to (10)]

1248 Hrs. 05 Mins.   TOTALS CARRIED FOR

The author's log for the period in which U-955 was attacked and sunk.

The Sinking of U-955

| | | | | | | | | | | |

FORM 414 (A)

SUMMARY of FLYING and ASSESSMENTS FOR YEAR COMMENCING 1st. JUNE *1943.
[* For Officer, insert " JUNE " ; For Airman Pilot, insert " AUGUST.") — JUNE 1944

| | S.E. AIRCRAFT | | M.E. AIRCRAFT | | TOTAL for year | GRAND TOTAL All Service Flying |
	Day	Night	Day	Night		
DUAL	—	—	—	—		99.10
PILOT CAPTAIN	—	—	398.35	112.50	511.25	929.15
PASSENGER 2ⁿᵈ PILOT	—	—	—	—	—	166.05

ASSESSMENT of ABILITY

(To be assessed as :—Exceptional, Above the Average, Average)

(i) AS A CAPTAIN † PILOT (F.B.) Sunderland ... Exceptional

(ii) AS PILOT-NAVIGATOR/NAVIGATOR ...

(iii) IN BOMBING ...

(iv) IN AIR GUNNERY ...

(v) IN S.B.A. ...

† Insert :—" F.", " L.B.", " G.R.", " F.B.", " Instructor ", etc.

ANY POINTS IN FLYING OR AIRMANSHIP WHICH SHOULD BE WATCHED

An experienced bad weather pilot

Date ...

Signature ...

Officer Commanding O.C. ... SQUADRON

	7.50		6.15	
	6.55		6.00	
	28.00		28.45	

| 34.50 | 26.35 | | | 64.20 | 176.15 | 43.10 | 13.10 | 183.10 | 122.45 | 26.45 | |
| (1) | (2) | (3) | (4) | (5) | (6) | (7) | (8) | (9) | (10) | (11) | (12) | (13) |

CLOUD [Incl. in to (10)] PILOT (13)

231

A feeling of elation and relief now came over the crew, with just about everyone coming onto the intercom. Anderson made us all laugh saying, 'By God, Skipper, I just can't stop my knees knocking together; it's a wonder you can't hear them from there.' The truth was that I was nearly as bad, as I had the shakes in my left knee caused by the excitement of the last few hectic minutes. Even now, it is hard to appreciate that not a single shell had hit us from the streams of flak that came at us from just about point-blank range. Fate had surely been completely on our side.

Climbing to a safe height, and bringing in our two remaining DCs, we trimmed the aircraft for normal flight. Turning around we spotted the flame float that had been dropped from the galley at the same time as the depth-charges. We were also surprised to see one of our earlier flame floats still burning not more than a mile from our original position where the U-boat had dived more than three hours previously. His batteries must have been really low. We now sent off another coded message. It read, 'Have attacked fully surfaced U-boat with six DCs. Position 45° 13' North, 03° 30' West. Estimate straddle, flak experienced, nothing further seen. PLE (prudent limit of endurance) 04.00 hours.'

We flew around for about twenty minutes but saw nothing more, and were now quite convinced that our enemy had been sunk. So, at 03.20 hours, we resumed our patrol, and at 03.59 hours we set course for home. We were all in high spirits and, strangely enough, nobody felt tired. For, after months and months of uneventful patrols, we had been lucky to find a U-boat and carry out a successful attack. Best of all, our long training sessions and the efforts of hundreds of ground-crew and factory workers in providing us with the 'tools' had not been in vain. I felt particularly elated, as every skipper had the nagging fear that, when it really came to the crunch, he might well make a mess of it.

Just before dawn, hot tinned soup was served; then at about 05.00 hours, the cold grey light of dawn broke over the sea. We now maintained a very vigilant lookout. We had sent four signals from the same area which no doubt would have been picked up by German listening posts in western France, and our position would have been established. Later we picked up the friendly radar beacon on the Scillies, and at 08.45 hours made a landfall off Milford Haven. Having landed in the upper half of the Haven, we were soon on our mooring. I left a skeleton crew on board to refuel and tidy up the aircraft. As our dinghy approached the jetty, I could see Wg Cdr Van der Kiste waiting for us, and smiling all over. We poured out our story to him as we walked up to the ops room for debriefing. Any feelings of fatigue we had had were now gone. This time we had no difficulty in convincing the Duty Intelligence Officer of the success of our patrol, as our own Intelligence Officer had been with us. From the astrodome he had witnessed the whole event.

After debriefing, we went over to the aircrew mess, where we were joined by the rest of the crew for breakfast. I was still feeling much too excited to really enjoy eating, but sat listening to the banter and light-hearted chatter of the crew. I felt absolutely as one with them and looked forward to our next trip together; but that trip never came.

War is a terrible and wasteful thing, for never once did we spare a thought for the crew of the U-boat who had lost their lives in the encounter. I could well remember the British submarine *Thetis* that had foundered with the loss of all but four of the crew who had died slowly in their steel tomb. Now, we had inflicted the same thing on forty or more individuals and I had been the man who flew the air-craft and pressed the button sending them all to their doom. Nor had we thought of the two Americans who had been taken on board the U-boat and who would have perished with their captors. Our months of training and our knowledge of the thousands of friendly lives lost at sea had brainwashed us into believing that we had done a good and honourable thing, of which we were both proud and happy.

Returning to the officers' mess, I was soon luxuriating in a lovely hot bath. Then for the first time in twenty-four hours, I thought of my father. The memory of his death two nights earlier had been almost completely blanked out from my mind. Now the two worlds of my family life in London and my life in the RAF seemed so unrelated that I was unable to come to grips with the situation as it then existed. I was confused and sad at one moment, then happy and elated at the next.

As I soaked in the bath, my reveries were suddenly cut short by a knock at the bathroom door. 'Are you there, Bav?' called the CO, and I shouted an acknowledgement. 'Come over to my office as soon as you can', he bellowed. 'The Photo Section has developed the film taken by your rear-facing camera.' (The camera operated automati-cally when the DCs were released, taking photos every two and a half seconds.) 'They are marvellous', he said. Hurriedly I left the comfort of the bath, dressed and almost ran over to the CO's office. The rear-facing camera had been loaded with ordinary day film and I had not thought that anything worthwhile would have come out of it. Yet the prints were excellent, the best one showing all of the U-boat from the conning tower back to the stern. One of the depth-charges could clearly be seen entering the water a short distance from the centre of the hull. The next picture showed a gigantic explosion with the nose of the submarine protruding through the rising column of water. The detail was so good that in the first picture it was possible, with a magnifying glass, to count the number of insulators on the U-boat's rear aerials. In the second picture, the bow wave could be seen breaking across the deck of the U-boat as it turned violently to starboard.

The final analysis made by the photographic experts indicated that our depth-charge straddle had been perfect. The third DC had entered the water on the port side of the submarine in such a position that its underwater travel would cause it to explode directly under the centre of the hull. The fourth DC appeared to have been a 'dry hit' on the conning tower, falling alongside and exploding prematurely. This could have explained the severe shock felt in the aircraft during the attack. Taking account of the fact that no further sightings were made of the U-boat, Group assessed the attack as 'Almost certainly sunk'. The Admiralty, on the other hand, were more sceptical and gave us a 'Probable'.

The CO now agreed that I should go to London the following day for my father's funeral. That evening we all turned in early, having been on the go for almost thirty-six hours. Next morning we were up early, and with Colin, Peter Hunt and Tony Philip, who shared one large room with me, I went over to breakfast. Afterwards, we joined the rest of the crew in the flight office and stood around chatting together. Our attack had obviously welded us into an effective crew, and I felt that I was now accepted as their skipper, not just a temporary stand-in for Longland. In fact, they were most disappointed that I was going away for a few days.

I attended the CO's morning conference, and after it was over, he asked me if I would give a talk to the groundcrews about my attack. He wished to involve them as much as possible in the squadron's activities and make them feel that our attack had only been made possible through their co-operation and hours of toil. Of course, I readily agreed with the CO's request, though I did not look forward to it very much. However, I had to admit that it was an excellent idea in the circumstances. Flying-boat crews did not have the direct contact with the servicing lads that existed, for example, between fighter pilots and the teams of armourers, fitters, riggers and refuelling crews who met their aircraft on the tarmac. They were all vitally interested in the pilots who flew them. Perhaps the morale of our groundcrew suffered to some extent in consequence.

The CO later accompanied me over to the flight office in the main hangar. So as not to cause any unnecessary waste of staff time, he had arranged for two members of every servicing section to attend my short talk. A large blackboard had been provided for me to sketch the outline of the attack relating to the photos that had been taken by the rear-facing camera. As the CO and I walked into the room, everybody stood to attention. Inviting them to be seated, the CO began with the following introduction:

> 'You all know Flt Lt Baveystock and that the crew of 'S' has made a successful attack on an enemy U-boat. He has asked me to call you together to thank you for the long hours of work your Sections have put in while servicing his aircraft. This one hundred per cent team effort has made a major contribution to this success.'

He then handed the meeting over to me.

As simply as I could, I outlined the events preceding the attack, and then the attack itself, taking care to emphasise how every piece of equipment on the aircraft had been 100 per cent efficient. I explained in detail the last few seconds of the attack, and the U-boat commander's tactics in trying to avoid us and to shoot us down before we reached him. The lads received the talk enthusiastically, and I finished off by asking them to convey my thanks to the other members of our groundcrew who were unable to hear the talk. There were nearly forty people present, representing engineers, riggers, armourers, radio and radar mechanics, and several more from the Marine Section and the ops room. There were numerous other sections on the squadron whose staff all worked with the sole purpose of making an attack such as ours possible. As I handed the meeting back to the CO, there was a round of applause. It was so spontaneous that I knew that I had managed to make them all feel that their efforts were not only appreciated, but also of vital importance to the war effort. As we left the hangar, the CO showed obvious pleasure that it had gone so well. 'They clapped,' he said, 'they actually clapped.'

That afternoon I boarded the train at Haverfordwest for London. My thoughts now were entirely about my family. Nevertheless, I could not completely shake off the feeling of elation that I had enjoyed during the previous couple of days. Nor the excitement that filled the air now that the long-awaited invasion of Europe was well under way. All of which helped to overcome the sadness of losing my father. I was looking forward to having Betty and Jill return with me to Pembroke Dock. I had found some good digs in the home of Mrs Lily Cooper in

PD itself. She appeared to be a most amiable person, a widow whose husband, a captain in the Army, had been killed in the fighting in Crete.

The next day I attended my father's funeral, and then, for the first time, it registered that I would never see him again. The feeling of loss was devastating, and I thought that I would never get over it. He was a soft-hearted man and the kindest of fathers possible. As well as being my 'boss', he was also my best friend.

After the funeral, we returned to my mother's house in Finchley, where I heard more bad news. The parents of Peter Hunt, my navigator, phoned to say that they had received a telegram stating that Peter was missing, his aircraft having failed to return from an operational patrol. They had phoned the parents of two other crew members who lived in London, only to find that they too had received similar telegrams. They were of course astounded to hear that I was in London, and had not been the skipper on that particular flight. Within seconds I was explaining the circumstances. I said I would find out what I could; though I knew that for security reasons I would not learn much on the phone.

I spoke to the squadron and was told that the crew had gone out in Sunderland 'S,' on an A/S patrol down in the Bay, with Sqn Ldr Ruth, our Flight Commander, as their captain. They had sent out a radio signal reporting that they had picked up a radar contact and were going to drop flares and make an attack if it proved to be a U-boat. There had been no further message. That their WOp had not sent out even the briefest SOS was almost certain proof that their end had been sudden and violent. They must have run into heavy flak as we had done earlier, but with tragic results.

The next day I went over to see Peter's parents to tell them what I had managed to find out, and about our successful attack on the eve of D-Day. I did my best to cheer them up, but I had little hope to offer them. The aircraft had been patrolling throughout the night close in to the French coast in company with many other aircraft attempting to seal off the invasion area from marauding U-boats. For obvious reasons, these patrols were known as Cork patrols. The loss of Peter to the Hunt family was indeed a savage blow. For they had four sons, all in the RAF, of whom two had already been killed. One had been lost over Germany on a bombing mission, and the other was killed in a tragic accident. He and the crew had returned from a bombing raid, and in the usual half deaf, half dazed manner of returning aircrew, had jumped from the aircraft in the dark as soon as the aircraft had reached its dispersal area. However, the outer engines had not been switched off and he had wandered under the wing and been struck by one of the propellers. The fourth son had barely finished his training when his mother had written to the Air Ministry, without telling her son about it, and had told them how they had already lost three of their sons. The Ministry staff must have been understanding and sympathetic, as the lad was withdrawn from operational flying. Whether he survived the war, I do not know, for like so many of us, I lost contact with nearly all my wartime friends after the war.

With a sad heart, I returned to Pembroke Dock, taking Betty and Jill with me. There I learned the whole sad story, as far as it could be ascertained. Any slight feelings of remorse for the German sailors that we had sent to their deaths left me completely. Another aircraft (a Catalina I believe) that was patrolling close to 'S' had seen tracer streaks and flares just after 'S' had sent out their first sighting report. This was

Flight Lieutenant Longland and his crew photographed before the author became their skipper. Longland is seated in the centre of the front row and the warrant officer pilot to his right on the photograph is unknown, but all the other crew flew with the author on the night of 6 June 1944 when U-955 was attacked and sunk. Shortly after that success the entire crew were killed whilst flying with Squadron Leader 'Babe' Ruth as skipper.
Front, left to right: Flg Off Peter Hunt, Flg Off Colin Griffith, Flt Lt Longland, Unknown and Flg Off Philip.
Back: Flight Sergeants Currie, Humphrey, Sharland, Watson, Foster and South. The only identification that can be made is that Hobson is on the extreme right.

followed by an explosion that appeared to be from an aircraft hitting the sea. Having gone over to investigate, they saw some fuel burning on the surface of the sea and some small white lights, but no sign of a U-boat or an aircraft.

I was dismayed at the news, for I could only think that the lights meant that some of the crew had survived the crash and had switched on the battery-operated lights on their Mae Wests. That had been several days previously, and all hope of them had already been given up. With the crash so close to the French coast, it had been impossible to send out search aircraft, as during daylight hours the area was under the control of enemy fighters. For days I hoped that they had managed to get into a dinghy and perhaps reached the coast, or been picked up by a fishing boat. Sadly, that turned out to be the unfortunate end of 'S for Sugar', and the nicest and most efficient crew with whom I had been privileged to fly. They could not have had a more skilled pilot than Sqn Ldr Ruth as their skipper. He had been decorated during his first operational tour in Bomber Command. So, had it not been for the death of my father, I felt certain that I would have been flying the aircraft that night in the same area, and would have met the same fate as my crew.

Chapter 16

THE SINKING OF U-107

With no crew, I hung around the station for a few days quite aimlessly. During that time, a signal was received from Group stating that I had been awarded a Bar to my DFC. Also, my two radar operators, Dennis South and Duncan Currie, had each been awarded the DFM. It was a sad and hollow occasion, as they did not live to learn of the honours awarded them. It was one of the few occasions that a wild party did not follow an award to a member of the squadron.

Then, on 16 June I went with Flg Off Mold and a skeleton crew to collect a new aircraft from Wig Bay. On 24 June we test-flew another new Sunderland. It was EJ 150 and bore the Squadron letter 'W.' I took it up with a crew made up of members of Flt Lt Bent's crew. Bent was a Canadian, known to all as 'Badly Bent'. He had just finished his operational tour and was going on rest (often a bloody sight more dangerous than ops!) I took over his crew to complete my own tour with another 200 flying hours.

The next day we did our first ops trip together – another Cork patrol. It was a long trip of just over fourteen hours, during which I got to know the crew quite well. My second pilot, Flg Off Brian Landers, was younger than I was. Somewhat quiet, he was a good steady pilot whom I felt was sufficiently confident to take over the controls whenever I left the bridge. My navigator was a New Zealander named Ian Riddell. Like most short people, he worked all the harder and more efficiently to compensate for his lack of height. We also carried a third pilot: a Canadian Flying Officer named MacGregor, known to all of us as 'Danny'. The rest of the crew were Plt Off Macaree, a newly commissioned WOp, WO Parsons, Flt Sgts Paton, Cottrell and Perran, and Sgts Bulloch and Howat.

We now entered a very busy period, flying whenever we could. However, we had a lot of trouble with our now obsolescent Pegasus engines, in which the valve guides wore out quickly. We hardly ever did a long trip without afterwards having to change at least one complete cylinder. After one epic trip, the ground engineers had to

239

The crew that sank U-107 on 18 August 1944, taken before Bav took over from Bent.
Back Row – left to right: Flt Sgt Cottrel, WO Parsons, Flg Off McGregor, Plt Off Macaree and Flt Sgt Bullock
Middle Row: Flg Off Ivor Wiles, Flg Off Ian Riddell, Flt Lt Bent, Flg Off Landers and Flt Lt Baveystock
Front Row: Sgt Howat, Flt Sgt Paton and Flt Sgt Perran.

change eighteen of our thirty-six cylinders (nine cylinders per engine). This was usually carried out while the aircraft was at its mooring, with the maintenance engineers working from small hanging platforms suspended below the engines – not an easy or pleasant job above a boisterous sea. This was a sobering thought when carrying out a fully laden night take-off, when one hoped and prayed that nothing had been left undone. True, we often did a short air test in the afternoon or morning before a flight, but this was with an unladen aircraft, which on full power lifted off on quite a short run.

On Cork patrols, we were briefed to stay on patrol at all costs. Even if our bomb gear proved faulty, it was imperative to stay on the job to ensure that no U-boat was able to sneak through into the Channel. If we were unable to attack, we had to remain to home in other aircraft that could. On 5 July, we did have to abort a patrol, jettison fuel and return to PD. As soon as we got airborne and had climbed to cruising height (usually 1,000 feet) it was the custom to test-fire the guns and run out the depth-charges to test the circuits. However, when I

240

signalled the crew to bring in the DCs and close the bomb doors, I could hardly have imagined the result. For, as they did so, three almighty bumps vibrated through the hull and the aircraft yawed to starboard. Hastily correcting the yaw, I shouted on the intercom to ask what the hell was going on. One of the crew in the bomb room replied, 'Christ, Skipper, three of the DCs have fallen off the racks and two of the bastards have gone through the floor. Others look like falling off at any moment.'

Hurriedly I handed over to Landers and went below. Sure enough, the three DCs had wrecked the floor panels, and two others were swinging loosely. Worst of all, one of the DCs in falling had wrenched the starboard bomb door from its tracks. About seven feet long and three feet wide, it was left jammed half in and half out of the aircraft, having the effect of a rudder. I was scared stiff that it would suddenly be torn away in the 115 knot slipstream, and possibly hit the tailplane or elevators. This might well throw the aircraft out of control. So I dare not free it, or risk getting it back into the aircraft. One of the crew got a length of anchor rope and together we secured the door as best as we could, still sticking out of the aircraft. Finally, I decided to abort the patrol, and signalled base, alerting them to our early return. As we were too heavy for a landing, we jettisoned a thousand gallons of fuel from the main tanks.

Landing back at base I could see our CO standing in the dinghy that had come out to meet us, but this time there was no smile on his face. The dinghy came alongside our rear door, and while we were still taxiing, the CO came aboard. When he saw the damage and the bomb door sticking out of the side of the aircraft he was very relieved. He admitted to me that he had come out prepared to give me 'one hell of a rocket', but was pleased to find that we did not deserve it. The outcome was not so good, however, for the armourer whose negligence was responsible.

During the immediate post-Invasion period, both air and ground crews were pushed to their limit. Years later, I read that on D-Day itself over 32,000 aircrew had been airborne over France and the Channel. The crews of my former squadron, No. 461, with us at PD, were really busy. They sighted seven U-boats during the period June to September, attacking six and destroying three of them. Our squadron did quite well, and it fell to Flt Lt 'Wally' Walters to make a successful attack on a submerged U-boat 'snorkelling'. The *schnorkel*, or 'Snort' as it was nicknamed, was a new device; had it come earlier in the war, it would have been a serious menace. U-boats equipped with it could stay under water at periscope depth, sucking in air through the Snort

241

from above the surface. This enabled them to run their diesel engines without having to surface for the regular charging of their batteries. The size of the Snort that was exposed above the surface of the sea was so small that our radar was unable to obtain a response from it. So a U-boat could cruise at night without any danger of being attacked and maintain a diesel-engine speed of 10 knots indefinitely.

Wally Walters had joined the pre-war RAF as a Boy Entrant way back in 1929. Like me, he had come up through the ranks, becoming a non-commissioned pilot, and was married. His attack, confirmed by a series of excellent pictures taken by the rear-facing camera, showed his depth charges straddling the U-boat. Subsequent photographs displayed much wreckage, and the attack earned him a Bar to his DFC. Its destruction was confirmed from German records after the war. I did not see him again for 32 years, until one day he appeared on the TV News in connection with a flying incident that I had read about in the Press the previous day. I was delighted to learn that he was the Director of Civil Aviation here in New Zealand. I met him several times later and he was just the same old Wally, apart from the thin white hair and a few facial lines.

As July 1944 passed into August, we entered the busiest flying period I had known throughout the war. From 8 to 18 August we flew six operational trips totalling seventy-six hours. As most of the German fighters had been moved into the Invasion battle areas, we were now operating close in to the French coast. Nevertheless, there were still some fighters around, which made it more nerve-racking and tiring than when one was expecting to be jumped by a fighter at any moment.

By the time our sixth flight came up on 18 August, we were very jaded and just about worn out through sheer lack of sleep. Fortunately, the weather was perfect both at base and in the patrol area. Our brief was to scour the water between Brest and Bordeaux. The American Army had encircled Brest, and key German personnel and 'top brass' were being ferried by sea down to Bordeaux to escape the net. It was known that some U-boats had, with their crew, almost a hundred men on board. These were the U-boats we had to search for. We were airborne as dawn broke and soon reached our starting point just south-west of Brest. The weather was clear, with visibility more than fifteen miles, and there wasn't a ripple on the water. After turning onto our new course, I handed the controls over to Brian Landers, with MacGregor, our third pilot, occupying the second dickey's seat. Then I went below, not just to stretch my legs but rather to answer a some-what urgent call of nature. I had barely finished the job in hand and was sitting quietly when I was shaken out of my wits by the blaring of the alarm hooters.

At first, I thought that we were under attack by a JU 88, but the hooters were sounding three short blasts, which was the signal for a U-boat sighting. I literally leapt to my feet and snatched up my trousers, pulling the braces over my shoulders. With my shirt-tails flying, I tore up the companionway to the bridge, where Ian Riddell shouted that we had just passed a submarine that was clearly showing its periscope. It had been spotted simultaneously by MacGregor and Flt Sgt Paton in the front turret. Paton had been the first to report on the intercom, but it had already been spotted by MacGregor. He pointed it out to Landers, who had it under observation through the binoculars.

I told Landers to continue flying the aircraft and to turn around to port to get into a position to attack. He had already run out the DCs, but before taking over, I rechecked our 'Mickey Mouse' release mechanism to ensure that the 'live' position had been correctly set. As it was a daylight attack, I decided to shorten the stick spacing so that the DCs would explode at fifty-foot intervals instead of the normal sixty feet. I knew that as long as I dropped the stick down in the correct place we would have more chance of hitting our prey with two DCs instead of just one. Motioning MacGregor to move, I took his place in the second pilot's seat. One of the crew stuck my flying helmet on my head while another plugged it into the intercom. I could now hear the mid-upper gunner reporting that the U-boat's periscope would soon come into our view on the port side.

With Landers still flying the aircraft, anxiously I waited for it to appear. Suddenly it came into view, and I couldn't believe what I was seeing. The lookout on the periscope must have been blind not to see us. I can only imagine that he had been searching the horizon for surface ships (we had destroyers in the area) and had neglected the sky above. The periscope could clearly be seen with its long feathery wake trailing behind it. Best of all, Landers had positioned the aircraft just perfectly for an attack. Having already lost much of our height, a steep dive in the last few seconds of our run-in was avoided. So I gave him a thumbs-up and took control from the second pilot's position.

It feels quite different to fly from the righthand side of an aircraft, and some pilots admit that they never quite get used to it. However, I was quite at home in this position, having given a fair amount of dual instruction to other members of the squadron who had flown with me. I reduced height to less than fifty feet and began to line up on a point just ahead of the U-boat's track. Compared with our previous night attack, it could not have been easier.

The U-boat was almost beam on to us, and I had no difficulty in getting the run-in just right. At the precise moment I pressed the 'bomb tit' and held the aircraft steady as the stick went down. We passed across the U-boat's track slightly ahead of the periscope. Thus, the forward speed of the U-boat would just cancel out the time lag between our DCs dropping and completing their thirty feet of underwater travel before exploding. Ian was watching from the astrodome and, together with our mid-upper and rear gunners, clearly saw the stick drop across the U-boat's track, three on each side.

After almost skimming the sea before the attack, I climbed away after it. (Far too dangerous to come so low in a land-plane, but quite normal in a flying-boat whose pilots are practised at landing the aircraft on the sea.) As we turned to port, the rear gunner shouted excitedly that the U-boat was attempting to surface as the explosions erupted on both sides. However, I believed that he was not trying to surface, but had been lifted by the force of the explosions. We reset the bomb release unit to select the two remaining DCs in case the U-boat did surface, and we needed to deliver the *coup de grâce*; but we had no need to use them. Where the periscope had last been seen, a massive disturbance was raging just under the surface. The sea was boiling with the vast amount of compressed air that was coming to the surface, and was white over an area fully one hundred feet in diameter. As we passed over it, taking photographs from the galley hatch, the sun shining deep down into the dense rising column of air bubbles caused it to take on a brilliant light green appearance. This eruption of escaping air continued for the best part of twenty minutes, bringing up thick oil and debris that spread out over an ever-widening circle.

Following our first sighting report, we now sent Group a signal reporting the attack and that we were circling the aftermath. Gradually, the major eruption of air and debris subsided, leaving two separate locations about fifty feet apart from which two thinner streams of air bubbles continued to surface. This made us believe that the third DC in the stick had actually split the U-boat into two sections.

We then received a signal instructing us to tune our IFF to the band reserved for air-to-ship recognition. This enabled us to identify ourselves on the radar screens of our naval vessels in the area. We then increased our altitude to facilitate reception by ships that were still below the horizon. Our position was 46° 46' North, 03° 39' West, south-west of Belle Isle. This was just about where one would expect a U-boat to be while in transit between Brest and Bordeaux. Although it was fairly close to the coast, there would have been ample depth to crash-dive, if necessary, the sea being between 150 and 600 feet in depth.

This photo, taken with a hand-held camera, was taken at 500 feet, and shows escaping oil and air from U-107 one minute after the attack.

About one hour after our attack we received a signal instructing us to return to base because of weather deterioration expected there. Before leaving, we took one more photograph of the oil and debris that littered the area. We also dropped another flame float to mark the position for the Navy, who were appearing on the horizon. The oil slick now extended for about two miles, with oil still coming up from the same spot; the slick widened out to about half a mile at its furthest point. Amongst the debris were about forty large sheets of white paper some three or four feet square. We guessed these were plotting sheets

Oil and debris from U-107 spreading over the sea.

or charts from the navigator's position. Finally, we left the area and set course for home, hardly able to believe our obvious success.

We landed well ahead of the approaching bad weather and were met by our CO. This was not my friend Van der Kiste, but a new wing commander known as 'Jasper' Coates. He was a colourful character of the pre-war breed, and a very good and understanding commander. By the time we got ashore and into the ops room for debriefing, a signal from the naval vessels we had homed to our position had been relayed from Group to our ops room. They had picked up some of the debris and scooped up oil still rising to the surface, together with some of the charts that we had seen from the air. The oil was diesel of the type used in submarine engines. No Asdic returns had been obtained from the surrounding area, which indicated that the hull of the U-boat was lying at the bottom of the sea.

Unfortunately, our rear-facing camera had not functioned; so we had no photographs of the DCs straddling the path of the periscope. The camera was fitted with a waterproof cover over the lens to keep it clear of spray thrown up during the aircraft's take-off. As the DCs were released, a small spring opened the cover, and the camera then operated continuously until it was switched off. For some unknown reason the cover had stuck. However, we had taken many photos of the debris and oil on the surface of the sea. These and the photos taken immediately after the attack showing the massive surge of compressed air coming up from the hull were all very clear.

Once again the RAF were certain that the U-boat had been destroyed, and even the remarks of the Admiralty Assessment Board were quite enthusiastic. The report published in the September 1944 issue of the *Coastal Command Review* said: 'Photographs confirm an excellent attack. In view of the evidence from surface wreckage, the attack is assessed as "U-boat probably sunk"': high praise indeed from the Admiralty. After the war, this was confirmed as a 'kill', the submarine being U-107, captain 2nd Lt Fritz, on passage from Lorient to La Pallice.

Somehow, this success did not give me the kick I had expected. I liked Brian Landers and Ian Riddell, my navigator, a lot, and had absolute confidence in Landers as my co-pilot. But I truly missed

NS-W (EJ 150) of No. 201 Sqn that sank U-107 seen on the slip at Castle Archdale.

YEAR 1944		AIRCRAFT		PILOT, OR	2ND PILOT, PUPIL	DUTY
MONTH	DATE	Type	No.	1ST PILOT	OR PASSENGER	(INCLUDING RESULTS AND REMAR
—	—	—	—	—	—	—— TOTALS BROUGHT FORWA
JULY	5	SUNDERLAND	EJ.150	SELF.	F/O LANDERS & CREW	A/S PATROL. returned U.S.
"	7.	"	EJ.150	SELF.	" " " "	A/S PATROL.
"	14.	"	EJ.150	SELF.	" " " "	TRANSIT to CASTLE ARCHDAL
"	14.	"	EJ.150	SELF.	" " " "	RETURN FROM "
"	15.	"	EJ.150	SELF.	" " " "	AIR TEST.
"	18	"	EJ.150	SELF.	" " " "	OASTHOUSE.
		SUMMARY	FOR	JULY 1944	AIRCRAFT	1. SUNDERLAND.
		UNIT.	201 SQO.			
		DATE	JULY 31st			
		SIGN				
AUG	8	SUNDERLAND.	EJ.150.	SELF.	F/O LANDERS & CREW	A/S PATROL. (BREST
	10.	"	EJ.150	SELF.	" " " "	A/S PATROL. (BELLE
	12.	"	EJ.150	SELF.	" " " "	A/S PATROL. (BREST)
	14.	"	EJ.150	SELF.	" " " "	AIR TEST.
	14	"	EJ.150	SELF.	" " " "	A/S PATROL.
	18	"	EJ.150	SELF	" " " "	1 A/S PATROL.
	18.	"	EJ.150	SELF	F/O LANDERS,	A/S PATROL. SIGHTED U/B
					RIDDLE, MACGREGOR.	PERISCOPE. ATTACKED WITH
	U BOAT WAS	U/107.			P/O MACAREE.	6x250 lb. TORPEX. OBTAINED
	KILL CONFIRMED	BY AIR			A/S.PATON. HOWAT.	STRADDLE, CONSIDERABLE DE
	HISTORICAL	BRANCH.			COTTRELL. PERRAN.	& OIL. & GERMAN CHARTS.
					W/O PARSONS.	
					SGT. BULLOCH.	

GRAND TOTAL [Cols. (1) to (10)]

1350 Hrs 40 Mins.

TOTALS CARRIED FORWA

Baveystock's log, showing the sinking of U-107 on 18 August 1944.

SINGLE-ENGINE AIRCRAFT				MULTI-ENGINE AIRCRAFT						PASS-ENGER	INSTR/CLOUD FLYING [Incl. in cols. (1) to (10)]	
DAY		NIGHT		DAY			NIGHT					
DUAL	PILOT	DUAL	PILOT	DUAL	1ST PILOT	2ND PILOT	DUAL	1ST PILOT	2ND PILOT		DUAL	PILOT
(1)	(2)	(3)	(4)	(5)	(6)	(7)	(8)	(9)	(10)	(11)	(12)	(13)
·50	26·35		\	64·20	716·15	43·10	13·10	183·10	122·45	26·45		
					·40			1·30				
					10·45			3·05				
					4·35							
					2·10							
					·35							
					2·55							
					21·40			4·35				
					12·55							
					13·25							
					9·00			4·10				
					·30							
					5·35			8·30				
					5·00			8·30				
					8·45							
50	26 35			64·20	953·05	43·10	13·10	208·55	122·45	26·45		
(1)	(2)	(3)	(4)	(5)	(6)	(7)	(8)	(9)	(10)	(11)	(12)	(13)

Longland's crew, and the thought of them perishing in the sea, perhaps over the course of a few terrible drawn-out hours, still preyed on my mind. I missed Colin Griffiths and Peter Hunt especially, and could not forget the grief of the Hunt family. When a few days later I learned that I had been awarded an immediate DSO, it did not bring me the thrill that I might have expected.

I took the entire crew for a booze-up in a local pub, but somehow things did not seem right in our crew; later, Ian Riddell told me why. It appeared that some of the crew thought that as two of my previous crew had been awarded DFMs, then perhaps one of them might also

Flight Lieutenant L. H. Baveystock, DSO, DFC*, DFM, in 1944, at the end of his operational tour.

have been singled-out in this way, following our successful attack. Flight Sergeant Paton, who had first reported seeing the wake of the periscope, thought that this might well have been him. In fact, it was our third pilot, MacGregor, who had spotted it first and had pointed it out to Landers. I suppose it had been difficult for the CO to select a second member of the crew to recommend for an award. Consequently, the rest of them missed out.

In retrospect, the man who should perhaps have received some sort of recognition, a Mention in Despatches at least, was Brian Landers, for he had been the perfect second pilot during my absence from the bridge, and had brought the aircraft into the ideal position for me to make the final attack. However, it was not to be, and a sort of gloom descended on our celebration. Perhaps I had not really gelled with Bent's crew as successfully as I had done with my two earlier crews. As we were still so very busy after this particular patrol, I soon forgot about it, as did most of the crew.

Chapter 17

INSTRUCTIONAL FLYING
AT ALNESS

etween 8 August and 29 September we did over two hundred hours' flying, of which sixty-eight were at night. Although we never picked up any more U-boat contacts, we got our fair share of false alarms. Usually, our contacts turned out to be Spanish fishing boats. A low-level run-in at night on an unidentified contact was a nerve-racking experience for all pilots. Many RAF aircraft were lost through homing onto specially prepared flak ships, and this danger was forever on our minds. I remember one particular night when there was heavy rain and poor visibility, our radar had picked up a contact and I homed in to investigate, ready to attack if necessary. When the flares went down, I could not see a thing for the bright reflection of the flares from the rain. I had dived as low as I dared, fearing all the time that we might hit the sea or run into a sudden hail of point-blank shellfire. But we saw nothing, and I climbed away again.

Then our radar operator reported another contact from the same position, and again we made a low-level run-in. The flares went down but we were unable to get the slightest glimpse of anything through the murk and heavy rain. During every second of the manoeuvre, I fully expected to be suddenly shot out of the sky. As we switched off the flare chute and climbed away again, the tension that I had endured during both run-ins proved too much for me and I started to tremble violently. It took a short while before I regained control of myself. So I abandoned further attempts to identify the contact that our radar operator later admitted was a rather hazy one.

In retrospect, with the knowledge of how modern commercial aircraft use radar to avoid flying into large dangerous clouds, our contact was probably the centre of the large rain-filled cloud that we had been in. It could not have been a surfaced U-boat, for it would surely have opened fire on us. Afterwards, I felt that maybe I had been somewhat cowardly in not pursuing this elusive radar blip.

Flying home, I had been reminded of a contact that had been picked up by our squadron's American pilot, Lt Glen Ferguson. He had homed onto it during a night patrol and, ready to attack, he had trimmed his aircraft with forward trim to offset the drag of the DCs. Half a mile from the target, flares were dropped, and bang in front of them, broadside on, was an RN destroyer. Ferguson held his breath, wondering at first if it was a German flak ship and his end was nigh. Immediately, he stopped the flares and brought in the DCs to begin climbing away. But with the tension of the previous few seconds, he had forgotten the forward trim that he had wound onto the elevator trimming tabs. In total darkness the aircraft went into a dive and hit the sea at about 150 knots. By an absolute miracle, the Sunderland bounced off the surface like a huge cork, and Ferguson managed to regain control. He then abandoned the patrol as the aircraft had lost a wing float, and also was difficult to fly; some hours later he landed back at base. When the Sunderland was taken up onto the hard, it was found that the hull was so twisted that the tailplane was several degrees out of line with the mainplane. As a result, the aircraft had to be scrapped.

On 29 September 1944, I returned from what was to be my last operational flight. Then on 1 October, I flew with Flg Off Lillingstone on a night exercise in order to give him the benefit of my experience. This was followed by some well-earned leave, which the crew undoubtedly needed. In fact, Ian Riddell, who was not a very strong person at the best of times, had become an absolute 'cot case'. There was only one navigator in a Sunderland crew, and he worked with his head down on every trip. He had to keep a continuous DR plot, taking a wind check every fifteen minutes, and working out our new position each time. This was not too difficult perhaps when flying from 'A' to 'B', but on patrol when we were flying a 'pattern', with continuing changes of course having to be worked out, he was as busy as a one-armed paper-hanger. The squadron doctor had ordered Ian into hospital for a few days' rest. Instead, I persuaded the Doc that I should invite him to spend his leave with Betty and me in London. Having completed 800 hours of operational flying, I was due for a rest and would be posted elsewhere at the end of the leave.

We caught the night train to London, and during the journey Ian remarked that he would hope to see a 'Doodlebug' while in London. 'It would be great to see one going over,' he remarked. 'Something to tell the folks about when I get back to New Zealand.' Two nights later, he was to change his mind. We had gone to bed in our house in Friern Barnet at about ten-thirty when quite soon afterwards we were awakened by the sound of an air-raid siren going off in the distance. Betty and I stayed in bed straining our ears to hear if another siren might sound closer to where we were, since, with the advent of Doodlebugs, the air-raid warning system had been modified. Once a 'plot' had been worked out on the flight path of the Bug, the sirens were only sounded along its route. The ARP Centre notified direct any factories employing a large staff.

The next siren that sounded was the one in our district, to be followed almost at once by the siren at the Standard Telephone Cable Company's factory only about a mile away from us. Immediately, we jumped out of bed and pulled on some clothes that we always laid out at the foot of the bed. Then I picked up Jill, and together with Betty and Ian we ran down to our air-raid shelter at the bottom of the garden. Once Betty and Jill were safely inside, Ian and I remained outside, straining our ears and eyes for the approaching Doodlebug.

Our next-door neighbour, Joan Hotten, then joined Betty and Jill in the shelter, telling us that her husband and daughter were following. However, before he arrived, we heard the Doodlebug in the distance, and then, about half a mile away, we spotted it as it came into view above the rooftops. We could clearly see the flame from its jet motor, and the familiar chugging sound got ever louder. We knew, of course, that while its motor continued to run the Bug would maintain its course until its fuel ran out. We could then see that it would pass directly over us. Charles, with his daughter in his arms, had by now reached the gate in our garden fence. Ian was now pointing at the thing saying, 'It's going right over us'. Suddenly the flame from its motor went out and a second or so later the sound of its motor stopped. It was only a few hundred yards from where we stood, and probably no more than 400 or 500 feet high. Ian and I literally threw ourselves down the concrete steps into our shelter. For a few seconds there was a terrifying silence and then 'Boom!' as it hit the ground and exploded. Charles, with his daughter still in his arms, threw himself to the ground some way from our shelter, fully expecting to be blown sky high. However, as was often the way with Doodlebugs, once the engine stopped the gyro toppled; the Bug then no longer kept flying straight-ahead and crashed out of control. As it turned to starboard during its final dive, it fell a little way up Oakleigh Road. It demolished six houses and broke windows all around the area, killing many people who had not bothered to leave their beds and go down to their shelters. Fortunately for us, there was a small hill between our house and where it exploded, and we suffered no damage from the blast. Ian had got his wish; but the next morning, when he saw the damage, he confessed that he did not want to see another Doodlebug, and luckily enough, he didn't.

At the end of the leave, Ian and I returned to Pembroke Dock, leaving Betty and Jill in our home. A couple of days later the squadron held a dinner in the mess to celebrate its Thirtieth Anniversary. The dinner was quite a formal affair and gave us wartime officers our first real taste of what service in a peacetime squadron would be like. Afterwards, when we had drunk the Royal Toast, the formality disappeared at about the same rate as the beer, and we had a most enjoyable evening. Following general practice, we signed the menus as keepsakes, and thirty years later I found that my spidery signature still adorned the menu that had been kept in the 'Squadron Line Book' (the unofficial historic record).

During my last few days with the squadron, I flew only three more times. The first lasted three and a half hours, giving dual instruction to our third pilot MacGregor, and to a Flg Off Coffey and a Flt Sgt Beck. We did nothing but practise landings and take-offs. I was now becoming quite adept at giving dual instruction in the Sunderland, which was a good thing, as I guessed that would most likely be my job while on rest. When I returned to the mess, I had a call from the Station Adjutant telling me that Gp Capt Bolland, the Station Commander, wished to see me in his office. When I arrived there he bade me to sit down opposite his desk and to make myself comfortable. Then he told me that in view of my record on the squadron, Group had arranged a special job for me and I would not therefore have to go off on some routine job as I had expected. I was going to be the personal pilot to Air Marshal Sir Arthur Longmore. It was a great 'leg up', and the group captain assured me that the air marshal was an extremely good chap. He was an old 'boat' man himself, having earlier formed 201 Squadron as its first CO in 1914.

Before I left the Station Commander, he asked me if I would take him and Wg Cdr Coates down to Plymouth for an appointment at Group HQ. So, on 24 October, with a 'scratch crew' in Sunderland DP196, I flew down to Mount Batten for the last time. On arrival, we went to the group ops room, where I was delighted to see my old CO, Wg Cdr Van der Kiste. I was introduced to AVM Brian Baker, who congratulated me on my DSO and on my coming appointment with Air Marshal Longmore.

We were not due to return to PD until the following day, so I set off to visit my Uncle Alfred at Plymstock. Walking along the country lanes that led to 'Four Winds', his house on the hill, I mused on my continuous good luck since joining the RAF in 1940. It seemed hard to believe that I had nearly been 'scrubbed' off my initial pilot's course, and I would have dearly loved to meet my instructor Messiter to flaunt my success in his face. But I doubt whether he ever paid any interest to his former pupils.

After about half an hour's walk, I was again seated in my uncle's comfortable house. He asked me innumerable questions, and I don't think that I had ever seen him so enthusiastic and excited. So we had a most happy and enjoyable evening. The next day I took leave of him and his tranquil home, which I never visited again.

Back at Mount Batten, I picked up my crew, and after a visit to the ops room, we went out to our Sunderland moored on the Cattewater. Group Captain Bolland and Wg Cdr Coates joined us, and taking off from Plymouth Sound we flew across Devon and the Severn estuary back to PD. I knew that this would be my last flight with 201, and I felt sorry that I would be leaving them. However, my future looked to be of such interest that it was of little consequence. In fact, of course, it was not to be my final flight with the squadron, for I flew with them again just thirty years later when I was a grandfather, and the world an altogether different place. Again, I found myself bound for London to report to Coastal Command HQ at Northwood. After spending the night at home with Betty and Jill, I arrived at the HQ for an interview with the postings officer, who outlined my future job with AM Longmore. I was told that first I would go to a conversion unit to learn to fly the York aircraft. This sounded fine, for the York was the transport version of the famous Lancaster, and being without armament should be a responsive aircraft to fly. The best part would be getting the acting rank of squadron leader. This was quite something, as at that time I was only an acting flight lieutenant faced with the possibility, despite my four gongs, of having to drop back to the rank of flying officer. This would have been the normal procedure had I gone to an RAF station that already had its full complement of flight lieutenants.

When my interview was almost at an end, I was asked if I had applied for a permanent commission in the RAF, and of course, I had not done so. A few months earlier, the RAF had asked interested aircrew to apply for permanent commissions when the war ended. I had thought the matter over as I guessed that I had a very good chance of being selected. However, taking account of my position back in our business, which I had inherited with my brother, and the fact that both Betty and I wished to return to our own home permanently, I had decided not to apply. So, reluctantly I admitted that I had not done so, stating that I had no wish to remain in the Air Force after the war.

The postings officer was very disturbed by this admission. Wagging his head from side to side, he pointed out that the job with the air marshal would be a terrible waste for someone not wishing to make a career out of the RAF. He then said that he would have to think the whole thing over and consult his superiors about the matter. Finally, he told me that he would post me to the OTU at Alness (where I had done my skipper's course in early 1943) while a decision was made regarding my future.

Naturally, I was very disappointed with this news and I told him so. I pointed out the large difference there was between being an instructor at Alness and the job with AM Longmore. He nodded in agreement and said that I would go to Alness only while some other posting was found for me. But I knew from the tone of his voice that I had shot my bolt, and nothing worthwhile would be found for me now. Later, when I looked back, I realised that his decision was the correct one, for the RAF had so many good young pilots with no job to return to in Civvy Street, who would have given half an arm to have the chance that had been offered to me. Somewhat crestfallen, I returned to Raleigh Drive to await the posting notice and railway warrant to take me back up to Scotland and Alness.

After another long journey north, I was pleased to find that I was not a complete stranger, for the Deputy Chief Flying Instructor was my old friend Raban, now a squadron leader, who had sent me solo when I first joined 461 Squadron. There were more old-timers, including Australian gunner Peter Jensen, and 'Smithy', Flt Lt Gordon Smith-Gander, both of whom had been with me in Dudley Marrows's crew.

From Peter I learned the story of what had befallen them after I had gone to 201. They had flown together for many months without seeing anything of consequence. Then on 3 July 1943, while on patrol in the Bay of Biscay, they picked up a message from a Liberator of 53 Squadron reporting a pack of three U-boats travelling west on the surface together. Their position was some 200 miles away from their aircraft position so Marrows had ignored it. He expected the U-boats would have submerged long before they had time to get there. However, they remained on the surface, fighting off any attempt to attack them. Suddenly, Marrows received a signal from Group ordering him to proceed to the position and join in the mêlée. On arrival, they found the U-boats in formation still heading west. Marrows made a few attempts to attack, but had to break off owing to the intensity of the combined firepower thrown up at him. One should bear in mind the fact that the three U-boats had a combined firepower of at least twelve 20 mm cannon, each firing explosive shells, any one of which hitting the pilot's cockpit, or one of the ten fuel tanks, would bring the aircraft down. While at that time during the war, the Sunderland had only a single .303 machine-gun in the front turret, with just 100 rounds of ammunition. The U-boat's cannon had a range of some 2,000 yards against the 600 yards of the Sunderland's front gun.

At last, Marrows got his chance when the Liberator made an attack. He had got to within a thousand yards before the U-boat opened fire, hitting the aircraft's starboard wing. When they were close enough, Marrows's front gunner opened fire and was lucky enough to knock out the entire gun crew of the submarine. Just at the right moment, Marrows had released the DCs, straddling the U-boat just forward of the conning tower with seven of his eight depth-charges. There was an enormous eruption from around the sub. and the hull appeared to break in half. Again Marrows brought his aircraft round for a further attack with the remaining DC, but there was no need. The sea where the U-boat had been was now a mass of wreckage and oil, and struggling in it were many of the submarine's crew. His job now done, Marrows had no hate left in his heart for the men who minutes before might well have killed him and all his crew. Typically of this big-hearted man, he again brought his Sunderland down low over the struggling men, and this time, instead of death-dealing explosives, he dropped one of the aircraft's dinghies. Among the many men who clung to it was the U-boat's captain, and, he, with the other survivors, was picked up later by the Royal Navy.

The outcome of the battle was that all three U-boats were sunk, the second by a Halifax aircraft flown by a Dutchman, and the third by ships of the Escort Group that arrived just as Marrows was leaving. Jubilant at having seen three U-boats on the same day, Marrows and his crew set course for home.

About an hour later their front gunner, Paddy Watson announced in an excited voice, 'U-boat on the starboard bow'. The entire crew burst out laughing, thinking that it was a joke. But sure enough, it was another U-boat. Marrows ran out his remaining DC and dived in to attack. On their run-in they again met a hail of flak and were hit in the wing, setting fire to the motor that operated the bomb racks. Unknowingly, Marrows, in selecting 'bomb doors open', had in-advertently pushed against the control that operated the automatic pilot. So, when he started to pull out of his initial dive just before reaching the target, he was unable to do so, for the aircraft was locked into the diving angle. With the Sunderland now plunging straight for the sea, Marrows yelled at his co-pilot to pull back on the control column. With their feet pressed hard against the rudder controls, they pulled back with all their strength. Slowly, the aircraft came out of its headlong dive. Nevertheless, Marrows pressed the bomb tit to release the DC, but their luck had run out, for the release gear had been damaged by enemy flak and would not function. By the time they had discovered the fact that the automatic pilot was engaged and had brought the aircraft around, the U-boat had crash-dived.

They were now running short of fuel and doubted if they could reach base. So they set course for the Scilly Islands and landed just off St Mary's Bay. Later, when they finally reached base, the Escort Group, who had picked up seventy survivors, had reported the full story. Among them was the captain of the U-boat that Marrows had sunk who asked the Navy to convey his thanks for the humane action of dropping a life-saving dinghy to his crew. The Fickle Finger of Fate (to quote an RAF saying) became apparent when later it was found that the U-boat Marrows had sunk was U-461, and Marrows's aircraft was 'U' of 461 Squadron. Truly a case of the saying (modified) that, 'You only get hit by the depth-charge with your number on it.'

I started with a few local trips, including one to Sullom Voe. Then, on 16 November, I was given a night-flying check by Sqn Ldr Dagg. This struck me as somewhat unnecessary, as the last two flying assessments in my log book were 'Exceptional', with the remark, 'A First Class bad weather pilot'. However, I suppose it was the usual procedure for new pilots joining the unit. A few days later two more old friends joined me at Alness. One was my last CO on 201 Squadron, Wg Cdr Coates, who had been promoted to group captain and appointed as the new Station Commander at Alness. The other was Sqn Ldr Flint who had flown with me several times in June 1943. He was now a wing commander and took over as Chief Instructor. I felt quite happy in my new surroundings until one morning the CO called me into his office regarding my acting rank of flight lieutenant. I knew of course that there were more substantive flight lieutenants on the station than the establishment allowed for, and that my 'second ring' was in dire peril. The CO explained that I would have to have my pay reduced to that of a flying officer, but he would ask Group to allow me to wear my second ring until my substantive rank came through a few weeks later (two years from the date of commissioning). For this, I was grateful. The CO felt sure that, taking account of my decorations, this minor face-saving request would be granted. It wasn't, and two days later, I had to unstitch my second ring, leaving obvious marks where it had been. This was a tremendous blow to my ego, especially as only weeks before I had been told that I was to be promoted to squadron leader. I still had high hopes that I would soon hear from Coastal Command HQ, and a better posting would turn up.

At the end of the month, together with several other pilots on rest, I received instructions to attend a course at No. 12 (Operational) Flying

Instructors School at Killadeas on Lough Erne, some four miles south of Castle Archdale. Again, I had to pack up all my gear and begin the long journey to Killadeas. There was just a small staff there and eleven 'pupils'. We were all on rest, with at least one operational tour behind us. Three were from the RAAF, including a fellow named Livermore from 461 Squadron whom I knew quite well. He and I flew together, taking turns in dual instruction from a young chap named Parkinson, who, in spite of his lowly rank of flying officer, was a 'red-hot' pilot.

We flew a total of thirty-six hours, learning the instructional patter and the various procedures required of an adept Sunderland skipper. Long before the course finished, to my great surprise I found that, despite my squadron assessment of 'Exceptional', in reality I never knew what a Sunderland was actually capable of – in particular, the manoeuvres that a knowledgeable pilot could perform with a lightly laden aircraft. Discounting a slow roll or a loop, the old Sunderland could do just about anything without getting into trouble. On the squadron we had got so used to flying fully laden aircraft that we rarely, if ever, did anything risky or out of the ordinary.

We were shown all manner of tricks that the aircraft would do, in spite of its huge size and weight. For example, how you could dive the aircraft with the engines throttled back and then pull the nose up into a steep climb. With the stick right back in your stomach, you sat and waited for the aircraft to stall. And stall it did, falling clean out of the sky, the like of which we had never seen since our Tiger Moth days. Much to our surprise, recovery from the stall was just as straight-forward as it had been with the Tiger.

At a safe height with full power on all engines and with one-third flap to simulate a take-off, our instructor showed us just what would happen if two engines on one side failed together. With hands off the stick, the aircraft immediately dropped the 'dead' wing and rolled over into a frightening spiral dive. But with corrective action, it could be brought back into straight and level flight without opening up the dead engines or shutting down the live ones. Previously we had heard so many old wives' tales, such as 'if we stalled, the floats would fall off', that in the past we had never experimented at all. One of the most useful things that we learned was that if we needed to lose height in an emergency from high altitude, the best thing was not to throttle back the engines and go into a dive, but to throttle back and pull the control column right back into one's stomach. In this attitude the aircraft stalled, with the nose a little below the horizon and the speed dropping off to about 50 knots. By vigorous use of the rudder, the wings were easily kept level and height was lost at over 2,000 feet per minute.

To recover, the nose was eased down to increase speed, the engines opened up and bingo, everything was back to normal in no time at all.

Finally, by the end of the course I had gained unlimited faith in the Sunderland, and I looked forward to imparting the knowledge to others. I left Killadeas having gained a Category 'B' Instructor's Certificate, with an assessment of 'Average' as an instructor and 'Above Average' as a pilot. Four months later, I was re-examined by officers of the RAF Central Flying School and was upgraded to Category 'A2' Instructor. With the course ending on 22 December I was given leave and had Christmas with Betty (who had just confirmed her pregnancy) and Jill in our home in Friern Barnet. I returned to Alness and began flying again on 23 January 1945.

The officers' mess at Alness was in a beautifully built stone hunting lodge, known as Dalmore House, set in lovely grounds through which ran a trout stream. Of course, there was insufficient room in the house to accommodate all the many officers on the station, and I was given a tiny bedroom in an unheated Nissen hut in the grounds. It was miserably cold at night, and owing to the shortage of hot water in the mess, we had to take cold showers in a toilet block in another unheated Nissen hut.

Being so far north, the hours of daylight were very much shorter than down in London, and with just nothing to do during off-duty hours, the life was meagre indeed. Again, I began to search for digs for Betty and Jill. These were most difficult to find, and it was the end of March before I had any success.

Meanwhile, I had become adjusted to giving dual instruction. Yet, it was not very enjoyable as most of the time the weather was terrible. Nothing out of the ordinary ever seemed to happen, apart from a few of the new Mark V Sunderlands arriving on the unit. These aircraft were fitted with Pratt and Whitney Twin Wasp radial engines that not only had fully feathering propellers, but produced some 200 extra horsepower each. The initial credit for fitting these engines went to 10 Squadron, the Australian unit based at Mount Batten in Plymouth Sound. They had obtained four engines from the company and made up all the necessary parts to fit them into a standard Pegasus-engined aircraft. All the work was done in their station workshops. This proved so successful that the necessary instructions were given to Short and Harland in Belfast to switch assembly to this new version.

I first flew in one on 7 February with Lt Cdr Abildsoe, who was the Assistant Chief Flying Instructor. Bill Abildsoe was a Norwegian naval officer, aged about 38 to 40 years, who had been instructing for almost the whole of the war, for which he had been awarded an Air Force

261

Cross. We stayed up for about two hours and I found the aircraft just marvellous to fly. Boy, how I wished that we had been equipped with them while I was with 201. However, it was a great consolation to know that if I ever returned to ops again it would be on one of these new machines.

At last, the day came for Betty and Jill to join me in Scotland. As she was now six months pregnant she managed to get a night sleeper to Inverness. We took the Highland train to Invergordon, where I had managed to rent a small cottage close to the RN hospital, which belonged to an elderly widow who now lived with her sister. It had been built during the 1914–18 War, when Invergordon was a large naval base, and after the war had been sold with the others in the street for the princely sum of £80. It was warm and cosy, and like every other place we ever lived in, Betty soon made it feel like home. I was also very pleased that Jock Wright, who had been my flight engineer in my first crew on 201, had also been posted to Alness on completion of his tour on the squadron. His wife Agnes got on well with Betty and the four of us became firm friends. Our different status, commissioned and non-commissioned, was of absolutely no consequence.

As the days lengthened and the weather improved, life became very enjoyable. I had now got over my disappointment at losing the job with Air Marshal Longmore and had found full-time instructing to be easy and satisfying. The job was never irksome, as the instructors did not have to do the working jobs such as staying on board to refuel after a flight, or having to do duty on the aircraft while a gale warning was in force. About midway through April, a team of specialists from the Empire Central Flying School arrived on the station to check all the instructors and to consider any necessary regrading. As I mentioned earlier, I had been given a 'B' Category grading at Killadeas.

I flew with a Flt Lt Monk and gave him an hour's instruction in the same way as I would with a trainee course pilot. The following day I had an informal oral examination from a squadron leader who questioned me for over two hours. We went through every damn thing possible, from the effects of icing on a Sunderland to details of engines and airframes. I was particularly glad that I had done the Engine course at the Bristol works in Filton. However, there was one question that I could not answer in complete detail. That was why, in conditions of high humidity, did small vapour trails sometimes appear off the wingtips during a steep turn? I knew that it was the high-pressure air from under the wing spilling off the end of the wingtip and mixing with the low-pressure air from above the wing. But this simple

262

explanation was not enough to satisfy my examiner, who wanted to know exactly why this should cause the phenomenon. When I admitted that this was something that I had never learned about, he admitted that he too did not know and had only the vaguest idea.

Altogether about forty instructors were tested, including our Chief Flying Instructor and Assistant Chief Flying Instructors. Then, to my surprise, two days later their findings were published on the main notice board. There, in black and white for all to see, only Bill Abildsoe and I had been upgraded to 'A2' Category. I was pleased indeed, though many others were plainly disappointed. To add to my pleasure was the news that my substantive rank of flight lieutenant had finally come through.

The war in Europe was going well, and with the spring turning into summer, there was not a blot on the horizon. The war with Germany ended at the beginning of May and we were all jubilant. I would have liked to be in London at this time with our friends and neighbours, as in our remote corner of the world the celebrations could hardly have been quieter. However, our jubilations were soon to take a nosedive, for all sorts of rumours were flying around that the whole unit was soon to move out to the Far East. It turned out to be nonsense, but we did all begin to wonder if we would soon be involved in the war against the Japs. To be honest, the prospect appealed to none of us. It was not the thought of more fighting, but rather the idea of having to learn a whole new ball game. Like most of the other instructors at Alness, I had been in the RAF for nearly five years, and well over half of this time I had spent under training. Learning never really stopped, for there was always something new to swot up in order to keep apace of developments that were coming through continuously.

During the time we had been on boats, we had become familiar with most of the flying-boat bases around the British Isles and had enough experience to land at any of them in bad or marginal weather. To go to the Far East would be to put us back to square one again. Obviously, we would be working in the American sphere of operations and would be just like new boys. We knew nothing about Jap aircraft or ships and it would be like starting from scratch to fight another war. Learning to fly an operational aircraft is only a very small part of learning how to use it as an effective war machine.

Now with my thirtieth birthday only five months away, I felt that I had had enough. I would willingly have done another tour of operations on Sunderlands or any other type of aircraft, which would have been a continuation of what had gone before. But the Far East was another kettle of fish, too complicated to even think about. Like most of us, I longed for a miracle to finish Japan off quickly. Meanwhile, life as a flying instructor continued to be interesting and enjoyable, and sometimes we did manage to have quite a bit of fun. Very often we would take up passengers, and on one occasion I took up thirty-two Air Training Corps cadets. The aircraft just swarmed with them and it made me think of an old wooden house full of borer beetles. Having got airborne I sat in the second pilot's seat and gave as many as there was time for a brief few minutes in the skipper's seat, and I let them fly the aircraft and try a few turns. It was great to see the look of excitement on their faces when they had the stick in their hands. Some of them were very good and better than I had been on my first trip in a Tiger Moth. Quite often we found three or four sailors waiting on the quay trying to cadge a flight on a local trip that was going up for only an hour or two. Provided they had a 'Blood Chit' from their CO, it was left to our discretion as to whether we took them up or not. Back in 1943 when I did my skipper's course at Alness, one of my instructors had shown me how to have a little bit of fun with newcomers. A few miles west of Alness on the northern side of Cromarty Firth, Fyrish Hill rose sharply from the shore to a height of about a thousand feet. At the top of the hill was an almost level plateau extending back some way until it rose further into a mountain. My instructor had taken the aircraft up a little higher than the plateau itself. He then turned the aircraft around at the top end of the plateau and brought it down as low as was safe over the ground. Then he turned to the south, and flying very low from the high ground he headed towards the edge of the hill where the ground fell away steeply. This gave a most uncanny feeling: hurtling along close to the ground and seeing the edge of the cliff coming towards you, felt rather like being in a motor car in a similar situation. As the aircraft zoomed out into space, the instructor thrust the stick suddenly forward, giving a feeling as if one had jumped off a cliff into space. Even as an experienced pilot it had given me a feeling of fear, and to anyone not used to flying, the effect was a never-to-be-forgotten experience. This was pure showmanship that I sometimes indulged in on a good day.

Another amusing incident that stuck in my memory was the day we tried to beat up a Mosquito. We had been doing some 'engine failure' practice up at three thousand feet, which was pretty high for us. We had spotted a 'Mossie' flying east along the Black Isle about a couple of thousand feet below us. As no one on the Sunderland had seen a Mossie close up, I opened the throttles and put the aircraft into a fairly steep dive. Even in a steep dive the speed built up very slowly in a Sunderland, owing to the 'drag' caused by its huge hull and thick wings.

Slowly we overtook the Mossie, our speed increasing to its maximum of 200 knots. As we passed him a few feet at a time, I did my best to waggle our wings. However, at high speed there is so much pressure over the control surfaces, which unlike more modern aircraft did not have hydraulic assistance, that the effort required to move the ailerons was almost superhuman. So it took twenty seconds or more to produce even the slightest suggestion of a wing waggle. The pilot of the Mosquito looked at us in amazement as we inched past him, not knowing of course of our dive from above, or the fact that we were just about at our maximum speed. So, with a good laugh we continued on our way, taking ages to get rid of the surplus speed.

A couple of minutes later, our lookout in the astrodome came on the intercom to say that the Mossie was approaching fast on our starboard side. We turned our heads and waited for him to appear ahead of our wing. Lo and behold, when he did, his aircraft was flying on one engine with the other fully feathered and the prop stationary. He was much closer to us than we had been to him, and the pilot and navigator were laughing their heads off, giving us the 'V for Victory' sign in a most derisive and energetic manner.

The days passed quickly and Betty's time came near. We had arranged for her to have her baby in the Ross Memorial Hospital in Dingwall, about ten miles away towards Inverness. On 23 June at just the expected time, I took her into the hospital in a hired car. I was told to phone the Matron the next morning for any news. On returning to the mess, I found that I was flying the next morning. Rising early, I cycled from Invergordon to Alness and rang the hospital. I contacted the Matron and she told me that Betty had had a baby girl and both were well.

In high spirits I told some of the boys and then left the mess to go flying. We hadn't been airborne much more than an hour when our WOp received a message telling me to land and phone the mess. We landed, and having signalled a dinghy to come alongside the rear door, I left my pupil to moor the aircraft. Arriving at a barge used as a staging post *en route* to the shore, I was able to call the mess to discover what the fuss was about. I was amazed to hear that the Matron had been on the phone in a high state of anxiety to say that she had made a mistake and that Betty had in fact produced a boy. It caused a lot of fun in the mess, and a number of members wondered whether it was one of those babies that might turn out later to be of either sex. Actually, what had happened was that two babies, a boy and a girl, had been born the previous night and both were safe with their respective mothers. The Matron had not confused the babies, but the names of the mothers, and didn't discover her error until she made her rounds the following morning after she had already given me the good news.

While Betty was in hospital Jock Wright and his wife moved into our cottage to look after Jill. Then Jill not only caught the measles, but also suffered a disastrous nosebleed. I will not bore readers with the unpleasant details of the frightful trauma I had with both the Chief Medical Officer at the RN hospital and the local civilian doctor. Fortunately, I managed to get the RAF doctor at Alness to come and have a look at Jill, whose bleeding had not stopped and who was now in quite a bad way. However, using yards of gauze packing the doctor was able to staunch the flow of blood. He was a very kind and sympathetic man, but the events that night dispelled for ever my previous notion that all doctors are kind and understanding people whose one aim in life is to help those in need. Hippocratic oath, my bloody foot!

Betty came home again with our new son Robert Charles. The elderly spinster who owned our cottage (whom we had never met) wrote to us in all seriousness suggesting that we name our son 'Victor Spitfire'. A few days later Betty's mother came to stay with us. She was a great help to Betty, as I had to spend a lot of time away from home. This was despite the fact that I now had less flying to do, as we had an excess of pilots on rest to share the instructional duties.

During July, I flew only six times, mostly on night dual instruction. I had in fact been selected, together with two other senior pilots, for the job of Duty Commander. We took it in turns every three days to deputise for the Station Commander and take charge of all flying on the station. Our tour of duty lasted for 24 hours and required us to be in the ops room while any flying was in progress. Much of the flying at Alness entailed long flights of a semi-operational nature out over the sea, as part of the final training of new crews. It was our responsibility to supervise these flights, keeping a special eye on the weather, and to recall or divert them if necessary. Particularly adverse conditions could result in cancelling the flights altogether. This routine meant that, in addition to my night flying, I had to spend every third night sleeping in a small room off the ops room.

July passed into August, and the fateful dropping of Atom Bombs on Hiroshima and Nagasaki was followed by the complete capitulation of Japan. As luck would have it, I was giving night dual to a Flt Lt Wickman and Captain Phelan, a South African, when the official news of Japan's surrender was announced. We were doing circuits and bumps, and our WOp, listening to the BBC, joyfully gave me the news. We had been flying for over four hours, and although our stint was not really over, I felt that in the circumstances I had had enough. By the time we had landed, moored the aircraft and then got ashore, it was 2 o'clock in the morning. There was no visible sign of celebrations, and the entire countryside was as quiet as a graveyard as I cycled back to our cottage. Betty of course was tucked up in bed, but unable to sleep until I was safely home. From our cottage, which overlooked the flying area of the Cromarty Firth, she could hear the droning of our engines as we carried out one take-off and landing after another. When finally the noise stopped, she knew I would soon be home. Sleepily, she asked, 'Have you heard the news? Isn't it wonderful?' Then I tumbled into bed and was soon asleep. We had always said what a wonderful time we would have when the war was finally over, never dreaming that when the day came how quiet and what an anticlimax it would be. The next day, the finality that the war was over dawned on us, and all we could think about was just how soon we could get to our own home again.

Although life continued on the station, all the urgency had gone from our work. I did another thirteen hours of instructing, and then heard that I had been detailed to fly to Stavanger in Norway. We left on 30 August in Sunderland ML 739, taking Wg Cdr Flint with us. Our task was to escort a single-engined Northrop seaplane over the North Sea to Norway. Being a small aircraft, its navigation equipment was of an elementary nature and its range only just adequate. The crew were due to rejoin the Norwegian Air Force. The weather was perfect, and our charge flew comfortably about a hundred yards out from our starboard wing. We were of course flying straight and level, having engaged 'George', our automatic pilot. Anxious to show his skill, the Norwegian pilot left his station and moved in closer. Soon our wings were overlapping as he tucked himself in alongside our fuselage. I think he was trying to scare us, which he certainly did. We tried to ignore him, afraid to break away and demonstrate our nervousness. Also, if we broke away, we might have clobbered him with our tailplane. So we just stuck it out and continued to ignore him until he eventually broke away.

We arrived off the Norwegian coast dead on track and landed safely after a flight of three hours. Going ashore, we spotted a Fieseler Storch circling around and then landing in a small field close by. Who should be in it but our old friend Lt Cdr Bill Abildsoe, who had been posted back to Norway a few days after the fall of Germany. He had learned of our visit and had turned up to welcome his old colleagues. Later we were taken to have a look at the airfield at Stavanger, near the seaplane base at Solo where we had landed. On Stavanger airfield and its satellite field nearby, there were just hundreds of German aircraft that had been surrendered to the Norwegians. In the evening, we went with the two crew members of the Northrop to one of their friend's apartments, where they did their best to drink us under the table. We returned to Alness the following day.

In September, I flew on only eight days, giving some twenty hours of dual instruction. The last of these flights was on 21 September 1945, and I did not fly again until 22 October. Between these dates I went on leave, taking Betty and the family back to London. We stopped in Edinburgh for two nights and saw Scotland's Victory Parade. At the same time, there was an Investiture at Holyrood House where I went to receive my DSO and DFC and Bar from the King.

Leaving Betty and the family at our home in Raleigh Drive, I returned to Alness for just one more month. There I continued giving dual instruction to several different pilots. The final flight, I believe, deserves a special mention, being the one that I had always dreamed of, but was never sure in what manner it would occur. It is described in my final chapter.

Chapter 18

LAST FLIGHT

On the night of 15 November 1945 I took up Sunderland ML 866 for a night flight lasting two hours and forty minutes. It was my last ever flight as captain of an RAF aircraft. As it was a dark and dirty night, I took the precaution of carrying out the initial take-off myself. My task was to give instruction in circuits and bumps to two young pilot officers named Priest and Clarke. They had both been up with me before, the last time being a flight of over four hours' duration, and they had become quite confident. I doubt, however, if they ever became aircraft skippers, as, like the other Services, the RAF was reducing its manpower as rapidly as possible.

When our flight was over and the aircraft safely back on its buoy, I breathed my usual sigh of relief. I had got quite used to night flying, and the Sunderland was an easy aircraft to land if conditions were okay. However, it was an aircraft that, in the final stage before touchdown, had to be landed almost entirely by attention to the instruments. As with all flying-boats, the pilot gets no indication of height above the landing surface as a land-plane does when it lands on a well-lit flare-path, with its angle-of-approach lights for guidance. In the Sunderland, the second pilot's position, where the instructor sits, does not have a full blind-flying instrument panel. Also, having a wide-bodied fuselage, it is very difficult to see the first pilot's panel from the instructor's position. So it was always with a certain measure of relief that I finished giving night dual instruction, and this flight was extra special. This was the flight that I had often thought would end with me not being 'in one piece'.

The date of my 'demob' had now come through and soon I would be going home for good. Later, when I entered the flight in my flying log book, its significance really dawned on me. Before leaving, I was told to hand the log book into the flight office for the addition of the final assessment of my flying ability. There, I was alarmed to discover that log books were the property of the Air Ministry, and were being retained when the holders left the Service. This I just could not stomach at all, for my log book was the record of my life in the RAF, and it contained the names of so many people who had flown with me. So I took the only course open to me and recovered the book from the pile in the flight office awaiting endorsement. How very, very glad I am that I did do so, for without this log book to jog my fading memory, this story would never have been written.

Looking back through it now, I am surprised at the actual number of separate aircraft in which I flew. In the faithful and ever youthful Tiger Moth (some of which still fly today), I made ninety-eight flights in twenty different aircraft. In the Airspeed Oxford (in the design of which Nevil Shute played a large part), I flew eighty-nine flights, using forty-one aircraft to do so. In the tricky Handley Page Hampden, in which so many of my friends had been killed at the Cottesmore OTU, I flew some forty flights in twenty-two different aircraft. The ugly and ill-fated Manchester carried me on twenty-five trips in fifteen different aircraft. In the Avro Anson, I flew twenty-four trips in fourteen aircraft. Finally, came the wonderful old Sunderland. Designed by Sir Arthur Gouge of Short Brothers and built in a variety of UK locations, I believe that some 748 were completed altogether. I flew in eighty-two of them for a total of 311 flights.

Thus, I flew a grand total of 587 flights in ninety-four separate aircraft. If I include the miscellaneous trips I did, mainly acting as navigator on cross-country exercises at the training school in Canada, my total flying hours were just over 1,800. Not many hours perhaps, when judged against today's airline pilots, but many more than those flown by the vast majority of RAF aircrew who never lived to see the final entry in their flying log books.

Appendix I
THE ESCAPE REVISITED

Andrée Dumont
(Code name
'Nadine'), also
known as Dédée,
seen with Bav in
1946. She took
him and Bob
Horsley from
Brussels to Paris,
part of the escape
route used in
1942.

After the war, Bav visited the grave of Flying Officer Les Manser, VC, the heroic pilot who captained the Avro Manchester from which Bav baled-out in 1942. He remained at the controls to keep the damaged aircraft flying so that the crew could exit the stricken aircraft, an act that cost him his life.

A wartime photograph of Dédée and her father Frédéric de Jongh. *(Comtesse de Jongh)*

Gisèle Salpetier (née Evrard).

Bav and Bob Horsley photographed with Dédée (Andrée Dumont) and Gisèle (Evrard) at a reunion in Canberra, Australia.

INDEX

The index is arranged alphabetically, except for entries under Leslie and Betty Baveystock, and Bob Horsley, which are in chronological order. Page numbers in *italics* refer to illustrations.

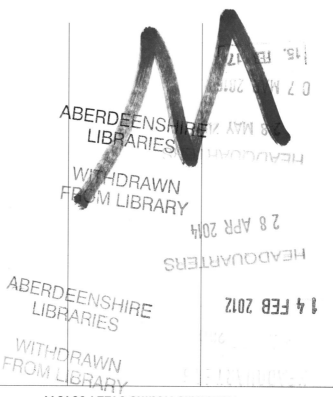